Dataset Shift in Machine Learning

Neural Information Processing Series

Michael I. Jordan and Thomas Dietterich, editors

Advances in Large Margin Classifiers, Alexander J. Smola, Peter L. Bartlett, Bernhard Schölkopf, and Dale Schuurmans, eds., 2000

Advanced Mean Field Methods: Theory and Practice, Manfred Opper and David Saad, eds., 2001

Probabilistic Models of the Brain: Perception and Neural Function, Rajesh P. N. Rao, Bruno A. Olshausen, and Michael S. Lewicki, eds., 2002

Exploratory Analysis and Data Modeling in Functional Neuroimaging, Friedrich T. Sommer and Andrzej Wichert, eds., 2003

Advances in Minimum Description Length: Theory and Applications, Peter D. Grunwald, In Jae Myung, and Mark A. Pitt, eds., 2005

Nearest-Neighbor Methods in Learning and Vision: Theory and Practice, Gregory Shakhnarovich, Piotr Indyk, and Trevor Darrell, eds., 2006

New Directions in Statistical Signal Processing: From Systems to Brains, Simon Haykin, José C. Prncipe, Terrence J. Sejnowski, and John McWhirter, eds., 2007

Predicting Structured Data, Gökhan Bakır, Thomas Hofmann, Bernhard Schölkopf, Alexander J. Smola, Ben Taskar, and S. V. N. Vishwanathan, eds., 2007

Toward Brain-Computer Interfacing, Guido Dornhege, José del R. Millán, Thilo Hinterberger, Dennis J. McFarland, and Klaus-Robert Müller, eds., 2007

Large-Scale Kernel Machines, Léon Bottou, Olivier Chapelle, Denis DeCoste, and Jason Weston, eds., 2007

Dataset Shift in Machine Learning, Joaquin Quiñonero-Candela, Masashi Sugiyama, Anton Schwaighofer, and Neil D. Lawrence, eds., 2009

Dataset Shift in Machine Learning

Joaquin Quiñonero-Candela
Masashi Sugiyama
Anton Schwaighofer
Neil D. Lawrence

The MIT Press
Cambridge, Massachusetts
London, England

Typeset by the authors using LATEX 2_ε
Library of Congress Control No. 2008020394

Library of Congress Cataloging-in-Publication Data
Dataset shift in machine learning / edited by Joaquin Quiñonero-Candela ... [et al.].
    p. cm. — (Neural information processing)
  Includes bibliographical references and index.
  ISBN 978-0-262-17005-5 (hardcover : alk. paper), 978-0-262-54587-7 (pb)
  1. Machine learning.   I. Quiñonero-Candela, Joaquin.
  Q325.5.D37 2009
  006.3'1–dc22

                                    2008020394

Contents

7 A Conditional Expectation Approach to Model Selection and Active Learning under Covariate Shift   **107**

Masashi Sugiyama, Neil Rubens, Klaus-Robert Müller

8 Covariate Shift by Kernel Mean Matching   **131**

Arthur Gretton, Alex Smola, Jiayuan Huang, Marcel Schmittfull, Karsten Borgwardt, Bernhard Schölkopf

9 Discriminative Learning under Covariate Shift with a Single Optimization Problem   **161**

Steffen Bickel, Michael Brückner, Tobias Scheffer

Series Foreword

The yearly Neural Information Processing Systems (NIPS) workshops bring together scientists with broadly varying backgrounds in statistics, mathematics, computer science, physics, electrical engineering, neuroscience, and cognitive science, unified by a common desire to develop novel computational and statistical strategies for information processing and to understand the mechanisms for information processing in the brain. In contrast to conferences, these workshops maintain a flexible format that both allows and encourages the presentation and discussion of work in progress. They thus serve as an incubator for the development of important new ideas in this rapidly evolving field. The series editors, in consultation with workshop organizers and members of the NIPS Foundation Board, select specific workshop topics on the basis of scientific excellence, intellectual breadth, and technical impact. Collections of papers chosen and edited by the organizers of specific workshops are built around pedagogical introductory chapters, while research monographs provide comprehensive descriptions of workshop-related topics, to create a series of books that provides a timely, authoritative account of the latest developments in the exciting field of neural computation.

Michael I. Jordan and Thomas G. Dietterich

Preface

Systems based on machine learning techniques often face a major challenge when applied "in the wild": The conditions under which the system was developed will differ from those in which we use the system. An example could be a sophisticated email spam filtering system that took a few years to develop. Will this system be usable, or will it need to be adapted because the types of spam have changed since the system was first built? Probably any form of real world data analysis is plagued with such problems, which arise for reasons ranging from the bias introduced by experimental design, to the mere irreproducibility of the testing conditions at training time.

In an abstract form, some of these problems can be seen as cases of *dataset shift*, where the joint distribution of inputs and outputs differs between training and test stage. However, textbook machine learning techniques assume that training and test distribution are identical. Aim of this book is to explicitly allow for dataset shift, and analyze the consequences for learning.

In their contributions, the authors will consider general dataset shift scenarios, as well as a simpler case called *covariate shift*. Covariate (input) shift means that only the input distribution changes, whereas the conditional distribution of the outputs given the inputs $p(y|x)$ remains unchanged.

This book attempts to give an overview of the different recent efforts that are being made in the machine learning community for dealing with dataset and covariate shift. The contributed chapters establish relations to transfer learning, transduction, local learning, active learning, and to semisupervised learning. Three recurrent themes are how the *capacity* or complexity of the model affects its behavior in the face of dataset shift (are "true" conditional models and sufficiently rich models unaffected?), whether it is possible to find projections of the data that attenuate the differences in the training and test distributions while preserving predictability, and whether new forms of importance reweighted likelihood and cross-validation can be devised which are robust to covariate shift.

Overview

Part I of the book aims at providing a general introduction to the problem of learning when training and test distributions differ in some form.

Amos Storkey provides a general introduction in chapter 1 from the viewpoint of learning transfer. He introduces the general learning transfer problem, and formulates the problem in terms of a change of scenario. Standard regression and classification models can be characterized as conditional models. Assuming that the conditional model is true, covariate shift is not an issue. However, if this assumption does not hold, conditional modeling will fail. Storkey then characterizes a number of different cases of dataset shift, including simple covariate shift, prior probability shift, sample selection bias, imbalanced data, domain shift, and source component shift. Each of these situations is cast within the framework of graphical models and a number of approaches to addressing each of these problems are reviewed. Storkey also introduces a framework for multiple dataset learning that also prompts the possibility of using hierarchical dataset linkage.

Dataset shift has wider implications beyond machine learning, within philosophy of science. David Corfield in chapter 2 shows how the problem of dataset shift has been addressed by different philosophical schools under the concept of "projectability." When philosophers tried to formulate scientific reasoning with the resources of predicate logic and a Bayesian inductive logic, it became evident how vital background knowledge is to allow us to project confidently into the future, or to a different place, from previous experience. To transfer expectations from one domain to another, it is important to locate robust causal mechanisms. An important debate concerning these attempts to characterize background knowledge is over whether it can all be captured by probabilistic statements. Having placed the problem within the wider philosophical perspective, Corfield turns to machine learning, and addresses a number of questions: Have machine learning theorists been sufficiently creative in their efforts to encode background knowledge? Have the frequentists been more imaginative than the Bayesians, or vice versa? Is the necessity of expressing background knowledge in a probabilistic framework too restrictive? Must relevant background knowledge be handcrafted for each application, or can it be learned?

Part II of the book focuses on theoretical aspects of dataset and covariate shift.

In chapter 3, Matthias Hein studies the problem of binary classification under sample selection bias from a decision-theoretic perspective. Starting from a derivation of the necessary and sufficient conditions for equivalence of the Bayes classifiers of training and test distributions, Hein provides the conditions under which –asymptotically– sample selection bias does not affect the performance of a classifier. From this viewpoint, there are fundamental differences between classifiers of low and high capacity, in particular the ones which are Bayes consistent. In the second part of his chapter, Hein provides means to modify existing learning algorithms such that they are more robust to sample selection bias in the case where one has access to an unlabeled sample of the test data. This is achieved by constructing a graph-based regularization functional. The close connection of this approach to semisupervised learning is also highlighted.

Lars Kai Hansen provides a Bayesian analysis of the problem of covariate shift in chapter 4. He approaches the problem starting with the hypothesis that it is possible to recover performance by tracking the nonstationary input distribution. Under the average log-probability loss, Bayesian transductive learning is generalization optimal (in terms of the conditional distribution $p(\text{label} \,|\, \text{input})$). For realizable supervised learning –where the "true" model is at hand– all available data should be used in determining the posterior distribution, including unlabeled data. However, if the parameters of the input distribution are disjoint of those of the conditional predictive distribution, learning with unlabeled data has no effect on the supervised learning performance. For the case of unrealizable learning –the "true" model is not contained in the prior– Hansen argues that "learning with care" by discounting some of the data might improve performance. This is reminiscent of the importance-weighting approaches of Kanamori et al. (chapter 6) and Sugiyama et al. (chapter 7).

In chapter 5, the third contribution of the theory part, Shai Ben-David provides a theoretical analysis based around "domain adaptation": an embedding into a feature space under which training and test distribution appear similar, and where enough information is preserved for prediction. This relates back to the general viewpoint of Corfield in chapter 2, who argues that learning transfer is only possible once a robust (invariant) mechanism has been identified. Ben-David also introduces a taxonomy of formal models for different cases of dataset shift. For the analysis, he derives error bounds which are relative to the best possible performance in each of the different cases. In addition, he establishes a relation of his framework to inductive transfer.

Part III of the book focuses on algorithms to learn under the more specific setting of covariate shift, where the input distribution changes between training and test phases but the conditional distribution of outputs given inputs remains unchanged.

Chapter 6, contributed by Takafumi Kanamori and Hidetoshi Shimodaira, starts with showing that the ordinary maximum likelihood estimator is heavily biased under covariate shift if the model is *misspecified*. By misspecified it is meant that the model is too simple to express the target function (see also chapter 3 and chapter 4 for the different behavior of misspecified and correct models). Kanamori and Shimodaira then show that the bias induced by covariate shift can be asymptotically canceled by weighting the training samples according to the importance ratio between training and test input densities. However, the weighting is suboptimal in practical situations with finite samples since it tends to have larger variance than the unweighted counterpart. To cope with this problem, Kanamori and Shimodaira provide an information criterion that allows optimal control of the bias-variance trade-off. The latter half of their contribution focuses on the problem of active learning where the covariate distribution is designed by users for better prediction performances. Within the same information-criterion framework, they develop an active learning algorithm that is guaranteed to be consistent.

In chapter 7 Masashi Sugiyama and coworkers also discuss the problems of model selection and active learning in the covariate shift scenario, but in a slightly different framework; the conditional expectation of the generalization error given training inputs is evaluated here, while Kanamori and Shimodaira's analysis is in terms of the full expectation of the generalization error over training inputs and outputs. Sugiyama and coworkers argue that the conditional expectation framework is more data-dependent and thus more accurate than the methods based on the full expectation, and develop alternative methods of model selection and active learning for approximately linear regression. An algorithm that can effectively perform active learning and model selection at the same time is also provided.

In chapter 8 Arthur Gretton and coworkers address the problem of distribution matching between training and test stages, which is similar in spirit to the problem discussed in chapter 5. They propose a method called *kernel mean matching*, which allows direct estimation of the importance weight *without* going through density estimation. Gretton et al. then relate the re-weighted estimation approaches to *local learning*, where labels on test data are estimated given a subset of training data in a neighborhood of the test point. Examples are nearest-neighbor estimators and Watson-Nadaraya-type estimators. The authors further provide detailed proofs concerning the statistical properties of the kernel mean matching estimator and detailed experimental analyses for both covariate shift and local learning.

In chapter 9 Steffen Bickel and coworkers derive a solution to covariate shift adaptation for arbitrarily different distributions that is purely discriminative: neither training nor test distribution is modeled explicitly. They formulate the general problem of learning under covariate shift as an integrated optimization problem and instantiate a kernel logistic regression and an exponential loss classifier for differing training and test distributions. They show under which condition the optimization problem is convex, and empirically study their method on problems of spam filtering, text classification, and land mine detection.

Amir Globerson and coworkers take an innovative view on covariate shift: in chapter 10 they address the situation where training and test inputs differ by adversarial *feature corruption*. They formulate this problem as a two-player game, where the action of one player (the one who builds the classifier) is to choose robust features, whereas the other player (the adversary) tries to corrupt the features which would harm the current classifier most at test time. Globerson et al. address this problem in a minimax setting, thus avoiding any modeling assumptions about the deletion mechanism. They use convex duality to show that it corresponds to a quadratic program and show how recently introduced methods for large-scale online optimization can be used for fast optimization of this quadratic problem. Finally, the authors apply their algorithm to handwritten digit recognition and spam filtering tasks, and show that it outperforms a standard support vector machine (SVM) when features are deleted from data samples.

In chapter 11 some of the chapter authors are given the opportunity to express their personal opinions and research statements.

Acknowledgements

The idea of compiling this book was born during the workshop entitled "Learning When Test and Training Inputs Have Different Distributions" that we organized at the 2006 Advances in Neural Information Processing Systems conference. We would like to thank the PASCAL Network of Excellence for supporting the organization of this workshop.

The majority of the chapter authors either gave a talk or were present at the workshop; the few that weren't have made major contributions to dealing with dataset shift in machine learning. Thanks to all of you for making this book happen!

Joaquin Quiñonero-Candela
Masashi Sugiyama
Anton Schwaighofer
Neil D. Lawrence

Cambridge, Tokyo, and Manchester, 15 July 2008

I Introduction to Dataset Shift

1 When Training and Test Sets Are Different: Characterizing Learning Transfer

Amos Storkey

In this chapter, a number of common forms of dataset shift are introduced, and each is related to a particular form of causal probabilistic model. Examples are given for the different types of shift, and some corresponding modeling approaches. By characterizing dataset shift in this way, there is potential for the development of models which capture the specific types of variations, combine different modes of variation, or do model selection to assess whether dataset shift is an issue in particular circumstances. As an example of how such models can be developed, an illustration is provided for one approach to adapting Gaussian process methods for a particular type of dataset shift called mixture component shift. After the issue of dataset shift is introduced, the distinction between conditional and unconditional models is elaborated in section 1.2. This difference is important in the context of dataset shift, as it will be argued in section 1.4 that dataset shift makes no difference for causally conditional models. This form of dataset shift has been called covariate shift. *In section 1.5, another simple form of dataset shift is introduced: prior probability shift. This is followed by section 1.6 on sample selection bias, section 1.7 on imbalanced data, and section 1.8 on domain shift. Finally, three different types of source component shift are given in section 1.9. One example of modifying Gaussian process models to apply to one form of source component shift is given in section 1.10. A brief discussion on the issue of determining whether shift occurs (section 1.11) and on the relationship to transfer learning (section 1.12) concludes the chapter.*

1.1 Introduction

A camera company develops some expert pattern recognition software for their cameras but now wants to sell it for use on other cameras. Does it need to worry about the differences?

The country Albodora has done a study that shows the introduction of a particular measure has aided in curbing underage drinking. Bodalecia's politicians are impressed by the results and want to utilize Albodora's approach in their own country. Will it work?

A consultancy provides network intrusion detection software, developed using machine learning techniques on data from four years ago. Will the software still work as well now as it did when it was first released? If not, does the company need to do a whole further analysis, or are there some simple changes that can be made to bring the software up to scratch?

In the real world, the conditions in which we use the systems we develop will differ from the conditions in which they were developed. Typically environments are nonstationary, and sometimes the difficulties of matching the development scenario to the use are too great or too costly.

In contrast, textbook predictive machine learning methods work by ignoring these differences. They presume either that the test domain and training domain match, or that it makes no difference if they do not match. In this book we will be asking about what happens when we allow for the possibility of *dataset shift*. What happens if we are explicit in recognizing that in reality things might change from the idealized training scheme we have set up?

The scenario can be described a little more systematically. Given some data, and some modeling framework, a model can be learned. This model can be used for making predictions $P(\mathbf{y}|\mathbf{x})$ for some targets $\mathbf{y}$ given some new $\mathbf{x}$. However, if there is a possibility that something may have changed between training and test situations, it is important to ask if a different predictive model should be used. To do this, it is critical to develop an understanding of the appropriateness of particular models in the circumstance of such changes. Knowledge of how best to model the potential changes will enable better representation of the result of these changes. There is also the question of what needs to be done do to implement the resulting process. Does the learning method itself need to be changed, or is there just post hoc processing that can be done to the learned model to account for the change?

The problem of dataset shift is closely related to another area of study known by various terms such as *transfer learning* or *inductive transfer*. Transfer learning deals with the general problem of how to transfer information from a variety of previous different environments to help with learning, inference, and prediction in a new environment. Dataset shift is more specific: it deals with the business of relating information in (usually) two closely related environments to help with the prediction in one given the data in the other(s).

Faced with the problem of dataset shift, we need to know what we can do. If it is possible to characterize the types of changes that occur from training to test situation, this will help in knowing what techniques are appropriate. In this chapter some of the most typical types of dataset shift will be characterized.

The aim, here, is to provide an illustrative introduction to dataset shift. There is no attempt to provide an exhaustive, or even systematic literature review: indeed the literature is far too extensive for that. Rather, the hope is that by taking a particular view on the problem of dataset shift, it will help to provide an organizational structure which will enable the large body of work in all these areas to be systematically related and analyzed, and will help establish new developments in the field as a whole.

Gaussian process models will be used as illustrations in parts of this chapter. It would be foolish to reproduce an introduction to this area when there are already very comprehensible alternatives. Those who are unfamiliar with Gaussian processes, and want to follow the various illustrations, are referred to Rasmussen and Williams [2006]. Gaussian processes are a useful predictive modeling tool with some desirable properties. They are directly applicable to regression problems, and can be used for classification via logistic transformations. Only the regression case will be discussed here.

1.2 Conditional and Generative Models

This chapter will describe methods for dataset shift using probabilistic models. A probabilistic model relates the variables of interest by defining a joint probability distribution for the values those variables take. This distribution determines which values of the variables are more or less probable, and hence how particular variables are related: it may be that the probability that one variable takes a certain value is very dependent on the state of another. A good model is a probability distribution that describes the understanding and the occurrence of those variables well. Very informally, a model that assigns low probability to things that are not observed and relationships that are forbidden or unlikely and high probability to observed and likely items is favored over a model that does not.

In the realm of probabilistic predictive models it is useful to make a distinction between conditional and generative models. The term *generative model* will be used to refer to a probabilistic model (effectively a joint probability distribution) over all the variables of interest (including any parameters). Given a generative model we can generate artificial data from the model by sampling from the required joint distribution, hence the name. A generative model can be specified using a number of conditional distributions. Suppose the data takes the form of covariate $\mathbf{x}$ and target $\mathbf{y}$ pairs. Then, by way of example, $P(\mathbf{y}, \mathbf{x})$ can be written as $P(\mathbf{x}|\mathbf{y})P(\mathbf{y})$, and may also be written in terms of other hidden *latent* variables which are not observable. For example, we could believe the distribution $P(\mathbf{y}, \mathbf{x})$ depends on some other factor $\mathbf{r}$ and we would write

$$P(\mathbf{y}, \mathbf{x}) = \int d\mathbf{r} \, P(\mathbf{y}, \mathbf{x}|\mathbf{r})P(\mathbf{r}) \,, \tag{1.1}$$

where the integral is a *marginalization* over the $\mathbf{r}$, which simply means that as $\mathbf{r}$ is never known it needs to be integrated over in order to obtain the distribution for the observable quantities $\mathbf{y}$ and $\mathbf{x}$. Necessarily distributions must also be given for any latent variables.

Conditional models are not so ambitious. In a conditional model the distribution of some smaller set of variables is given for each possible known value of the other variables. In many useful situations (such as regression) the value of certain variables (the covariates) is always known, and so there is no need to model them. Building a conditional model for variables $\mathbf{y}$ given other variables $\mathbf{x}$ implicitly factorizes the joint probability distribution over $\mathbf{x}$ and $\mathbf{y}$, as well as parameters (or latent variables) Θ_x and Θ_y, as $P(\mathbf{y}|\mathbf{x}, \Theta_y)P(\mathbf{x}|\Theta_x)P(\Theta_y)P(\Theta_x)$. If the values of $\mathbf{x}$ are always given, it does not matter how good the model $P(\mathbf{x})$ is: it is never used in any prediction scenario. Rather, the quality of the conditional model $P(\mathbf{y}|\mathbf{x})$ is all that counts, and so conditional models only concern themselves with this term. By ignoring the need to model the distribution of $\mathbf{x}$ well, it is possible to choose more flexible model parameterizations than with generative models. Generative models are required to tractably model both the distributions over $\mathbf{y}$ and $\mathbf{x}$ accurately. Another advantage of conditional modeling is that the fit of the predictive model $P(\mathbf{y}|\mathbf{x})$ is never compromised in favor of a better fit of the unused model $P(\mathbf{x})$ as they are decoupled.

If the generative model actually accurately specifies a known generative process for the data, then the choice of modeling structure may fit the real constraints much better than a conditional model and hence result in a more accurate parameterization. In these situations generative models may fare better than conditional ones. The general informal consensus is that in most typical predictive modeling scenarios standard conditional models tend to result in lower errors than standard generative models. However this is no hard rule and is certainly not rigorous.

It is easy for this terminology to get confusing. In the context of this chapter we will use the term *conditional model* for any model that factorizes the joint distribution (having marginalized for any parameters) as $P(\mathbf{y}|\mathbf{x})P(\mathbf{x})$, and the term *unconditional model* for any other form of factorization. The term *generative model* will be used to refer to any joint model (either of conditional or unconditional form) which is used to represent the whole data in terms of some useful factorization, possibly including latent variables. In most cases the factorized form will represent a (simplified) causal generative process. We may use the term *causal graphical model* in these situations to emphasize that the structure is more than just a representation of some particular useful factorization, but is presumed to be a factorization that respects the way the data came about.

It is possible to analyze data using a model structure that is not a causal model but still has the correct relationships between variables for a static environment. One consequence of this is that it is perfectly reasonable to use a conditional form of model for domains that are not causally conditional: many forms of model can be statistically equivalent. If the $P(\mathbf{x})$ does not change, then it does not matter. Hence conditional models can perform well in many situations where there is no dataset shift regardless of the underlying beliefs about the generation process for the data. However, in the context of dataset shift, there is presumed to be an interventional change to some (possibly latent) variable. If the true causal model is not a conditional model, then this change will implicitly cause a change to the relationship $P(\mathbf{y}|\mathbf{x})$. Hence the learned form of the conditional model will no longer be valid. Recognition of this is vital: just because a conditional model performs well in the context of no dataset shift does not imply its validity or capability in the context of dataset shift.

1.3   Real-Life Reasons for Dataset Shift

Whether using unconditional or conditional models, there is a presumption that the distributions they specify are static; i.e., they do not change between the time we learn them and the time we use them. If this is not true, and the distributions change in some way, then we need to model for that change, or at least the possibility of that change. To postulate such a model requires an examination of the reasons why such a shift may occur.

Though there are no doubt an infinite set of potential reasons for these changes, there are a number of ways of collectively characterizing many forms of shift into qualitatively different groups. The following will be discussed in this chapter:

Simple covariate shift is when only the distributions of covariates $\mathbf{x}$ change and everything else is the same.

Prior probability shift is when only the distribution over $\mathbf{y}$ changes and everything else stays the same.

Sample selection bias is when the distributions differ as a result of an unknown sample rejection process.

Imbalanced data is a form of deliberate dataset shift for computational or modeling convenience.

Domain shift involves changes in measurement.

Source component shift involves changes in strength of contributing components.

Each of these relates to a different form of model. Unsurprisingly, each form suggests a particular approach for dealing with the change. As each model is examined in the following sections, the particular nature of the shift will be explained, some of the literature surrounding that type of dataset shift will be mentioned, and a graphical illustration of the overall model will be given. The graphical descriptions will take a common form: they will illustrate the probabilistic graphical (causal) model for the generative model. Where the distributions of a variable may change between train and test scenarios, the corresponding network node is darkened. Each figure will also illustrate data undergoing the particular form of shift by providing samples for the training (light) and test (dark) situations. These diagrams should quickly illustrate the type of change that is occurring. In the descriptions, a subscript tr will denote a quantity related to the training scenario, and a subscript te will denote a quantity relating to the test scenario. Hence $P_{\mathrm{tr}}(\mathbf{y})$ and $P_{\mathrm{te}}(\mathbf{y})$ are the probability of $\mathbf{y}$ in training and test situations respectively.

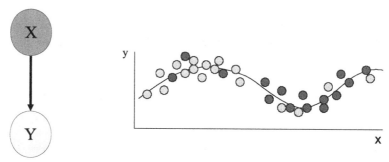

Figure 1.1   Simple covariate shift. Here the causal model indicated the targets **y** are directly dependent on the covariates **x**. In other words the predictive function and noise model stay the same, it is just the typical locations **x** of the points at which the function needs to be evaluated that change. In this figure and throughout, the causal model is given on the left with the node that varies between training and test made darker. To the right is some example data, with the training data in shaded light and the test data shaded dark.

1.4   Simple Covariate Shift

The most basic form of dataset shift occurs when the data is generated according to a model $P(\mathbf{y}|\mathbf{x})P(\mathbf{x})$ and where the distribution $P(\mathbf{x})$ changes between training and test scenarios. As only the covariate distribution changes, this has been called covariate shift [Shimodaira, 2000]. See figure 1.1 for an illustration of the form of causal model for covariate shift.

A typical example of covariate shift occurs in assessing the risk of future events given current scenarios. Suppose the problem was to assess the risk of lung cancer in five years (**y**) given recent past smoking habits (**x**). In these situations we can be sure that the occurrence or otherwise of *future* lung cancer is not a causal factor of *current* habits. So in this case a conditional relationship of the form $P(\mathbf{y}|\mathbf{x})$ is a reasonable causal model to consider.[1] Suppose now that changing circumstances (e.g., a public smoking ban) affect the distribution over habits **x**. How do we account for that in our prediction of risk for a new person with habits $\mathbf{x}^*$?

It will perhaps come as little surprise that the fact that the covariate distribution changes should have no effect on the model $P(\mathbf{y}|\mathbf{x}^*)$. Intuitively this makes sense. The smoking habits of some person completely independent of me should not affect my risk of lung cancer if I make no change at all. From a modeling point of view we can see that from our earlier observation in the static case this is simply a conditional model: it gives the same prediction for given **x**, $P(\mathbf{y}|\mathbf{x})$ regardless of

---

1. Of course there are always possible confounding factors, but for the sake of this illustration we choose to ignore that for now. It is also possible the samples are not drawn independently and identically distributed due to population effects (e.g., passive smoking) but that too is ignored here.

the distribution $P(\mathbf{x})$. Hence in the case of dataset shift, it still does not matter what $P(\mathbf{x})$ is, or how it changes. The prediction will be the same.

This may seem a little labored, but the point is important to make in the light of various pieces of recent work that suggest there are benefits in doing something different if covariate shift occurs. The claim is that if the class of models that is being considered for $P(\mathbf{y}|\mathbf{x})$ does not contain the true conditional model, then improvements can be gained by taking into account the nature of the covariate shift. In the next section we examine this, and see that this work effectively makes a change of global model class for $P(\mathbf{y}|\mathbf{x})$ between the training and test cases. This is valuable as it makes it clear that if the desire is (asymptotic) risk minimization for a constant modeling cost, then there may be gains to be made by taking into account the test distribution. Following this discussion we show that Gaussian processes are nonparametric models that truly are conditional models, in that they satisfy Kolmogorov consistency. This same characteristic does not follow for probabilistic formulations of support vector classifiers.

1.4.1 Is There Really no Modeling Implication?

There are a number of recent papers that have suggested that something different does need to be done in the context of covariate shift. For example, in Shimodaira [2000], the author proposes an importance reweighting of data points in their contribution to the estimator error: points lying in regions of high test density are more highly weighted that those in low-density regions. This was extended in Sugiyama and Müller [2005a], with the inclusion of a generalization error estimation method for this process of adapting for covariate shift. In Sugiyama et al. [2006, 2007], the importance reweighting is made adaptable on the basis of cross-validation error.

The papers make it clear that there *is* some benefit to be obtained by doing something different in the case of covariate shift. The argument here is that these papers indicate a computational benefit rather than a fundamental modeling benefit. These papers effectively compare different global model classes for the two cases: case one, where covariate shift is compensated for, and case two where covariate shift is not compensated for. This is not immediately obvious because the apparent model class is the same. It is just that in compensating for covariate shift the model class is utilized locally (the model does not need to account for training data that is seen but is outside the support of the test data distribution), whereas when not compensating the model class is used globally.

As an example, consider using a linear model to fit nonlinear data (figure 1.2(a)). When not compensating for covariate shift, we obtain the fit given by the dashed line. When compensating for covariate shift, we get the fit given by the solid line. In the latter case, there is no attempted explanation for much of the observed training data, which is fit very poorly by the model. Rather the model class is being used locally. As a contrast consider the case of a local linear model (figure 1.2(b)). Training the local linear model explains the training data well, and the test data

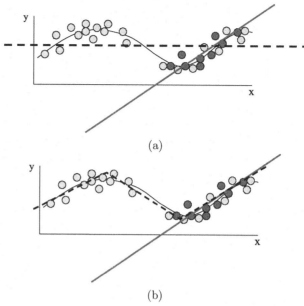

(a)

(b)

Figure 1.2 Covariate shift for misspecified models: *(a)* The linear model is a poor fit to the global data (dashed line). However by focusing on the local region associated with the test data distribution the fit (solid line) is much better as a local linear model is more appropriate. *(b)* The global fit for a local linear model is more reasonable, but involves the computation of many parameters that are never used in the prediction.

well. However only one of the local linear components is really used when doing prediction. Hence the effort spent computing the linear components for regions outside of the support of the test data was wasted.

There are a number of important contributions that stem from the recent study of covariate shift. It clarifies that there are potential computational advantages of adjusting for covariate shift due to the fact that it may be possible to use a simpler model class but only focus on a local region relevant to the test scenario, rather than worrying about the global fit of the model. There is no need to compute parameters for a more complicated global model, or for a multitude of local fits that are never used. Furthermore it also makes use of an issue in semisupervised learning: the nature of the clusters given by the test distribution might be an indicator of a data region that can be modeled well by a simple model form.

There is a another contention that is certainly worth considering here. Some might argue that there are situations where there can be strong a priori knowledge about the model form for the test data, but very little knowledge about the model form for the training data, as that may, for example, be contaminated with a number of other data sources about which little is known. In this circumstance it seems that it is vital to spend the effort modeling the known form of model for the test region, ignoring the others. This is probably a very sound policy. Even so, there is still the possibility that even the test region is contaminated by these other sources. If it is possible to untangle the different sources, this could serve to improve things further. This is discussed more in the context of source component shift.

1.4.2   Gaussian Processes and Conditional Modeling

Suppose instead of using a linear model, a Gaussian process is used. How can we see that this really is a conditional model where the distribution of the covariates has no effect on the predictions? This follows from the fact that no matter what other covariate samples we see, the prediction for our current data remains the same; that is, Gaussian processes satisfy Kolmogorov consistency:

$$P(\{y_i\}|\{\mathbf{x}_i\}, \{\mathbf{x}^k, y^k\}) = \int dy^* P(\{y_i\}, y^*|\{\mathbf{x}_i\}, \mathbf{x}^*, \{\mathbf{x}^k, y^k\}) \tag{1.2}$$

$$= P(\{y_i\}|\{\mathbf{x}_i\}, \mathbf{x}^*, \{\mathbf{x}^k, y^k\}) \tag{1.3}$$

where (1.2) results from the definition of a Gaussian process, and (1.3) from basic probability theory (marginalization). In this equation the y_i are the test targets, $\mathbf{x}_i$ the test covariates, $\mathbf{x}^k$ and y^k the training data, and $\mathbf{x}^*, y^*$ a potential extra training point. However, we never know the target y^* and so it is marginalized over. The result is that introducing the new covariate point $\mathbf{x}^*$ has had no predictive effect.

Using Gaussian processes in the usual way involves training on all the data points: the estimated conditional model $P(\mathbf{y}|\mathbf{x})$ has made use of all the available information. If one of the data points was downweighted (or removed altogether) the effect would simply be greater uncertainty about the model, resulting in a broader posterior distribution over functions.

It may be considered easier to specify a model class for a local region than a model class for the data as a whole. Practically this may be the case. However by specifying that a particular model may be appropriate for any potential local region, we are effectively specifying a model form for each different region of space. This amounts to specifying a global model anyway, and indeed one derivation of the Gaussian process can be obtained from infinite local radial basis function models [Gibbs and MacKay, 1997].

Are all standard nonparametric models also conditional models? In fact some common models are not: the support vector machine (SVM) classifier does not take this form. In Sollich [1999, 2002], it is shown that in order for the support vector machine to be defined as a probabilistic model, a global compensation factor needs to be made due to the fact that the SVM classifier does not include a normalization term in its optimization. One immediate consequence of this compensation is that the probabilistic formulation of the SVM does not satisfy Kolmogorov consistency. Hence the SVM is dependent on the density of the covariates in its prediction.

This can be shown, purely by way of example, for the linear SVM regression case. Generalizations are straightforward. We present an outline argument here, following the notation in Rasmussen and Williams [2006]. The linear support vector classifier maximizes

$$\exp\left(-\sum_{i=1}^{N}(1-y_i(\mathbf{w}^T.\mathbf{x}_i)_+)\right)\exp\left(-\frac{1}{2C}|\mathbf{w}|^2\right),\qquad(1.4)$$

where C is some constant, y_i are the training targets, $\mathbf{x}_i$ are the covariates (augmented with an addition unit attribute), and $\mathbf{w}$ the linear parameters. The $(.)_+$ notation is used to denote the function $(x)_+ = x$ iff $x > 0$ and is zero otherwise.

Equation (1.4) can be rewritten as

$$\left[\prod_{i=1}^{N}\frac{1}{Z_i(\mathbf{w})}\exp(-(1-y_i(\mathbf{w}^T\mathbf{x}_i)_+))\right]Z(\mathbf{w})\exp\left(-\frac{1}{2C}|\mathbf{w}|^2\right),\qquad(1.5)$$

where $Z_N = \prod_{i=1}^{N}Z_i(\mathbf{w})$, and $Z_i(\mathbf{w}) = \sum_{y_i=\pm1}\exp(-(1-y_i(\mathbf{w}^T\mathbf{x}_i)_+))$ is a normalization constant, so now

$$\frac{1}{Z_i(\mathbf{w})}\exp(-(1-y_i(\mathbf{w}^T\mathbf{x}_i)_+))\overset{\text{def}}{=}P(y_i|\mathbf{w})\qquad(1.6)$$

can be interpreted as a probability. Hence the support vector objective can be written

$$\left[\prod_{i=1}^{N}P(y_i|\mathbf{w})\right]Z_N(\mathbf{w})\exp\left(-\frac{1}{2C}|\mathbf{w}|^2\right).\qquad(1.7)$$

Consider the cases $N = N^*$ and $N = N^* + 1$. Starting with the latter, marginalization over y_{N^*+1} is now straightforward as it only occurs as a probability. So the marginal objective is now

$$\left[\prod_{i=1}^{N^*}P(y_i|\mathbf{w})\right]Z_{N^*+1}(\mathbf{w})\exp\left(-\frac{1}{2C}|\mathbf{w}|^2\right).\qquad(1.8)$$

However $Z_{N^*+1}(\mathbf{w}) \neq Z_{N^*}(\mathbf{w})$ due to the extra product term. Specifically the dependence on $\mathbf{w}$ is different, so the objective (1.8) does not match the objective (1.7) for $N = N^*$. Hence the support vector objective for the case of an unknown value of target at a given point is different from the objective function without considering that point. The standard probabilistic interpretation of the support vector classifier does not satisfy Kolmogorov consistency, and seeing a covariate at a point will affect the objective function even if there is no knowledge of the target at that point. Hence the SVM classifier is in some way dependent on the covariate density, as it is dependent purely on the observation of covariates themselves.

1.5   Prior Probability Shift

Prior probability shift is a common issue in simple generative models. A popular example stems from the availability of naive Bayes models for the filtering of spam

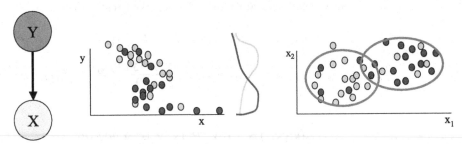

Figure 1.3   Prior probability shift. Here the causal model indicated the covariates **x** are directly dependent on the predictors **y**. The distribution over **y** can change, and this effects the predictions in both the continuous case *(left)* and the class conditional case *(right)*.

email. In cases of prior probability shift, an assumption is made that a causal model of the form $P(\mathbf{x}|\mathbf{y})P(\mathbf{y})$ is valid (see figure 1.3) and the Bayes rule is used to inferentially obtain $P(\mathbf{y}|\mathbf{x})$. Naive Bayes is one model that makes this assumption. The difficulty occurs if the distribution $P(\mathbf{y})$ changes between training and test situations. As **y** is what we are trying to predict it is unsurprising that this form of dataset shift will affect the prediction.

For a known shift in $P(\mathbf{y})$, prior probability shift is easy to correct for. As it is presumed that $P(\mathbf{x}|\mathbf{y})$ does not change, this model can be learned directly from the training data. However the learned $P_{\mathrm{tr}}(\mathbf{y})$ is no longer valid, and needs to be replaced by the known prior distribution in the test scenario $P_{\mathrm{te}}(\mathbf{y})$.

If, however, the distribution $P_{\mathrm{te}}(\mathbf{y})$ is not known for the test scenario, then the situation is a little more complicated. Making a prediction

$$P(\mathbf{y}|\mathbf{x}) = \frac{P(\mathbf{x}|\mathbf{y})P(\mathbf{y})}{P(\mathbf{x})} \tag{1.9}$$

is not possible without knowledge of $P(\mathbf{y})$. But given the model $P(\mathbf{x}|\mathbf{y})$ and the covariates for the test data, certain distributions over **y** are more or less likely. Consider the spam filter example again. If in the test data, the vast majority of the emails contain spammy words, rather than hammy words, we would rate $P(\mathrm{spam}) = 0$ as an unlikely model compared with other models such as $P(\mathrm{spam}) = 0.7$. In saying this we are implicitly using some a priori model of what distributions $P(\mathrm{spam})$ are acceptable to us, and then using the data to refine this model.

Restated, to account for prior probability shift where the precise shift is unknown a prior distribution over valid $P(\mathbf{y})$ can be specified, and the posterior distribution over $P(\mathbf{y})$ computed from the test covariate data. Then the predicted target is given by the sum of the predictions obtained for each $P(\mathbf{y})$ weighted by the posterior probability of $P(\mathbf{y})$.

Suppose $P(\mathbf{y})$ is parameterized by θ, and a prior distribution for $P(\mathbf{y})$ is defined through a prior on the parameters $P(\theta)$. Also assume that the model $P_{\mathrm{tr}}(\mathbf{x}|\mathbf{y})$ has been learned from the training data. Then the prediction taking into account the parameter uncertainty and the observed test data is

$$P(\mathbf{y}_1|\{\mathbf{x}_i\}) = \int d\theta P(\mathbf{y}_1|\mathbf{x}_1, \theta) P_{\text{te}}(\theta|\{\mathbf{x}_i\}) \tag{1.10}$$

$$= \int d\theta \frac{P_{\text{tr}}(\mathbf{x}_1|\mathbf{y}_1) P(\mathbf{y}_1|\theta)}{P_{\text{tr}}(\mathbf{x}_1|\theta)} P_{\text{te}}(\theta|\{\mathbf{x}_i\}) \,, \tag{1.11}$$

where

$$P_{\text{te}}(\theta|\{\mathbf{x}_i\}) \propto \prod_i \sum_{\mathbf{y}_i} P_{\text{tr}}(\mathbf{x}_i|\mathbf{y}_i) P(\mathbf{y}_i|\theta) P(\theta) \tag{1.12}$$

and where i counts over the test data, i.e., these computations are done for the targets $\mathbf{y}_i$ for test points $\mathbf{x}_i$. The ease with which this can be done depends on how many integrals or sums are tractable, and whether the posterior over θ can be represented compactly.

1.6   Sample Selection Bias

Sample selection bias is a statistical issue of critical importance in numerous analyses. One particular area where selection bias must be considered is survey design. Sample selection bias occurs when the training data points $\{\mathbf{x}_i\}$ (the sample) do not accurately represent the distribution of the test scenario (the population) due to a selection process for each item i that is (usually implicitly) dependent on the target variable $\mathbf{y}_i$.

In doing surveys, the desire is to estimate population statistics by surveying a small sample of the population. However, it is easy to set up a survey that means that certain groups of people are less likely to be included in the survey than others because either they refuse to be involved, or they were never in a position to ask to be involved. A typical street survey, for example, is potentially biased against people with poor mobility who may be more likely to be using other transport methods than walking. A survey in a train station is more likely to catch people engaging in leisure travel than busy commuters with optimized journeys who may refuse to do the survey for lack of time.

Sample selection bias is certainly not restricted to surveys. Other examples include estimating the average speed of drivers by measuring the speeds of cars passing a stationary point on a motorway; more fast drivers will pass the point than slow drivers, simply on account of their speed. In any scenario relying on measurement from sensors, sensor failure may well be more likely in environmental situations that would cause extreme measurements. Also the process of data cleaning can itself introduce selection bias. For example, in obtaining handwritten characters, completely unintelligible characters may be discarded. But it may be that certain characters are more likely to be written unclearly.

Sample selection bias is also the cause of the well-known phenomenon called "regression to the mean". Suppose that a particular quantity of importance (e.g.,

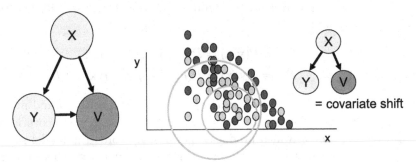

Figure 1.4 Sample selection bias. The actual observed training data is different from the test data because some of the data is more likely to be excluded from the sample. Here v denotes the selection variable, and an example selection function is given by the equiprobable contours. The dependence on $\mathbf{y}$ is crucial as without it there is no bias and this becomes a case of simple covariate shift.

number of cases of illness X) is subject to random variations. However, that circumstance could also be affected by various causal factors. Suppose also that, across the country, the rate of illness X is measured, and is found to be excessive in particular locations Y. As a result of that, various measures are introduced to try to curb the number of illnesses in these regions. The rate of illnesses are measured again and, lo and behold, things have improved and regions Y no longer have such bad rates of illnesses. As a result of that change it is tempting for the uninitiated to conclude that the measures were effective. However, as the regions Y were chosen on the basis of a statistic that is subject to random fluctuations, and the regions were chosen because this statistic took an extreme value, even if the measures had no effect at all the illness rates would be expected to reduce at the next measurement precisely because of the random variations. This is sample selection bias because the sample taken to assess improvement was precisely the sample that was most likely to improve anyway. The issue of reporting bias is also a selection bias issue. "Interesting" positive results are more likely to be reported than "boring" negative ones.

The graphical model for sample selection bias is illustrated in figure 1.4. Consider two models: P_{tr} denotes the model for the training set, and P_{te} the model for the test set. For each datum $(\mathbf{x}, \mathbf{y})$ in the training set

$$P_{\text{tr}}(\mathbf{y}, \mathbf{x}) = P(\mathbf{y}, \mathbf{x}|v = 1) = P(v = 1|\mathbf{y}, \mathbf{x})P(\mathbf{y}|\mathbf{x})P(\mathbf{x}) \qquad (1.13)$$

and for each datum in the test set

$$P_{\text{te}}(\mathbf{y}, \mathbf{x}) = P(\mathbf{y}, \mathbf{x}) = P(\mathbf{y}|\mathbf{x})P(\mathbf{x}). \qquad (1.14)$$

Here v is a binary selection variable that decides whether a datum would be included in the training sample process ($v = 1$) or rejected from the training sample ($v = 0$).

In much of the sample selection literature this model has been simplified by assuming

$$P(\mathbf{y}|\mathbf{x}) = P(\epsilon = \mathbf{y} - \mathbf{f}(\mathbf{x})) \text{ and} \tag{1.15}$$

$$P(v = 1|\mathbf{y}, \mathbf{x}) = P(\nu > g(\mathbf{x})|\mathbf{y} - f(\mathbf{x})) = P(\nu > g(\mathbf{x})|\epsilon) \tag{1.16}$$

for some densities $P(\epsilon)$ and $P(\nu|\epsilon)$, function g and map $\mathbf{f}$. The issue is to model $\mathbf{f}$, which is the dependence of the targets $\mathbf{y}$ on covariates $\mathbf{x}$, while also modeling for g, which produces the bias. In words the model says there is a (multivariate) regression function for $\mathbf{y}$ given covariates $\mathbf{x}$, where the noise is independent of $\mathbf{x}$. Likewise (1.16) describes a classification function for the selection variable v in terms of $\mathbf{x}$, but where the distribution is dependent on the deviation of $\mathbf{y}$ from its predictive mean. Note that in some of the literature, there is an explicit assumption that v depends on some features in addition to $\mathbf{x}$ that control the selection. Here this is simplified by including these features in $\mathbf{x}$ and adjusting the dependence encoded by $\mathbf{f}$ accordingly.

Study of sample selection bias has a long history. Heckman [1974] proposed the first solution to the selection bias problem which involved presuming $\mathbf{y} = y$ is scalar (hence also $\epsilon = \epsilon$ and $\mathbf{f} = f$), f and g are linear, and the joint density $P(\epsilon, \nu) = P(\epsilon)P(\nu|\epsilon)$ is Gaussian. Given this the likelihood of the parameters can be written down for a given complete dataset (a dataset including the rejected samples). However, in computing the maximum likelihood solution for the regression parameters, it turns out the rejected samples are not needed. Note that in the case that ϵ and μ are independent, and $P(\epsilon, \nu) = P(\epsilon)P(\mu)$, there is no predictive bias, and this is then a case of simple covariate shift.

Since the seminal paper by Heckman, many other related approaches have been proposed. These include those that relax the Gaussianity assumption for μ and σ, most commonly by mapping the Gaussian variables through a known nonlinearity before using them [Lee, 1982] and using semiparametric methods directly on $P(\epsilon|\nu)$ [Heckman, 1979]. More recent methods include Zadrozny [2004], where the author focuses on the case where $P(v|\mathbf{x}, \mathbf{y}) = P(v|\mathbf{y})$, Dudík et al. [2006], which looks at maximum entropy density estimation under selection bias; and Huang et al. [2007], which focuses on using additional unbiased covariate data to help estimate the bias. More detailed analysis of the historical work on selection bias is available in Vella [1998] and a characterization of types of selection bias is given in Heckman [1990].

1.7 Imbalanced Data

It is quite possible to have a multiclass machine learning problem where one or more classes are very rare compared with others. This is called the problem of *imbalanced data*. Indeed the prediction of rare events (e.g., loan defaulting) often provides the most challenging problems. This imbalanced data problem is a common cause of dataset shift *by design*.

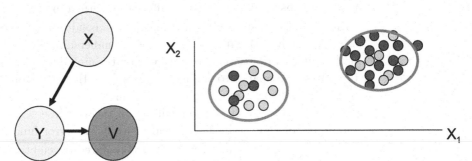

Figure 1.5 Imbalanced data: imbalanced data is sample selection bias with a designed known bias that is dependent on only the class label. Data from more common classes is more likely to be rejected in the training set in order to balance out the number of cases of each class.

If the prediction of rare events is the primary issue, to use a balanced dataset may involve using a computationally infeasible amount of data just in order to get enough rare cases to be able to characterize the class accurately. For this reason it is common to "balance" the training dataset by throwing away data from the common classes so that there is an equal amount of data corresponding to each of the classes under consideration. Note that here, the presumption is not that the model would not be right for the imbalanced data, rather that is is computationally infeasible to use the imbalanced data. However the data corresponding to the common class is discarded, simply because typically that is less valuable: the common class may already be easy to characterize fairly well as it has large amounts of data already.

The result of discarding data, though, is that the distribution in the training scenario no longer matches the imbalanced test scenario. However it is this imbalanced scenario that the model will be used for. Hence some adjustment needs to be made to account for the deliberate bias that is introduced. The graphical model for imbalanced data is shown in figure 1.5 along with a two-class example.

In the conditional modeling case, dataset shift due to rebalancing imbalanced data is just the sample selection bias problem with a known selection bias (as the selection bias was by design not by constraint or accident). In other words, we have selected proportionally more of one class of data than another precisely for no reason other than the class of the data. Variations on this theme can also be seen in certain types of stratified random surveys where particular strata are oversampled because they are expected to have a disproportionate effect on the statistics of interest, and so need a larger sample to increase the accuracy with which their effect is measured.

In a target-conditioned model (of the form $P(\mathbf{x}|\mathbf{y})P(\mathbf{y})$), dataset shift due to imbalanced data is just prior probability shift with a known shift. This is very simple to adjust for as only $P(\mathbf{y})$ needs to be changed. This simplicity can mean that some people choose generative models over conditional models for imbalanced data problems. Because the imbalance is decoupled from the modeling it is transparent that the imbalance itself will not affect the learned model.

In a classification problem, the output of a conditional model is typically viewed as a probability distribution over class membership. The difficulty is that these probability distributions were obtained on training data that was biased in favor of rare classes compared to the test distribution. Hence the output predictions need to be weighted by the reciprocal of the known bias and renormalized in order to get the correct predictive probabilities. In theory these renormalized probabilities should be used in the likelihood and hence in any error function being optimized.

In practice it is not uncommon for the required reweighting to be ignored, either through naivety, or due to the fact that the performance of the resulting classifier appears to be better. This is enlightening as it illustrates the importance of not simply focusing on the probabilistic model without also considering the decision-theoretic implications. By incorporating a utility or loss function a number of things can become apparent. First, predictive performance on the rare classes is often more important than that on common classes. For example, in emergency prediction, we prefer to sacrifice a number of false positives for the benefit of another true positive. By ignoring the reweighting, the practitioner is saying that the bias introduced by the balancing matches the relative importance of false positives and true positives. Furthermore, introduction of a suitable loss function can reduce the problem where a classifier puts all the modeling effort into improving the many probabilities that are already nearly certain at the sacrifice of the small number of cases associated with the rarer classes. Most classifiers share a number of parameters between predictors of the rare and common classes. It is easy for the optimization of those parameters to be swamped by the process of improving the probability of the prediction of the common classes at the expense of any accuracy on the rare classes. However, the difference between a probability of 0.99 and 0.9 may not make any difference to what we do with the classifier and so actually makes no difference to the real results obtained by using the classifier, if predictive probabilities are actually going to be ignored in practice.

Once again the literature on imbalanced data is significant, and there is little chance of doing the field great justice in this small space. In Chawla et al. [2004] the authors give an overview of the content of a number of workshops in this area, and the papers referenced provide an interesting overview of the field. One paper [Japkowicz and Stephen, 2002] from the AAAI workshops looks at a number of different strategies for learning from imbalanced datasets. SMOTE [Chawla et al., 2002] is a more recent approach that has received some attention. In Akbani et al. [2004] the authors look at the issue of imbalanced data specifically in the context of support vector machines, and an earlier paper [Veropoulos et al., 1999] also focuses on support vector machines and considers the issue of data imbalance while discussing the balance between sensitivity and specificity. In the context of linear program boosting, the paper by Leskovec and Shawe-Taylor [2003] considers the implications of imbalanced data, and tests this on a text classification problem. As costs and probabilities are intimately linked, the paper by Zadrozny and Elkan [2001] discusses how to jointly deal with these unknowns. The fact that adjusting class probabilities does make a practical difference can be found in Latinne et al. [2001]. Further useful analysis of the general problem can be found in Japkowicz and Stephen [2002].

1.8   Domain Shift

In life, the meaning of numbers can change. Inflation reduces the value of money. Lighting changes can effect the appearance of a particular color or the meaning of a position can change dependent on the current frame of reference. Furthermore, there is often the possibility of changes in measurement units. All of these can cause dataset shift. We call this particular form of dataset shift *domain shift*. This term is borrowed from linguistics, where it refers to changes in the domain of discourse. The same entity can be referred to in different ways in different domains of discourse: for example, in one context meters might be an obvious unit of measurement, and in another inches may be more appropriate.

Domain shift is characterized by the fact that the measurement system, or method of description, can change. One way to understand this is to postulate some underlying unchanging latent representation of the covariate space. We denote a latent variable in this space by $\mathbf{x}_0$. Such a variable could, for example, be a value in yen indexed adjusted to a fixed date. The predictor variable $\mathbf{y}$ is dependent on this latent $\mathbf{x}_0$. The difficulty is that we never observe $\mathbf{x}_0$. We only observe some map $\mathbf{x} = \mathbf{f}(\mathbf{x}_0)$ into the observable space. And that map can change between training and test scenarios, see figure 1.6 for an illustration.

Modeling for domain shift involves estimating the map between representations using the distributional information. A good example of this is estimating gamma correction for photographs. Gamma correction is a specific parametric nonlinear map of pixel intensities. Given two unregistered photographs of a similar scene from different cameras, the appearance may be different due to the camera gamma calibration or due to postprocessing. By optimizing the parameter to best match the pixel distributions we can obtain a gamma correction such that the two photographs are using the same representation. A more common scenario is that a single camera moves from a well-lit to a badly lit region. In this context, gamma correction is correction for changes due to lighting—an estimate of the gamma correction needed to match some idealized pixel distribution can be computed. Another form of explicit density shift includes estimating Doppler shift from diffuse sources.

1.9   Source Component Shift

Source component shift may be the most common form of dataset shift. In the most general sense it simply states that the observed data is made up from data from a

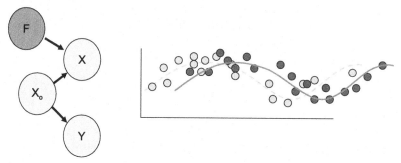

Figure 1.6   Domain shift: The observed covariates **x** are transformed from some idealized covariates $\mathbf{x}_0$ via some transformation F, which is allowed to vary between datasets. The target distribution $P(\mathbf{y}|\mathbf{x}_0)$ is unchanged between test and training datasets, but of course the distribution $P(\mathbf{y}|\mathbf{x}_0)$ does change if F changes.

number of different sources, each with its own characteristics, and the proportions of those sources can vary between training and test scenarios.

Source component shift is ubiquitous: a particular product is produced in a number of factories, but the proportions sourced from each factory vary dependent on a retailer's supply chain; voting expectations vary depending on type of work, and different places in a country have different distributions of jobs; a major furniture store wants to analyze advertising effectiveness among a number of concurrent advertising streams, but the effectiveness of each is likely to vary with demographic proportions; the nature of network traffic on a university's computer system varies with time of year due to the fact that different student groups are present or absent at different times.

It would seem likely that most of the prediction problems that are the subject of study or analysis involve at least one of

- samples that could come from one of a number of subpopulations, between which the quantity to be predicted may vary;

- samples chosen are subject to factors that are not fully controlled for, and that could change in different scenarios; and

- targets that are aggregate values averaged over a potentially varying population.

Each of these provides a different potential form of source component shift. The three cases correspond to *mixture component shift*, *factor component shift*, and *mixing component shift* respectively. These three cases will be elaborated further.

The causal graphical model for source component shift is illustrated in figure 1.7. In all cases of source component shift there is some changing environment that jointly affects the values of the samples that are drawn. This may sound indistinguishable from sample selection bias, and indeed these two forms of dataset shift are closely related. However, with source component shift the causal model states that the change is a change in the *causes*. In sample selection bias, the change

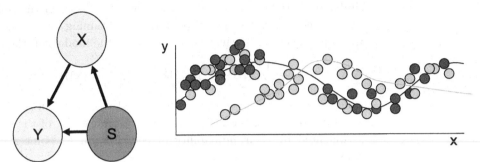

Figure 1.7 Source component shift. A number of different sources of data are represented in the dataset, each with its own characteristics. Here S denotes the source proportions and these can vary between test and training scenarios. In mixture component shift, these sources are mixed together in the observed data, resulting in two or more confounded components.

is a change in the *measurement process*. This distinction is subtle but important from a modeling point of view. At this stage it is worth considering the three different cases of source component shift.

Mixture Component Shift In mixture component shift, the data consists directly of samples of $(\mathbf{x}, \mathbf{y})$ values that come from a number of different sources. However for each datum the actual source (which we denote by s) is unknown. Unsurprisingly these different sources occur in different proportions $P(s)$, and are also likely to be responsible for different ranges of values for $(\mathbf{x}, \mathbf{y})$: the distribution $P(\mathbf{y}, \mathbf{x}|s)$ is conditionally dependent on s. Typically, it is presumed that the effects of the sources $P(\mathbf{y}, \mathbf{x}|s)$ are the same in all situations, but that the *proportions* of the different sources vary between training and test scenarios. This distinction is a natural extension to prior probability shift, where now the shift in prior probabilities is in a latent space rather than in the space of the target attributes.

Factor Component Shift Here the data is dependent on a number of factors that influence the probability, where each factor is decomposable into a form and a strength. For concreteness' sake, a common form of factor model decomposes $P(\mathbf{x}, \mathbf{y})$ as

$$P(\mathbf{x}, \mathbf{y}) = \frac{1}{Z} \exp \left(\sum_k \alpha_k \Phi_k(\mathbf{x}, \mathbf{y}) \right) \qquad (1.17)$$

for form exponents $\Phi_k(\mathbf{x}, \mathbf{y})$ and strength exponents α_k. Factor component shift occurs when the form of the factors remains the same, but the strength of the factors changes between training and test scenario.

Mixing Component Shift In mixing component shift, the scenario is the same as mixture component shift, but where the measurement is an aggregate: consider sampling whole functions independently from many independent and identically distributed mixture component shift models. Then, under a mixing component shift model, the observation at $\mathbf{x}$ is now an average of the observations at $\mathbf{x}$ for each of those samples. The probability of obtaining an $\mathbf{x}$ is as before. Presuming the applicability of a central limit theorem, the model can then be written as

$$P(\mathbf{y}|\mathbf{x}) = \frac{1}{Z} \exp\left((\mathbf{y} - \boldsymbol{\mu}(\mathbf{x}))\boldsymbol{\Sigma}^{-1}(\mathbf{x})(\mathbf{y} - \boldsymbol{\mu}(\mathbf{x})))\right), \tag{1.18}$$

where the mean $\boldsymbol{\mu}(\mathbf{x}) = \sum_s P(s|\mathbf{x})\boldsymbol{\mu}_s$ and the covariance $\boldsymbol{\Sigma} = \sum_s P(s|\mathbf{x})\boldsymbol{\Sigma}_s$ are given by combining the means $\boldsymbol{\mu}_s$ and covariances $\boldsymbol{\Sigma}_s$ of the different components s, weighted by their probability of contribution at point $\mathbf{x}$ (usually called the responsibility).

Although all three of these are examples of source component shift, the treatment each requires is slightly different. The real issue is being able to distinguish the different sources and their likely contributions in the test setting. The ease or otherwise with which this can be done will depend to a significant extent on the situation, and on how much prior knowledge about the form of the sources there is. It is noteworthy that, at least in mixture component shift, the easier it is to distinguish the sources, the less relevant it is to model the shift: sources that do not overlap in $\mathbf{x}$ space are easier to distinguish, but also mean that there is no mixing at any given location to confound the prediction.

It is possible to reinterpret sample selection bias in terms of source component shift if we view the different rejection rates as relating to different sources of data. By setting

$$P_{\text{te}}(s) \propto \int d\mathbf{x}d\mathbf{y}\, P(\mathbf{x}, \mathbf{y}| P(v=1|\mathbf{x}, \mathbf{y}) = s) \tag{1.19}$$

$$P(\mathbf{x}, \mathbf{y}|s) \propto P(\mathbf{x}, \mathbf{y}| P(v=1|\mathbf{x}, \mathbf{y}) = s) \tag{1.20}$$

$$P_{\text{tr}}(s) \propto s \int d\mathbf{x}d\mathbf{y}\, P(\mathbf{x}, \mathbf{y}| P(v=1|\mathbf{x}, \mathbf{y}) = s) \tag{1.21}$$

we can convert a sample selection bias model into a source component shift model. In words, the source s is used to represent how likely the rejection would be, and hence each source generates regions of $\mathbf{x}, \mathbf{y}$ space that have equiprobable selection probabilities under the sample selection bias problem. Figure 1.8 illustrates this relation. At least from this particular map between the domains, the relationship is not very natural, and hence from a generative point of view the general source component shift and general sample selection bias scenarios are best considered to be different from one another.

1.10 Gaussian Process Methods for Dataset Shift

Gaussian processes have proven their capabilities for nonlinear regression and classification problems. But how can they be used in the context of dataset shift? In this section, we consider how Gaussian process methods can be adapted for mixture component shift.

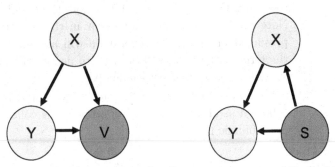

Figure 1.8 Sample selection bias *(left)* and source component shift *(right)* are related. The sources are equated to regions of $(\mathbf{x}, \mathbf{y})$ space with equiprobable sample rejection probabilities under the sample selection bias model. Then the proportions for these sources vary between training and test situations. Here $\mathbf{x}$ and $\mathbf{y}$ are the covariates and targets respectively, s denotes the different sources, and v denotes the sample selection variable.

1.10.1 Mixture Component Shift Model

In mixture component shift, there are a number of possible components to the model. We will describe here a two-source problem, where the covariate distribution for each source is described as a mixture model (a mixture of Gaussians will be used). The model takes the following form:

■ The distribution of the training data and test data are denoted P_{tr} and P_{te} respectively, and are unknown in general.

■ Source 1 consists of M_1 mixture distributions for the covariates, where mixture t is denoted $P_{1t}(\mathbf{x})$. Each of the components is associated[2] with regression model $P_1(\mathbf{y}|\mathbf{x})$.

■ Source 2 consists of M_2 mixture distributions for the covariates, where mixture t is denoted $P_{2t}(\mathbf{x})$. Each of the components is associated with the regression model $P_2(\mathbf{y}|\mathbf{x})$.

■ The training and test data distributions take the following form:

$$P_{\text{tr}}(\mathbf{x}) = \sum_{t=1}^{M_1} \beta_1 \gamma_{1t}^D P_{1t}(\mathbf{x}) + \sum_{t=1}^{M_2} \beta_2 \gamma_{2t}^D P_{2t}(\mathbf{x}) \text{ and } P_{\text{te}}(\mathbf{x}) = \sum_{t=1}^{M1} \gamma_{1t}^T P_{1t}(\mathbf{x}) \quad (1.22)$$

Here β_1 and β_2 are parameters for the proportions of the two sources in the training data, γ_{1t}^D are the relative proportions of each mixture from source 1 in the training data, and γ_{2t}^D are the relative proportions of each mixture from source 2 in the training data. Finally, γ_{1t}^T are the proportions of each mixture from source 1 in the

---

2. If a component i is associated with a regression model j, this means that any datum $\mathbf{x}$ generated from the mixture component i, will also have a corresponding $\mathbf{y}$ generated from the associated regression model $P_j(\mathbf{y}|\mathbf{x})$.

test data. Once again, D and T denote the training and test datasets respectively. Note that source 2 does not occur in the test dataset. All these parameters are presumed unknown. In general we will assume the mixtures are Gaussian, when the form $N(\mathbf{x}; \mathbf{m}, \mathbf{K})$ will be used to denote the Gaussian distribution function of $\mathbf{x}$, with mean $\mathbf{m}$ and covariance $\mathbf{K}$.

For Gaussian process models for $P_1(\mathbf{y}|\mathbf{x})$ and $P_2(\mathbf{y}|\mathbf{x})$, with mixture parameters collected as $\mathbf{\Omega}$, and the mixing proportions collected as $\boldsymbol{\gamma}$ and $\boldsymbol{\beta}$, we have the full probabilistic model

$$P(\{\mathbf{y}^\mu, \mathbf{x}^\mu | \mu \in D\}, \{\mathbf{x}^\nu | \nu \in T\} | \boldsymbol{\beta}, \mathbf{\Omega}) = \sum_{\{s^\mu\}, \{t^\mu\}} \prod_{\mu \in D} P(s^\mu | \boldsymbol{\beta})$$

$$P(t^\mu | \boldsymbol{\gamma}, s^\mu) P_{s^\mu t^\mu}(\mathbf{x}^\mu | \Omega_{t^\mu}) P_{s^\mu}(\mathbf{y}^\mu | \mathbf{x}^\mu) \prod_{\nu \in T} P(t^\nu | \boldsymbol{\gamma}) P_{1t^\nu}(\mathbf{x}^\nu | \mathbf{\Omega}) \quad (1.23)$$

where s^μ denotes the source, and t^μ denotes the mixture component. In words this model says:

- For each item in the training set:
  - Decide which source generated this datum.
  - Decide which of the mixtures associated with this source generated the covariates.
  - Sample the covariates from the relevant mixture.
  - Sample the target from the Gaussian process (conditioned on the covariates) associated with this source.
- For each item in the test set:
  - Decide which of the mixtures from source 1 generated the covariates (source 2 is not represented in the test data).
  - Generate the covariates from that mixture.

1.10.2   Learning and Inference

The primary computational issue in learning and inference in this model is the difficulty of summing over all the allocations of data points to mixture components. For Gaussian processes, this computation is harder than in most parametric models as we cannot expect to be able to do standard expectation maximization. Expectation maximization algorithms involve iterative computation of responsibilities $P(s^\mu)$ for each data point μ and then a maximum-likelihood parameter estimation for the parameters given the responsibilities. However as Gaussian processes are nonparametric, the distribution is not independent of the allocation. Hence whether one point is allocated to one mixture or not will immediately affect the distribution over all other mixtures.

Here, a variational approximation is proposed, which enables a variational expectation maximization procedure to be used. The approximation takes the form of an intermediate approximating Gaussian process for each mixture component and factorized responsibilities.

For simplicity, we will assume that the target is a scalar value: we are interested in regression. The issues of generalization to multidimensional targets are the same as in standard Gaussian process models. Furthermore, for ease of notations the targets for all of the N data points y^μ are collected into a vector $\mathbf{y} = (y^1, y^2, \ldots y^N)^T$. The same is done for all other relevant scalar quantities such as the indicators $\mathbf{s}$, etc. The quantities $\mathbf{f}_1$ and $\mathbf{f}_2$ denote the collections of values of each noise-free Gaussian process at all the points $\{\mathbf{x}^\mu\}$, and noise σ^2.

The Gaussian process mixture can be written as

$$P(\mathbf{y}|\{\mathbf{x}^\mu\}) = \sum_{\mathbf{s}} \int d\mathbf{f}_1 \; d\mathbf{f}_2 P(\mathbf{f}_1, \mathbf{f}_2, \mathbf{s}, \mathbf{y}|\{\mathbf{x}^\mu\}) \,, \tag{1.24}$$

where

$$P(\mathbf{f}_1, \mathbf{f}_2, \mathbf{s}, \mathbf{y}|\{\mathbf{x}^\mu\}) = P(\mathbf{f}_1|\{\mathbf{x}^\mu\})P(\mathbf{f}_2|\{\mathbf{x}^\mu\}) \times$$
$$\prod_\mu \frac{1}{\sqrt{2\pi\sigma^2}} \exp\left(-\frac{1}{2\sigma^2} \left[s^\mu(y^\mu - f^\mu)^2 + (1 - s^\mu)(y^\mu - f^\mu)^2\right]\right). \tag{1.25}$$

Note $P(\mathbf{f}_1|\{\mathbf{x}^\mu\})$ and $P(\mathbf{f}_2|\{\mathbf{x}^\mu\})$ are simply the prior Gaussian process regressors for the two sources.

By using a variational approximation of the form $Q(\mathbf{f}_1)Q(\mathbf{f}_2)\prod_\mu Q(s^\mu)$ and iteratively reducing the Kullback-Leibler (KL) divergence $KL(Q\|P)$ we obtain the following approximation procedure for an iterative solution of the covariate shift model. Here α_{st}^μ is used to denote the responsibility of mixture t of source s for point μ in the training set. The term $\alpha_s^\mu = \sum_t \alpha_{st}^\mu$ is the responsibility of source s for the point μ.

- Perform a standard Gaussian mixture model expectation maximization to initialize the responsibilities α_s^μ for each of the two sources.

- Iterate:

  □ Compute the pseudovariances σ^2/α_s^μ for each point and each source.

  □ Build the covariance C_1 for source 1 from the covariance of the Gaussian process, and an additive pseudonoise given by a matrix with the pseudovariances for source 1 down the diagonal.

  □ Do the same for source 2 to obtain C_2.

  □ Compute the mean predictions $(f_1^*)^\mu$ and $(f_2^*)^\mu$ at points $\{\mathbf{x}^\mu\}$ for Gaussian processes with training covariances C_1, and C_2, and prediction covariances given by the original covariance functions.

  □ Compute the parameter updates for the Gaussian processes using the usual hyperparameter optimizations, and the updates for the various mixture components using

$$\mathbf{m}_{st} = \frac{\sum_{\mu \in (D,T)} \alpha_{st}^{\mu} \mathbf{x}^{\mu}}{\sum_{\mu \in (D,T)} \alpha_{st}^{\mu}} \ , \ \mathbf{K}_{st} = \frac{\sum_{\mu \in (D,T)} \alpha_{st}^{\mu} (\mathbf{x}^{\mu} - \mathbf{m}_{st})(\mathbf{x}^{\mu} - \mathbf{m}_{st})^{T}}{\sum_{\mu \in (D,T)} \alpha_{st}^{\mu}} \ . \ (1.26)$$

▫ Compute the new responsibilities for each mixture, each source, and each data point using

$$\alpha_{st}^{\mu} = \frac{\beta_s \gamma_{st}^{D} P_{st}(\mathbf{x}^{\mu}|\mathbf{\Omega}) P(y^{\mu}|(f_s^*)^{\mu}, \sigma^2)}{\sum_{s,t} \beta_s \gamma_{st}^{D} P_{st}(\mathbf{x}^{\mu}|\mathbf{\Omega}) P(y^{\mu}|(f_s^*)^{\mu}, \sigma^2)} \text{ and } \alpha_{1t}^{\nu} = \frac{\gamma_{1t}^{T} P_{1t}(\mathbf{x}^{\mu}|\mathbf{\Omega})}{\sum_{t} \gamma_{1t}^{T} P_{1t}(\mathbf{x}^{\mu}|\mathbf{\Omega})}$$

$$(1.27)$$

$$\beta_s = \frac{1}{|D|} \sum_{\mu \in D, t} \alpha_{st}^{\mu} \ , \ \gamma_{st}^{D} = \frac{1}{|D|} \sum_{\mu \in D} \frac{\alpha_{st}^{\mu}}{\beta_s} \ , \ \gamma_{1t}^{T} = \frac{1}{|T|} \sum_{\nu \in T} \alpha_{1t}^{\nu} \ , \qquad (1.28)$$

where

$$P(y^{\mu}|(f_s^*)^{\mu}, \sigma^2) = \frac{1}{\sqrt{2\pi\sigma^2}} \exp\left(-\frac{1}{2\sigma^2}(y^{\mu} - (f_s^*)^{\mu})^2\right). \qquad (1.29)$$

■ Predict the result on the test data using the Gaussian process prediction with the covariance between data points given by C_1 and covariance between test and data given by the usual covariance function.

See Tresp [2001] for more details of this approach to Gaussian process mixtures. Intuitively, this process increases the noise term on data that is poorly explained by one of the mixtures. A datum with an increased noise term will have less influence on the overall Gaussian process regressor that is learned. This model is related to a mixture of experts model [Jacobs et al., 1991; Jordan and Jacobs, 1994], but where there is a coupling of the regression function between different mixtures and the covariate density itself is also modeled. A similar model was developed in Sung [2004], but only for linear regressors, and single Gaussian components per regressor. This model has the usual deficits associated with mixture models, including local minima issues, and the difficulties in deciding on a suitable number of mixtures. The infinite mixture of Gaussian process experts [Rasmussen and Ghahramani, 2002] is another mixture of experts model, but one that uses Gaussian processes and does not suffer from model size selection issues. However, it too does not have the distribution in covariate space (although this could be added to the model without major difficulties). The main issues of adapting this for use here are those of having to resort to Markov chain Monte Carlo methods rather than variational methods, and incorporating the match to the test dataset. These are surmountable issues. In the current context, a Bayesian information criterion method can be used [Storkey and Sugiyama, 2007] for selection of the number of mixtures, but it may not always work well as it is both approximate and a heuristic for latent variable problems. One other consequence of the model selection issue is that this implementation of the model may well perform more poorly than a straight Gaussian process in cases of no dataset shift. This issue is discussed more generally in the next section.

1.11 Shift or No Shift?

One big issue in all types of dataset shift is determining whether there is, in fact, any type of shift at all. It is possible that using a modeling method which can account for covariate shift may produce worse results than a standard model on data for which no shift occurs. This is first because introducing the possibility of shift allows for a large scope of possible representations that waters down the more concrete (but rigid) assumptions that presuming no shift makes. Second, the various methods used in modeling covariate shift may have their own deficiencies (such as local minima) that mean that they do not properly include the no-shift case: for a maximum likelihood solution may prefer to improve the likelihood by utilizing the freedom of the dataset shift model to overfit, even if presuming no shift would generalize better.

At this point, there are some real practicalities that should outweigh theoretical niceties. It may be interesting to consider how to determine whether covariate shift occurs on the basis of the training covariates, training targets, and test covariates alone. It may also be useful in making a choice about a limited number of models to consider. However, in many realistic scenarios (the main exceptions being single future prediction cases[3]), a practitioner would be negligent not to check a model in the actual environment in which it is being developed for before rolling out the use of the model. There must come a stage at which some test targets are obtained, and at which some assessment is done on the basis of those. Furthermore even a few test targets provide a large amount of information regarding dataset shift, in the same way that semisupervised learning can provide major benefits over unsupervised learning. It would also seem peculiar if a no-shift model was not one of the small basket of models considered at this stage, unless a particular form of dataset shift was guaranteed a priori. The major improvements available from a semisupervised approach in the test domain should never be neglected: targets in the test domain are very valuable information.

1.12 Dataset Shift and Transfer Learning

Dataset shift and transfer learning are closely related. Transfer learning considers the issue of how information can be taken from a number of only partially related training scenarios and used to provide better prediction in one of those scenarios than would be obtained from that scenario alone. Hence dataset shift consists of the case where there are only two scenarios, and one of those scenarios has no training targets. Multitask learning is also related. In multitask learning the response for a given input on a variety of tasks is obtained, and information between tasks is used

---

3. As an example, a pollster predicting election results has no recourse to the voting patterns of the population as a whole until it is too late.

to aid prediction. Multitask learning can be thought of a special case of transfer learning where there is some commonality in training covariates between tasks, and where the covariates have the same meaning across scenarios (hence domain shift is precluded).

There is recent work on utilizing Gaussian processes for multitask learning [Bonilla et al., 2007]. Unlike the methods developed here, this approach relies on having target data for all scenarios to help in relating them. Many approaches to document analysis (e.g., latent Dirichlet allocation [Blei et al., 2003] and many related techniques) are in fact methods for mixture component shift, applied to unsupervised problems in more general multidataset scenarios. The major advantage of having multiple datasets is that it is possible to characterize the differences between the datasets.

1.13   Conclusions

Modeling dataset shift is a challenging problem, but one with significant real-world consequence. The failures that arise from ignoring the possibility of dataset shift (e.g., sample selection bias) have been known for a long time. Furthermore, models that work well in static scenarios (such as the use of a conditional model) can fail in situations of shift. By characterizing the different forms of dataset shift, we can begin to get a handle on the ways the data can be expected to change. Though sample selection bias and imbalanced data have been studied for many decades as subjects in their own right, some common forms of shift, such as source component shift and domain shift, may also be worthy of further explicit study. Hopefully, by relating the different types of shift, more general methods will become available that can cope with a number of different forms of shift at the same time. Such methods may help automate the process of prediction even in the case of changing environments. The aim is to develop methods that are robust to, and automatically accommodate for, dataset shift.

One big question that should be considered is whether it is important to study dataset shift in its own right, or whether there is more to be gained by the general study of methods for learning transfer that could be directly applied to dataset shift. Though the basket of approaches in the two fields may well be similar, there are methods that will require either some test targets or multiple training domains to work, both of which may be unavailable in a standard dataset shift problem. One thing is certain though, study of dataset shift and transfer learning cannot be done in isolation of one another, and in a world of data abundance, it may well be worth asking whether a scenario with a single training dataset, as well as a single unlabeled test dataset, is really the best way of expressing a given problem.

2   Projection and Projectability

David Corfield

The problem of dataset shift can be viewed in the light of the more general problem of induction, in particular the question of what it is about some objects' features or properties which allow us to project correlations confidently to other times and places. We explore the varieties of background knowledge which philosophers have taken to warrant this confidence. Finally, we ask whether or not Bayesians have been inhibited by their need to encode such forms of background knowledge in the shape of probability distributions.

2.1   Introduction

Philosophers have not directly addressed the problems of *dataset shift* or *covariate shift*, but, as I shall argue, these problems are closely related to ones they have discussed. Indeed, much of the philosophical literature dealing with inductive reasoning has some bearing on these problems. For example, the "projection" of a regularity to times or places beyond those of the observed supporting instances involves a covariate shift when time or space is regarded as an independent variable.

What philosophers of science have found to be key in inductive reasoning is background knowledge. In the natural sciences this forms a highly complex web of practical and theoretic knowledge, and many have decided that little more than a qualitative description of plausible inference is possible. In the case of machine learning we still have to deal with background knowledge, or else we shouldn't be able to do any learning at all. However, this knowledge is typically simpler and thus more amenable to encoding in a learning algorithm. A point I shall consider in this chapter is whether Bayesians help or hinder themselves by requiring this knowledge to be construed in probabilistic terms.

In order to relate the thematic problem of this book to that of background knowledge, it will be convenient to establish what precisely is meant by the definition of dataset shift as a situation where the joint distribution of inputs and outputs differs between the training and test stages. What does it mean to say that the training data and test data come from a different distribution? In the first section we shall need to consider two words in this question – "data" and "distribution".

2.2   Data and Its Distributions

Despite its etymology, data is not just something given to us. Rather, it is the result of the framing and recording of some interaction with the world. Those famous handwritten digits of the MNIST dataset need not have been collected in the way they were. They never had to have been photographed, nor once photographed to be pixellated, nor if pixellated to be pixellated the way they were. Nor did they have to be centered or size-normalized. The time and place a digit was written, who wrote it, and the type of writing implement used need not have been forgotten. But for convenience, and in the hope that sufficient usable information was captured in the representation, decisions were taken to do so. It is important to remember that decisions of this kind do not take place in a vacuum. They arise on the basis of certain expectations and knowledge. We shall need to keep the existence of this background firmly in mind.

Now, given some data-collecting protocol, what does it mean to say that the vectors of chosen attributes of the entities of a sample come from a distribution, which may be compared to another distribution generating a different sample? Does this not presuppose some relatively stable random process, like a coin-tossing device whose settings don't change in important ways while a sample is generated? Could the MNIST dataset collection be viewed like this?

Consider the question I heard posed by Peter Grünwald as to whether we should take the writings of Tolstoy to be generated according to a probability distribution. Certainly we can use the apparatus of probability theory to model his writings, and perhaps to provide evidence whether or not some newly discovered work was written by him. We may choose to model *War and Peace* by a Markov chain of order two, then come to realize that one of order three is more accurate, but that little is gained by extending this to order four. But what does it mean to say we have the true distribution, or have come close to it?

Even those canonical coin toss samples are not viewed universally as the product of a random generating process. Certainly some prominent thinkers have had difficulty with the idea of randomness and probability distributions being out there in the world. Indeed, for people like Bruno de Finetti and Edwin Jaynes, there just is no randomness in the world, certainly not at the classical level; distributions are simply representations of our state of belief.

But de Finetti would need not have had to excuse himself politely from this book had he been asked to contribute. He could imagine himself in a situation where he would take each of the training data and test data individually as exchangeable sequences, but not both datasets taken together. Something we might seek, in his language, is a way to map these datasets such that the joint image dataset *is* exchangeable. I shall keep to the standard way of speaking throughout the chapter, as though distributions are things belonging to the world, bearing in mind that there are ways of rephrasing matters to keep the de Finettian happy.

2.3   Data Attributes and Projection

There are many reasons why training data might have a different distribution from test data. As I said in the previous section, the data has already been chosen to take on a specific form. Perhaps we included a variable which made no difference to the output, but in whose presence we detect covariate shift. It is possible then that with a better choice of variables, and a projection onto them, the shift would disappear.

Viewing matters the other way around, had a different choice been made and had we been less restrictive, what was not a case of dataset or covariate shift becomes one. In other words, if the term "input variable" were taken broadly enough, all learning confronts the problem of covariate shift, as we may consider in the case of, say, classification,

$$\Pr (\text{class} \mid \text{features, place of observation, time of observation,...}).$$

Sometimes it is obvious that some of the dimensions of the input space are irrelevant. Usually we ignore them without thinking about it. If we wish to model the running speed of individuals we may consider their age, height, and weight, but we typically won't think to count the number of whirls on the fingerprint of their left ring finger. But we can consider that already a projection has taken place onto the chosen set of input variables.

Leaving major projections of time and space to one side, imagine that on a digit recognition task I find the top left pixel doesn't matter to the classification. Yet the training data has 80% dark pixels in that position, while the test data has 20% dark pixels there. If the projected training distribution matches the projected test distribution, won't we proceed happily, unless we suspect a relevant reason for the incidence of this pixel's darkness?

Or, I want to predict people's preference for a film Y. In my training data I have an input distribution skewed to the extremes for the likes/dislikes of another film, X, but these are not found to be significant for the assessment of film Y. Now in the test data, many people are indifferent to film X. Do I confidently project out from that film preference feature?

Clearly our confidence must rely on background knowledge. Set the same problem, i.e., exactly the same numerical values, in an artificial setting with meaningless predicates, you will be much less confident. This must be due to prior beliefs about the length scales in such a direction, which could be encoded in an algorithm such as Gaussian process classification.

Dataset shift problems may come about from mistakenly ignoring some feature of the collection of data. Had we included this feature we would just have the covariate shift problem. Of course we will have to model this extra dimension somehow. If all we have is the extra tag of either being in the test sample or training sample, then if we devise a kernel which makes differently tagged members be seen as far apart in feature space, we won't be able to learn from the training data. If X is the input space and $P(X)$ differs for test and training samples, then we're looking to find a function $f : X \to X'$, such that the induced $P(X')$ is sufficiently similar for test and training data. But clearly the closeness of projected distributions is not sufficient for a projection to be counted as good, otherwise a mapping with X' a single point might qualify. We would also like $P(Y|X = x)$ to be reasonably uniform in the neighborhoods of training points with the same image in X'. Furthermore, we would need to control the class of such mappings, f, or, in other words, we would need to regularize the projection algorithm.

How much evidence we require to convince ourselves that we have a good projection naturally depends upon our prior expectations. And indeed in the whole process of inductive inference, background knowledge is vital. Even though I had never been to Canada before the 2006 conference on neural information processing systems, I had a good idea whether and when it mattered. I expected the snow to be like it is Europe, but the number of times per hour I heard "dude" to be different. Now the term philosophers have used for the activity of extending the domain of some observed regularity is precisely the same as the one I have been using, namely, *projection*. This is no mere coincidence.

2.4   The New Riddle of Induction

Nelson Goodman [1955] devised the "new riddle of induction" in the 1950s in the heyday of logical empiricism, when philosophers tried to formulate scientific reasoning with the resources of predicate logic and a Bayesian inductive logic. What he was challenging was a position that all could be achieved merely syntactically, that is, in terms of the logical form of the relevant statements. He famously presented the riddle by way of a paradox.

Grue Paradox   Suppose that at time t we have observed many emeralds to be green. We thus have evidence statements

emerald a is green,
emerald b is green,
etc.

and these statements support the generalization

All emeralds are green.

But now define the predicate "grue" to apply to all things observed before *t* just in the case that they are green, and to other things just in the case that they are blue. Then we have also the evidence statements

emerald *a* is grue,

emerald *b* is grue,

etc.

and these evidence statements support the hypothesis

All emeralds are grue.

Hence the same observations support incompatible hypotheses about emeralds to be observed for the first time in the future after *t*; that they will be green and that they will be blue. What is it about green, Goodman asks, which warrants our projecting it to as yet unobserved cases, which does not hold for grue?

One might hope to solve this paradox by pointing out that the definition of grue includes a time parameter, so is intrinsically more complicated syntactically. However, when we define green and blue in terms of grue and bleen, they appear equally complex:

"green" = "grue if observed before *t* and bleen if observed thereafter,"

"blue" = "bleen if observed before *t* and grue if observed thereafter."

Goodman's answer to the riddle was to say that the reason we confidently project green is that color terms are "entrenched" in our language and so "projectable" based on the success of their past projections. These terms have earned their right to be in our language through the service they have performed in the past. Perhaps, then, the very vocabulary we use is an encoding of a huge amount of background knowledge.

The roots of inductive inference are to be found in our use of language. A valid prediction is, admittedly, one that is in agreement with past regularities in what has been observed; but the difficulty has always been to say what constitutes such agreement. The suggestion I have been developing here is that such agreement with regularities in what has been observed is a function of our linguistic practices. Thus the line between valid and invalid predictions (or inductions or projections) is drawn upon the basis of how the world is and has been described and anticipated in words [Goodman, 1955, pp. 120–121].

Let's see if our intuitions accord with Goodman's. If I tell you that in a remote island, that thousands of "denkos" have been observed and all are "hesty" and "heslin," do you feel inclined to believe these?:

All denkos are hesty.

All denkos are heslin.

What if I tell you that "hesty" is a word in the local vocabulary, but that "heslin" is not, just being a concoction of "hesty" and "snublin"?

But the bare presence of concocted terms is not sufficient to rule out successful projection. If I define an "emeraphire" to be "either an emerald if observed before time t, and otherwise a sapphire", then we can form what we take to be the true general statement "All emeraphires are grue."

Goodman's grue example is sometimes mistakenly thought to be about objects changing color, when really the artificial predicate is creatively linking the color of an object to the time it is *first* observed. Of course on the subject of objects changing color, we do have background knowledge which will make us suspicious of projecting green in some situations.

All leaves observed this year are green

is a statement supported by observed green leaves in May, June, July, ..., but one we will not expect to hold in November. We don't have a single word to capture the color change from green to red or yellow, which at least could be useful; how less likely we would have a word for color-time of observation relations.

In the case of emeralds and color much more is at stake than the presence or absence of predicates in our language. It is the lack of conceivable connection between the time of first observation and the color which is at play. Our expectation that the projection of grue will fail derives from our background knowledge of mineralogy, optics, etc. In later writings, Goodman broadens the scope of his account:

Projection of "green" and familiar coordinate color predicates overrides introduction of novel color predicates like "grue." For "grue" cuts across our familiar categories and would require awkward revision of our practical and scientific vocabulary and our linguistic and cognitive practice [Goodman and Elgin, 1998, p. 14].

More than a matter of the mere appearance of a term in the vocabulary, we hope that it corresponds to a class of entities for which a deeper scientific knowledge is possible, perhaps of a mechanism acting behind the scenes. Philosophers have discussed this issue in terms of natural kinds and causes.

2.5   Natural Kinds and Causes

If I wander for the first time in a rainforest in Africa and see an animal whose fur is a strange color to me, with lengths of body parts never before seen, but I also note it is suckling its young, then I will already believe a huge amount about the animal's anatomy, physiology, and genetics:

Pr(anatomy, physiology, and genetics are mammalian | suckling young,
     place observed, time observed, length of body parts, color of fur)

is very high.

This plausibility has been made all the greater by our considerable background knowledge of evolutionary biology, plate tectonics, zoology, etc. We take this animal to be a member of a species, expecting similarities with animals of other species belonging to the same class, and more so to the same order or family. Other observed features typically won't feature. If all of the first 20 instances of this new species have a bald patch in their fur, we won't project this property too readily by taking it to be an attribute of the species, but rather imagine some local skin disease.

Now, animal species and mineral types are paradigmatic examples of what philosophers call *natural kinds*, categories of entities with modal implications. In other words, a member of a natural kind will necessarily have certain attributes. An emerald may *happen* to weigh 50 grams, but *necessarily* it is green. The revival of interest in natural kinds in the 1960s was seen as metaphysical by those of a more empiricist outlook, who had tried to reduce such notions to patterns of observation statements.

Natural kinds are generally treated in the context of causality. Consider the difference between these lawlike and accidental generalizations:

> All the coins in my pocket are silver.
> I can put a copper coin in my pocket.

> All emeralds are green.
> I cannot make a blue emerald.

So, our willingness to project to other emeralds is related to our inability to make them of a different color.

In recent years, the treatment of causality has been cast by Judea Pearl [2000] in terms of sparse Bayesian networks, and the "do" calculus, e.g., when $P(y|x) \neq P(y|do(x))$, then Y is causally dependent upon X. We suspect we have the causal picture right when we can represent it with many conditional independence relations. And when we suspect a causal relationship between a set of parent input variables and an output variable, we are more likely to believe that in novel situations our classifications will robustly transfer to new distributions of the nonparent variables.

It is worth noting that similar considerations occur outside the natural sciences, for example, in the noncausal world of mathematics. Pólya [1954] describes how Euler realized that the function $\frac{\sin x}{x}$ resembles a complex polynomial, and so expected it to factorize into linear factors as all complex polynomials do:

$$\frac{\sin x}{x} = \left(1 - \frac{x}{\pi}\right)\left(1 - \frac{x}{4\pi}\right)\left(1 - \frac{x}{9\pi}\right)\cdots$$

This allowed him to derive the correct result $\sum \frac{1}{n^2} = \frac{\pi^2}{6}$.

Now, why can this analysis not be applied to $\frac{\tan x}{x}$? Which properties "cause" or are "responsible" for factorization in the case of complex polynomials but only some nonpolynomial functions. It turns out that we can project away from the condition that the number of zeros of the function be finite, but not from the condition that there be no pole (infinite value). Pólya spoke of a "hope for a common ground" between analogous results over different domains, in this case the fact that $\frac{\sin x}{x}$ is what is called an entire function, having no pole over the complex plane.

In the rest of the book he develops a large number of Bayesian principles in the context of mathematics [Corfield, 2003, chap. 5], but these are written in loose terms such as

> If A is analogous to B,
> <u>and A is found to be true,</u>
> then B is somewhat more likely.

Deeper research into the history of scientific and mathematical practice revealed a far more complex picture of language dynamics and scientific progress. Indeed, Thomas Kuhn used his study of the shifting meaning of a word like "mass" as paradigms change to argue against Bayesian reconstructions of scientific inductive reasoning, charging them that they presupposed language stability, when we know that words radically change their meaning through revolutions. Imre Lakatos made similar points to Kuhn about science, and criticized Pólya's inductive account of mathematics, stressing the importance of changes in our concepts.

But perhaps this is taking us too far from the humbler tasks of machine learning. While there is much we might learn from the philosophy of science literature, we might say that machine learning presents us with the problem of modeling domains with limited information and in stable theoretical settings. We're often not looking to devise an algorithm to help us break out of some conceptual confines. We don't want a groundbreaking new theory about the evolution of the digits; we just want a good classifier. Still we require background knowledge, but in many problems this is much simpler, and perhaps amenable to formalization. This raises the following questions: Have machine learning theorists been sufficiently creative in their efforts to encode background knowledge? Have frequentists been more imaginative, or less constrained by a probabilistic framework?

2.6   Machine Learning

We need to find ways to encode background knowledge to allow the transfer of inferential steps, and perhaps even schemes to allow us to find what is common between two situations. Examples of encoding background knowledge to date might seem to favor the frequentists as the more imaginative:

Cluster Assumption   We can expect that the input variables of data points bearing the same label will lie close to one another. Imagine a dataset consisting of two interspersed crescent shapes. One point in crescent 1 is labeled red, one in crescent 2 is labeled blue. Intuitively you think to color each crescent the same as its labeled member. But if you relied only on the labeled data, commonly used algorithms would just drive a classifying line through the perpendicular bisector of the line joining them. To use the unlabeled data you must feed in an assumption that points with the same label will tend to cluster. Frequentists used this assumption to devise certain semisupervised learning algorithms. Lawrence and Jordan [2005] recently added the notion of the null category to the Gaussian process framework to the same end for the Bayesians.

Invariance under Small Changes   We can expect small translations, rotations, and thinning or thickening of lines of images of numbers to represent the same number. Frequentists got here first by finding support vectors, then forming *virtual* support vectors by making slight modifications to the originals [Decoste and Schölkopf, 2002]. This was copied in the Gaussian process setting in Lawrence et al. [2005].

Robustness under Adversarial Deletion   We may expect that informative inputs are robust enough that even if an adversary does its best to put us off with a given number of feature deletions, we'll still be able to classify (see chapter 10 in this book). It would be a bad symbol system if the removal of a single pixel from the image of a letter made it look like another. On the other hand, not many auditory features of "nineteen" need be removed before it sounds like "ninety", and letters are notoriously hard to hear over the telephone, such as "F" and "S."

Structural Correspondence   Sentences taken from a medical journal may be very different from sentences taken from the *Wall Street Journal*, but still we may expect that words close to certain "pivots" will be the same parts of speech [Blitzer et al., 2006]. So a word appearing after "a" and before "required by" will most likely be a noun in both financial and medical contexts. If we have tagged a large corpus of financial text, then an algorithm which has learned to classify these tags well on the basis of the selected pivots should continue to work well on untagged medical texts. Generalization guarantees relating to this structural correspondence learning can be given.

In all four cases we have frequentists making the running. In the first two cases it was possible for Bayesians later to give their own versions, although in the case of invariance under small changes it would be preferable to encode this knowledge in the kernel. The last two cases are too recent to have been imitated. Where frequentists might point to what they consider to be the unnecessary restrictiveness of having to encode knowledge via probability distributions, there is little evidence to suggest that any of their ideas escape possible probabilistic representation. A small test of this thesis would be to Bayesianize "robustness under adversarial deletion" and "structural correspondence."

Synthesizing some responses, made at the workshop and by one of the editors, to the charge of lack of imagination, perhaps it is because the frequentists are forced to look for novel means of addressing each new situation that they exploit background knowledge more inventively. The Bayesian may view these efforts as somewhat ad hoc, and prefer to devote his or her time to working out mathematically more elegant models believed to apply over a wider range of learning situations, but perhaps there is something to be said for extracting whatever a specific situation has to offer. After all, as suggested earlier, learning in the natural sciences, a very successful form of learning, is unthinkable without reliance on a vast range of disparate knowledge which is particular to the case in hand. General problem-solving strategies seem to be avoided.

2.7   Conclusion

I have argued throughout this chapter that the *dataset shift* and *covariate shift* problems can usefully be viewed as part of the general problem of inductive inference. Finding the relevant variables in a given situation already captures much of what is necessary to transfer observed regularities to new domains, or new parts of input space. The theme of this book raises the interesting question of how to encode further refined background knowledge to allow the accurate transfer of learning to take place. To do so in too domain-specific a way risks too much human involvement. We would prefer not to have to hand code background knowledge for each new situation. Ideally, we would even be able to learn the relevant invariances using general purpose algorithms.

The philosophy of science literature could well provide a useful resource for machine learning practitioners. Although typically large amounts of intricate background knowledge are at stake in episodes of scientific inference, some simpler aspects may be encodable in learning algorithms. It will be interesting to follow the future course of research in this area. Will hand-coded measures continue to win out, or will researchers find principled methods to learn and encode invariances? Will frequentist thinking continue to lead the way, or will Bayesians forge forward with their probabilistic machinery?

Acknowledgments

I would like to thank Bernhard Schölkopf and the Max Planck Gesellschaft for giving me the opportunity to carry out the research recorded in this chapter, and to the editors of the book for inviting me to contribute.

II Theoretical Views on Dataset and Covariate Shift

3   Binary Classification under Sample Selection Bias

Matthias Hein

The problem of general sample selection bias is studied from a decision-theoretic perspective in the case of binary classification. We show necessary and sufficient conditions for the equivalence of the Bayes classifiers of training and test distribution and give bounds for the excess risk if they disagree. Moreover, we show without any assumptions on the type of sample selection bias that the knowledge about unlabeled data allows one to identify regions where the sign of the regression functions of training and test is guaranteed to coincide. In the second part we use the insights gained from the theoretical analysis. We provide a nonparametric framework for learning under general sample selection bias motivated by a modified cluster assumption. The connection to semisupervised learning is discussed. Further, we present experimental results for datasets with explicit control of the selection bias.

3.1   Introduction

In econometrics and sociology it is widely accepted that often the sample one uses for learning or estimation comes from a different distribution than the one used in testing. In the machine learning community only very recently has this problem been discussed [Zadrozny, 2004; Smith and Elkan, 2004]. The reason for this might be that one can argue that sample selection bias only occurs due to a bad choice of the training set. We agree that this can be the reason for sample selection bias, but there are problems where even the most careful choice of the training set would not prevent sample selection bias. One example is the prediction of the income of people based on a questionnaire. Usually, the richer people are, the less likely they are to answer such a questionnaire. Clearly the prediction based on the data of the questionnaire will be biased toward low income. Another case is when we have only training data from some proportion of the test population. This occurs if a bank wants to predict if someone who is applying for a loan will eventually repay it. The credit bank has only data from customers whose loan has been approved. This set of customers will be generally a biased sample of the whole population or the set of potential customers.

In the machine learning literature so far the main emphasis has been laid on a special kind of sample selection bias, the so-called covariate shift [Shimodaira, 2000; Sugiyama and Müller, 2005a; Huang et al., 2007], where the conditional distribution $p(y|x)$ of training and test distribution is the same. For the general sample selection bias problem several parametric models have been proposed in the econometrics literature; see e.g., Heckman [1979]; Winship and Mare [1992]; Dubin and Rivers [1989]. In this chapter we study the general scenario of sample selection bias; in particular we derive necessary and sufficient conditions for the equivalence of the Bayes classifiers of training and test distributions. Moreover, we analyze the situation where one has access to an unlabeled sample of the test distribution which can be either a part of the training data which has not been labeled or an independent sample of the marginal test distribution. A similar approach with the goal of identifying the possible range of probability measures responsible for the training data without making any prior assumptions on the sampling process has been studied by Manski and Horowitz [Manski, 1989; Horowitz and Manski, 2006].

Originating from this analysis we propose a new nonparametric principle to deal with sample selection bias in the case where one has access to unlabeled test data. The setting where one has unlabeled test data is similar to semisupervised learning (SSL). However, in semisupervised learning one assumes that training and test data come from the same distribution. We show that implementing the new principle via adaptive regularization leads to an algorithm which is similar to existing ones for semisupervised learning [Zhu et al., 2003a; Zhou et al., 2004]. Whereas the performance is similar when training and test data come from the same distribution, the new algorithm performs better in cases where also the conditional distribution changes. Therefore this algorithm can also be seen as an extension of semisupervised learning which is robust to sample selection bias.

3.2 Model for Sample Selection Bias

In this chapter we consider binary classification. Our goal is to learn a classifier $f : \mathcal{X} \to \mathcal{Y}$, where $\mathcal{X}$ and $\mathcal{Y}$ are the input and output domain. For binary classification we have $\mathcal{Y} = \{-1, +1\}$. We assume that there exists a (stationary) distribution P on $\mathcal{X} \times \mathcal{Y}$, the true distribution of X and Y. However, we are only given a biased sample. This can be formally described using a random binary selection variable s, where $s = 1$ means that we accept the point for the training sample and $s = 0$ means that we will not observe it in the training phase. Of interest is how $p(y|x, s = 1)$, the conditional distribution of the training sample, behaves with respect to the true conditional distribution $p(y|x)$.

We always assume in the following that both probability measures P_{tr} and P_{te} have densities p_{tr} and p_{te} with respect to some dominating measure, e.g., if $\mathcal{X} = \mathbb{R}^d$

we take as the dominating measure the Lebesgue measure. Thus we avoid an overly technical presentation. However, the results still hold in the general case.

In order to keep the presentation as clear as possible we will keep the explicit dependency on the selection variable s. We give the following dictionary to be consistent with the notation in the rest of the book.

$$\text{training distribution} \qquad p_{\text{tr}}(y, x) = p(y, x | s = 1)$$
$$\text{test distribution} \qquad p_{\text{te}}(y, x) = p(y, x)$$

We further assume in the following that the sampling of training and test data is done i.i.d. from $p(y, x | s = 1)$ and $p(y, x)$ respectively.

A central role will be played by $p(s = 1 | x, y)$, that is, the probability that a given joint pair (x, y) is observed in the training sample. The following relationships can be derived by straightforward application of the Bayes rule,

$$p(y | x, s = 1) = \frac{p(y | x) p(s = 1 | x, y)}{p(s = 1 | +, x) p(+|x) + p(s = 1 | -, x) p(-|x)},$$
$$p(x | s = 1) = \frac{p(s = 1 | x, +) p(+, x) + p(s = 1 | x, -) p(-, x)}{\int_X p(s = 1 | x, +) p(+, x) + p(s = 1 | x, -) p(-, x) \, dx}, \qquad (3.1)$$

where we have introduced the shorthand notation $+$ and $-$ for $y = 1$ and $y = -1$, e.g., $p(+, x)$ for $p(y = 1, x)$ and $p(-, x)$ for $p(y = -1, x)$. Since we can estimate $p(y | x, s = 1)$ and $p(x | s = 1)$ from the training data, it is more interesting to express the quantities of the test data in terms of the training data.

$$p(y | x) = \frac{p(y | x, s = 1) p(x | s = 1) p(s = 1) + p(y | x, s = 0) p(x | s = 0) p(s = 0)}{p(x | s = 1) p(s = 1) + p(x | s = 0) p(s = 0)}$$
$$= \frac{p(s = 1 | x)}{p(s = 1 | y, x)} p(y | x, s = 1)$$
$$p(x) = p(x | s = 0) p(s = 0) + p(x | s = 1) p(s = 1) = \frac{p(s = 1)}{p(s = 1 | x)} p(x | s = 1). \qquad (3.2)$$

Using these relations one can characterize different special cases of sample selection bias.

Random Selection   This is the case we usually assume to be true in standard binary classification. The selection is completely random, that is, independent of x and y. This implies $p(s = 1 | y, x) = p(s = 1)$. Obviously we have in this case $p(y | x, s = 1) = p(y | x)$ and $p(x | s = 1) = p(x)$ so that the distributions of training and test data are identical.

Class-Conditional Independent Selection   In this case the selection is independent of the class label y given the feature x or equivalently given x the knowledge of the selection variable s gives no information about the class label y. Due to this property this scenario is sometimes called "missing at random (MAR)". We have

$$p(s|x,y) = p(s|x) \iff p(y|x,s) = p(y|x).$$

The conditional probabilities of training and test data agree and therefore also the Bayes classifiers of training and test data. However, the marginal distribution of the training data is in general different,

$$p(x|s=1) = \frac{p(s=1|x)p(x)}{\int_X p(s=1|x)p(x)\,dx}.$$

Sometimes this scenario is also called *covariate shift*; see Shimodaira [2000], and Sugiyama and Müller [2005a]. Note that the support of the training data has to be contained in the support of the test data. Under covariate shift we can trust the labels we are given, but the true/test marginal distribution is different from the training distribution. In this case often reweighting of the loss function is done in order to get an unbiased estimate of true loss; see, e.g., Manski [1977], and Shimodaira [2000]; Huang et al. [2007]. We will come back to this issue in a later section.

Class-Dependent Selection   In this case the selection variable s is independent of the feature x given the label y,

$$p(s|x,y) = p(s|y) \iff p(x|y,s) = p(x|y).$$

This means that the class-conditional distributions stay the same. However, the class probabilities $p(y|s=1)$ and $p(y)$ of training and test data differ and thus the class-conditional probabilities $p(y|x,s=1)$ and $p(y|x)$ are different as well. In particular one has

$$p(y|s=1) = \frac{p(s=1|y)p(y)}{p(s=1|+)p(+) + p(s=1|-)p(-)},$$
$$p(y|x,s=1) = \frac{p(s=1|y)p(y|x)}{p(s=1|+)p(+|x) + p(s=1|-)p(-|x)}.$$

Having knowledge about $p(s=1|y)$ or equivalently the true class probabilities $p(y)$ one can easily correct for the modification of $p(y|x,s=1)$. Namely by setting $p(+|x) = p(-|x) = \frac{1}{2}$ we observe that the threshold for a Bayes optimal decision with respect to the test distribution is given by

$$\gamma = \frac{p(s=1|+)}{p(s=1|+) + p(s=1|-)},$$

that is, we decide for $+$ if $p(+|x,s=1) > \gamma$ and for $-$ otherwise. This problem is closely related to cost-sensitive learning; see Elkan [2001]. Suppose that $c_{-1,1}$ denotes the cost of predicting the positive class when the negative is true and $c_{1,-1}$ the corresponding opposite cost. It is then easy to show that the Bayes optimal threshold γ, that is, one predicts $+$ if $p(+|x) > \gamma$, is given by

$$\gamma = \frac{c_{-1,1}}{c_{-1,1} + c_{1,-1}}.$$

We observe that both expressions are equal if we identify $c_{-1,1} = p(s = 1|+)$ and $c_{1,-1} = p(s = 1|-)$. Thus the costs tell us how we should change the training distribution such that for the test distribution we can decide with the normal threshold $\frac{1}{2}$.

Note that in practice one often artificially balances the classes for training in order to get a better estimate of the decision boundary, in particular if the classes are very unbalanced. The process of balancing can be equivalently seen as a class-dependent selection. However, the correction for this simple form of sample selection bias is straightforward using the modified threshold which we introduced above.

The General Case Sample selection bias is a very general model for differing training and test distributions. In these paragraphs, we will analyze conditions on the probability measures P_{tr} and P_{te} such that P_{tr} can be seen as selected from P_{te}. Not all different training and test distributions can be modeled in such a way. The first basic requirement is the *support condition*: the support of the probability measure of the training data has to be a subset of the support of the probability measure of the test data.

Suppose that the support condition holds and we are given the densities of the joint measures $p_{tr}(y, x)$ and $p_{te}(y, x)$ of training and test distribution. Does there exist a sampling mechanism such that one can see p_{tr} as $p_{tr}(y, x) = p(y, x|s = 1)$ and $p_{te}(y, x) = p(y, x)$? We can check this using

$$p(y, x) = p(y, x|s = 0)p(s = 0) + p(y, x|s = 1)p(s = 1).$$

The part $p(y, x|s = 0)p(s = 0)$ can be modeled arbitrarily. We are searching for a nontrivial solution with $p(s = 1) > 0$. For every $(y, x) \in \mathcal{Y} \times \mathcal{X}$, we require

$$p(y, x) - p(s = 1)p(y, x|s = 1) \geq 0.$$

Thus the *selection condition*, a necessary and sufficient requirement that p_{tr} can be seen as generated by selecting from p_{te}, can be stated as

$$\sup_{(y,x)\in\mathcal{Y}\times\mathcal{X}} \frac{p_{tr}(y, x)}{p_{te}(y, x)} < \infty,$$

where we are slightly sloppy regarding the supremum.[1] If the above condition holds, then we can model P_{tr} as being selected from P_{te}. The probability of selection

---

1. The support condition can be equivalently formulated that for any measurable set A it holds $P_{te}(A) = 0 \Rightarrow P_{tr}(A) = 0$. Thus P_{tr} is absolutely continuous with respect to P_{te} which implies by the Radon-Nikodym theorem that there exists a density $f \in L_1(\mathcal{X})$ such that $P_{tr}(A) = \int_A f \, dP_{te}$. Then the selection condition is given by, $\|f\|_\infty < \infty$.

$p(s=1)$ is upper-bounded as $p(s=1) \leq \inf_{y,x} \frac{p_{\text{te}}(y,x)}{p_{\text{tr}}(y,x)}$.

Note that the support condition already rules out some cases. Namely $p_{\text{tr}}(y|x) > 0$ is not possible if $p_{\text{te}}(y|x) = 0$. Secondly, suppose $\mathcal{X} = \mathbb{R}^d$ and both measures have a marginal density with respect to the Lebesgue measure. Then the selection condition rules out cases where $p_{\text{te}}(x) = 0$ and $p_{\text{tr}}(x) > 0$. But also the tails of training and test distribution have to be well behaved. Suppose both have a Gaussian density with different means but equal covariance. Then the quotient $\frac{p_{\text{tr}}(x)}{p_{\text{te}}(x)}$ cannot be upper-bounded on $\mathbb{R}^d$. On the positive side one can make the following statement.

Lemma 3.1 *Let $\mathcal{X}$ be a compact subset of $\mathbb{R}^d$ and suppose the probability measures P_{tr} and P_{te} have continuous marginal densities with respect to the Lebesgue measure. Let further the support condition hold. If $p_{\text{te}}(x) > 0$ for all $x \in \mathcal{X}$ and $\sup_{x \in \mathcal{X}} \max_{y \in \{-1,1\}} \frac{p_{\text{tr}}(y|x)}{p_{\text{te}}(y|x)} < \infty$, then P_{tr} and P_{te} can be modeled in the sample selection framework.*

Proof: We decompose the selection condition into

$$\sup_{(y,x) \in Y \times \mathcal{X}} \frac{p_{\text{tr}}(y,x)}{p_{\text{te}}(y,x)} \leq \sup_{x \in \mathcal{X}} \frac{p_{\text{tr}}(x)}{p_{\text{te}}(x)} \sup_{x \in \mathcal{X}} \max_{y \in \{-1,1\}} \frac{p_{\text{tr}}(y|x)}{p_{\text{te}}(y|x)}.$$

The first supremum is finite since both $p_{\text{tr}}(x)$ and $p_{\text{te}}(x)$ are continuous and therefore both achieve their maximum and minimum due to compactness of $\mathcal{X}$ with $\inf_x p_{\text{te}}(x) > 0$ by assumption. The second supremum is finite by assumption. Let us finally discuss the situation where the supports of training and test distribution differ. There are in principle two situations. If the training distribution has probability mass on a set where the test distribution has not, then the information about this set is completely useless for learning on the remaining test set without making assumptions on the relation of training and test distribution. For us this means that we can safely discard this information and instead work with the probability measure $P_{\text{tr}}\Big(y, x | x \in \text{supp}\,(P_{\text{te}})\Big)$, where supp (P_{te}) is the support of the test distribution. On the other hand, if the test distribution has probability mass where the training distribution has not, then we cannot hope to make any useful predictions on this portion of the test distribution without any further assumptions on how training and test data have been generated. The support condition seems therefore not to be too restrictive.

3.3   Necessary and Sufficient Conditions for the Equivalence of the Bayes Classifier

The essential element for classification is the conditional distribution $p(y|x)$ We have seen in the previous section that in the case of covariate shift one has $p(y|x, s = 1) = p(y|x)$. The goal of this section is to analyze the general case of sample selection bias. In particular, we are interested under which conditions the Bayes classifier of training and test data agree. Since this is a much weaker condition than equivalence of the conditional distribution $p(y|x)$, this is usually said to be the reason why classification is easier than regression. Moreover, we give an exact expression of the excess error of the Bayes classifier of the training distribution compared to the error of the Bayes classifier of the test distribution. This will allow us to characterize cases where sample selection bias does not matter substantially.

We define the regression functions η_{tr} and η_{te} and the Bayes classifiers b_{tr} of b_{te} of the training and test distribution as

$$\eta_{\mathrm{tr}}(x) = 2p(+|x, s = 1) - 1, \qquad\qquad \eta_{\mathrm{te}}(x) = 2p(+|x) - 1,$$
$$b_{\mathrm{tr}}(x) = \mathrm{sign}\,\eta_{\mathrm{tr}}(x) \qquad\qquad\qquad b_{\mathrm{te}}(x) = \mathrm{sign}\,\eta_{\mathrm{te}}(x).$$

A necessary and sufficient condition that the Bayes classifiers agree is

$$\eta_{\mathrm{tr}}(x)\,\eta_{\mathrm{te}}(x) \ge 0, \quad \forall\, x \in X.$$

Using essentially (3.2) one can then derive necessary and sufficient conditions for the equivalence of the Bayes classifiers of training and test distribution. We give all results in terms of quantities related to the training distribution since this is the distribution we have access to. The statement about equivalence will depend on the *selection index*, which measures the amount of bias in the labels at a given point.

Definition 3.2 *The **selection index** $s(x) : X \to [-1, 1]$ is defined as*

$$s(x) = \frac{p(s = 1|+, x) - p(s = 1|-, x)}{p(s = 1|+, x) + p(s = 1|-, x)}.$$

The following theorem will state the equivalence of the Bayes classifiers in terms of the selection index.

Theorem 3.3 *Let $p(s = 1|y, x) > 0$ for all $x \in X$ and $y \in \{-1, 1\}$. The regression function of the test data η_{te} can be expressed as*

$$\eta_{\mathrm{te}}(x) = \frac{\eta_{\mathrm{tr}}(x) - s(x)}{1 - s(x)\eta_{\mathrm{tr}}(x)}.$$

The Bayes classifiers b_{te} and b_{tr} of test and training distribution agree at x if and only if

$$\left|\eta_{\mathrm{tr}}(x)\right| \ge \mathrm{sign}\Big(\eta_{\mathrm{tr}}(x)\Big)\,s(x).$$

Moreover the risk of the Bayes classifier b_{tr} of the training distribution $p(y, x|s = 1)$ with respect to the test distribution $p(y, x)$ is given as

$$R(b_{\mathrm{tr}}) = R(b_{\mathrm{te}}) + \int_{\{x \mid |\eta_{\mathrm{tr}}(x)| < \mathrm{sign}(\eta_{\mathrm{tr}}(x))\, s(x)\}} \left|\frac{\eta_{\mathrm{tr}}(x) - s(x)}{1 - s(x)\eta_{\mathrm{tr}}(x)}\right| p_{\mathrm{te}}(x)\, dx.$$

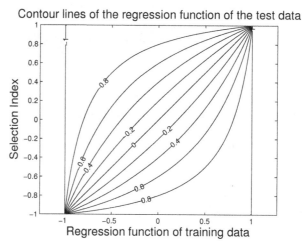

Figure 3.1 Contour lines of η_{te} in dependency of the selection index $s(x)$ and the regression function of the training data.

Proof: Using $p(+|x) = p(+|x, s = 1)\frac{p(s=1|x)}{p(s=1|+,x)}$ we arrive after a straightforward calculation at

$$p(+|x) = \frac{p(+|x, s = 1)p(s = 1|-, x)}{p(s = 1|+, x) - p(+|x, s = 1)[p(s = 1|+, x) - p(s = 1|-, x)]}.$$

Using now $p(+|x) = \frac{\eta_{\text{te}}(x)+1}{2}$ and $p(+|x, s = 1) = \frac{\eta_{\text{tr}}(x)+1}{2}$ we get the result

$$\eta_{\text{te}}(x) = \frac{\eta_{\text{tr}}(x) - s(x)}{1 - s(x)\eta_{\text{tr}}(x)}.$$

Equivalence of the Bayes classifiers is given if $\eta_{\text{tr}}(x)\eta_{\text{te}}(x) \geq 0$ for all $x \in \mathcal{X}$. Since $s(x) \in [-1, 1]$, we have $s(x)\eta_{\text{tr}}(x) \leq 1$ and thus,

$$\eta_{\text{tr}}(x)\eta_{\text{te}}(x) \geq 0 \quad \Leftrightarrow \quad \eta_{\text{tr}}(x)^2 \geq \eta_{\text{tr}}(x)s(x),$$

which gives the desired result. Finally, the risk $R(f)$ of a function $f : \mathcal{X} \to \{-1, +1\}$ with respect to the test distribution is given as

$$R(f) = R(b_{\text{te}}) + \mathbf{E}_X \left[I_{f(X)\eta_{\text{te}}(X)<0}|\eta_{\text{te}}(X)| \right].$$

Note that $\eta_{\text{tr}}(x)\eta_{\text{te}}(x) < 0$ is equivalent to $b_{\text{tr}}(x)\eta_{\text{te}}(x) < 0$. Plugging in $b_{\text{tr}}(x)$ for the function f and the expressions for η_{te} and $\eta_{\text{tr}}(x)\eta_{\text{te}}(x) < 0$ finishes the proof.

The interpretation of theorem 3.3 is not straightforward. From the form of the regression function η_{te} of the test distribution it becomes clear that $s(x)$ quantifies the amount of bias in the labels. If $s(x) \to \pm 1$ (we do not allow $s(x) = \pm 1$), then the training data is maximally biased. If $s(x)$ is positive, one has a bias toward the positive class and vice versa. Figure 3.1 shows the dependency of η_{te} on the selection index $s(x)$ and the regression function of the training data. Two statements can be made. We have $p(+|x) = p(+|x, s = 1)$ or equivalently $\eta_{\text{tr}}(x) = \eta_{\text{te}}(x)$ if and only if the selection index $s(x)$ is zero, that is, $p(s = 1|+, x) = p(s = 1|-, x)$. This is the special case of sample selection bias often called covariate shift, where the labels are missing at random. However, this is a much stronger condition then the derived condition for the equivalence of the Bayes classifiers. There, as one could have expected, we only need that the selection index $s(x)$ is zero at the decision boundary defined as $\{x \in \mathcal{X} \mid p(y|x) = \frac{1}{2}\}$. Away from the decision boundary one can allow for nonzero values of the selection index $s(x)$, that is, $p(s = 1|+, x) \neq p(s = 1|-, x)$. In the "easy" regions where the training distribution is noise-free, that is, $\eta_{\mathrm{tr}}(x) = \pm 1$, all nonzero values for $p(s = 1|y, x)$ are allowed. However, note that, e.g., $\eta_{\mathrm{tr}}(x) = 1 \Leftrightarrow p(+|x, s = 1) = 1$ is only equivalent to $p(+|x) = 1$ if $p(s = 1|-, x) > 0$. In general, if $p(s = 1|+, x) = 0$ or $p(s = 1|-, x) = 0$, then no statements about the conditional test distribution $p(y|x)$ can be made using knowledge about the conditional training distribution $p(y|x, s = 1)$.

If one has upper and lower bounds on $p(s = 1|y, x)$, one can derive the following corollary which gives an easier bound on the excess risk $R(b_{\mathrm{tr}}) - R(b_{\mathrm{te}})$ than theorem 3.3.

Corollary 3.4 *Assume* $|s(x)| \leq \delta$ *for all* $x \in X$. *Then the Bayes classifiers* b_{te} *and* b_{tr} *agree at* x *if* $|\eta_{\mathrm{tr}}| \geq \mathrm{sign}\Big(\eta_{\mathrm{tr}}(x)\Big)\delta$. *The risk of the Bayes classifier of the training distribution* b_{tr} *with respect to the test distribution can be upper-bounded as*

$$R(b_{\mathrm{tr}}) \leq R(b_{\mathrm{te}}) + \delta \, \mathrm{P}_{\mathrm{te}}\Big(|\eta_{\mathrm{tr}}| < \delta\Big) .$$

Proof: The Bayes classifier b_{tr} makes an error if $|\eta_{\mathrm{tr}}| \geq \mathrm{sign}\Big(\eta_{\mathrm{tr}}(x)\Big)\delta$. Suppose $\eta_{\mathrm{tr}}(x) > 0$, then an error happens if $\eta_{\mathrm{tr}}(x) < s(x)$ and $s(x) > 0$. We have $|\eta_{\mathrm{te}}(x)| = \frac{s(x) - \eta_{\mathrm{tr}}(x)}{1 - s(x)\eta_{\mathrm{tr}}(x)}$. A straightforward analysis shows that $|\eta_{\mathrm{te}}(x)|$ is monotonically decreasing with increasing $\eta_{\mathrm{tr}}(x)$. Therefore the maximum of $|\eta_{\mathrm{te}}(x)|$ is attained at $\eta_{\mathrm{tr}}(x) = 0$ and its value is δ. The same bound can be derived for the other case, which finishes the proof.

This corollary has a nice and easy interpretation. If the sampling process is not too nasty, that is, δ is small, and the probability mass of the test distribution around the decision boundary of the training distribution is small, then using the Bayes classifier of the training distribution is not much worse than the Bayes classifier of the test distribution.

One can also tackle the problem from a different direction. Similar to cost-sensitive learning the optimal decision threshold under sample selection bias for $p(y|x, s = 1)$ with respect to the test distribution will in general not be $\frac{1}{2}$. In other words one can also define a new threshold function which leads then to an optimal decision with respect to the test distribution but *not* with respect to the training distribution. This can be done through knowledge about $p(s = 1|y, x)$.

Theorem 3.5 *Define the threshold function*

$$\mathrm{Thresh}(x) = \frac{2\,p(s=1|+,x)}{p(s=1|+,x) + p(s=1|-,x)},$$

and the new regression function $\overline{\eta}_{\mathrm{tr}}$ of the training distribution as

$$\overline{\eta}_{\mathrm{tr}}(x) = 2p(+|x,s=1) - \mathrm{Thresh}(x).$$

If $p(s=1|y,x) > 0$, $\forall x \in \mathcal{X}$, then the new Bayes classifier $\overline{b}_{\mathrm{tr}}(x) = \mathrm{sign}\,\overline{\eta}_{\mathrm{tr}}(x)$ of the training distribution and the Bayes classifier of the test distribution $b_{\mathrm{te}}(x)$ agree for all $x \in \mathcal{X}$.

Proof: Set $p(+|x) = p(-|x) = \frac{1}{2}$ in (3.1), then one has $p(+|x,s=1) = \mathrm{Thresh}(x)$. Of course given only information about the training distribution there is no way to get any information about $p(s=1|y,x)$. But this result indicates how one can improve the performance under sample selection bias if more information about the sampling mechanism is available.

3.4   Bounding the Selection Index via Unlabeled Data

In the last section we indicated how bounds on the selection index can help to identify parts of the regression function η_{te}. By identification we mean that given complete knowledge about $p(y|x,s=1)$ we can at least be sure about the sign of the regression function η_{te} of the test distribution in some regions and thus predict the correct label. The process of so-called partial identification of probability measures has been pioneered by [Manski, 1989] and Horowitz [Horowitz and Manski, 2006].

In this section we will analyze the value of unlabeled data in order to determine bounds on the selection index. We will distinguish two situations. In the first one we assume that we know $p(y,x|s=1)$ and we are given the marginal density $p(x)$ of the test distribution. Both quantities can be estimated consistently from a training sample $(X^{\mathrm{tr}}, Y^{\mathrm{tr}})$ and an independent unlabeled test sample X^{te}. In the second one we know $p(y|x,s=1)$, the marginal density $p(x|s=0)$ of the sample points which have not been selected to be labeled and the probability $p(s=1)$ of being selected. This corresponds to a setting where we have an unlabeled sample $\{X_i^{\mathrm{te}}\}_{i=1,\dots,T}$ of size T and then a subset of size S is being selected to be labeled yielding the training sample of labeled data $\{(X_j^{\mathrm{tr}}, Y_j^{\mathrm{tr}})\}_{j=1,\dots,S}$ and a set of unlabeled data $\{X_i\}_{i=S+1,\dots,T}$ where we assume without loss of generality that the data has been reordered after the selection. Note that $p(s=1)$ can then be estimated via the ration S/T.

This distinction seems at first to be rather artificial. We illustrate both cases with an example. The first one corresponds, e.g., to a test study of a new medical treatment. There one has information about the patients who decided to participate in the study. But usually no information is stored about the patients who refused to take part in the study. However, one might know the distribution of people where this medical treatment is supposed to be applied. This could be either the whole population or a certain subset. The second case, where one has unlabeled data, is usually more generic. Assume a credit bank wants to assess how well their selection of customers works out. Potential customers are all persons who applied for a loan in the bank. The bank has labeled data of the customers who have been given a credit and they also have data about the customers who did not get one.

We see that both cases can occur in practice. In the second case one has the probability of selection $p(s = 1)$ as an important additional piece of information. We will see that without this information the knowledge about the marginal density $p(x)$ does not help to gain information about the selection index. However, given that we know $p(s = 1)$ also in the first case, then both cases are completely equivalent. This can be easily seen from

$$p(x) = p(x|s = 0)p(s = 0) + p(x|s = 1)p(s = 1),$$

where knowledge about $p(x|s = 1)$, $p(x)$ and $p(s = 1)$ identifies $p(x|s = 0)$ and vice versa. The following lemma restricts the selection index using information about $p(x)$ and $p(s = 1)$.

Lemma 3.6 *The selection index $s(x)$ can be bounded as*

$$\text{sign}(\eta_{\text{tr}}(x))s(x) \geq \frac{1 - p(s = 1|x)}{p(s = 1|x)}.$$

Thus the Bayes classifier of training and test data agree at $x \in \mathcal{X}$, if

$$|\eta_{\text{tr}}(x)| \geq \frac{1 - p(s = 1|x)}{p(s = 1|x)}.$$

Proof: One can decompose

$$p(s = 1|x) = p(s = 1|+, x)p(+|x) + p(s = 1|-, x)p(-|x).$$

Thus with $\lambda = p(+|x)$ we get $p(s = 1|+, x) = \frac{1}{\lambda}[p(s = 1|x) - (1 - \lambda)p(s = 1|-, x)]$ and plugging this into the expression for the selection index we can lower-bound $s(x)$ for $\lambda \geq \frac{1}{2}$ as

$$s(x) = \frac{p(s = 1|x) - p(s = 1|-, x)}{p(s = 1|x) - (1 - 2\lambda)p(s = 1|-, x)} \geq \frac{p(s = 1|x) - p(s = 1|-, x)}{p(s = 1|x)}$$
$$\geq \frac{p(s = 1|x) - 1}{p(s = 1|x)}.$$

Therefore, for $\eta_{\text{te}} > 0$ the selection bias toward negative labels is lower-bounded by $\frac{p(s=1|x)-1}{p(s=1|x)}$. Thus, if $\eta_{\text{tr}} < 0$ and $\eta_{\text{tr}} < \frac{p(s=1|x)-1}{p(s=1|x)}$, then we can be sure that also $\eta_{\text{te}} < 0$. The other direction follows by considering the case $\eta_{\text{te}} < 0$.

The second assertion follows directly from theorem 3.3. However, the following proof is quite instructive. We have

$$p(+|x) = p(+|x, s = 0)p(s = 0|x) + p(+|x, s = 1)p(s = 1|x).$$

In particular,

$$p(+|x, s = 1)p(s = 1|x) \le p(+|x) \le 1 - p(s = 1|x) + p(+|x, s = 1)p(s = 1|x).$$

Thus, given that $p(+|x, s = 1) \ge \frac{1}{2}$, we have to ensure that $p(+|x) \ge \frac{1}{2}$, which using the inequality holds if $p(+|x, s = 1) \ge \frac{1}{2\,p(s=1|x)}$ or equivalently $\eta_{\mathrm{tr}}(x) \ge \frac{1-p(s=1|x)}{p(s=1|x)}$. The other direction can be done similarly.

Note that $p(s = 1|x) = \frac{p(x|s=1)}{p(x)}p(s = 1)$ and therefore the quantity in the lower bound can be computed using the available knowledge about the marginal test density and the selection probability. Further, note that the bound is only nontrivial given that $p(s = 1|x) < \frac{1}{2}$. At a first glance, it might seem odd why the bound for the selection index has this strange form. This has a simple explanation. If $\eta_{\mathrm{te}}(x) > 0$ and we have positive selection bias, then clearly $\eta_{\mathrm{tr}}(x) > 0$ and vice versa. Therefore the selection index needs only be bounded with respect to the label of the training data, e.g., if $\eta_{\mathrm{tr}}(x) > 0$, then it could be that $\eta_{\mathrm{te}} < 0$ and we have a positive selection bias. Thus only an upper bound on the positive selection bias is required.

Lemma 3.6 shows that using unlabeled data we can be sure about our estimated function wherever $|\eta_{\mathrm{tr}}|$ is sufficiently large. This result holds without making any assumption on the form of the selection. Unfortunately, the bound is only nontrivial if $p(s = 1|x) < \frac{1}{2}$ or equivalently $p(x) < 2\,p(x|s = 1)p(s = 1)$. This condition holds in regions where the marginal test density is rather small with respect to the marginal training density. Thus the total mass of the test distribution of the region where this condition holds might be quite small.

3.5 Classifiers of Small and Large Capacity

Until now we have analyzed how the Bayes optimal classifiers of training and test data are related. In this section we will discuss the difference of classifiers of small and large capacity in the case of sample selection bias. The first statement is an easy corollary of theorem 3.3. Let us first recall the definition of a Bayes consistent classifier.

Definition 3.7 *A **Bayes or universally consistent classifier** is a sequence of classifiers f_n for which for every $\epsilon > 0$ and every probability measure on $\mathcal{X} \times \mathcal{Y}$,*

$$\lim_{n \to \infty} \mathrm{P}(R(f_n) - R(b) > \epsilon) = 0,$$

where n denotes the sample size, f_n is the selected classifier for a sample of size n, and b is the Bayes classifier.

Corollary 3.8 *Let $p(s = 1|y, x) > 0$ for all $x \in \mathcal{X}$ and $y \in \{-1, 1\}$. Any Bayes consistent classifier trained on the biased sample is also Bayes consistent for the*

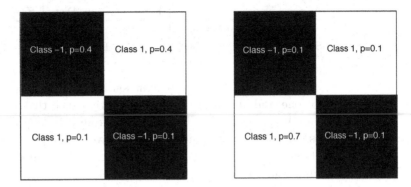

Figure 3.2 The checkerboard data as an example of covariate shift. *Left:* the training distribution. *Right:* the test distribution. Each square is sampled uniformly. The probability of each square is denoted by p.

test distribution if and only if

$$\forall x \in \mathcal{X}, \quad \left| \eta_{\text{tr}}(x) \right| \geq \text{sign}\left(\eta_{\text{tr}}(x) \right) s(x). \tag{3.3}$$

Formulating this (almost) trivial corollary in simple terms: at least in the asymptotic regime it does not matter if we train our classifier with the biased sample or the unbiased sample if condition (3.3) holds. The only criterion we have to fulfill is that we use a Bayes consistent classifier. For several classifiers Bayes consistency has been shown, e.g., K nearest-neighbors (KNN)-classifiers [Devroye et al., 1996] or the support vector machine (SVM) with a Gaussian kernel [Steinwart, 2002] and many more results are known. A Bayes consistent classifier has asymptotically maximal capacity because in the limit as the sample size goes to infinity any target function can be learned.

For the moment we assume that the Bayes classifiers of training and test distribution are equal, e.g., as in the covariate shift problem. What happens now if one uses a classifier of smaller capacity? A simple example shows that classifiers of small capacity can perform arbitrarily badly even if the conditional distribution of training and test data agrees. As a classifier of large capacity we take the SVM with a Gaussian kernel and for the one with small capacity the SVM with a linear kernel. We use the checkerboard data illustrated in figure 3.2. The sample selection bias is in this case just a covariate shift between training and test distribution. Since it is noise-free, the optimal Bayes error is zero in that case. We test the learned classifier once on samples drawn from the training distribution and once on samples from the test distribution. Table 3.1 shows the mean errors together with the standard deviation over 20 runs for 200 training points. The test error of the SVM with Gaussian kernel increases significantly but the performance is still reasonable. The results of the linear SVM are hopeless. The linear SVM is significantly worse than

Table 3.1   The mean error over 20 runs of the training and test data for the checkerboard data of figure 3.2 for an SVM with linear and Gaussian kernel with 200 data points.

	Error on Train. Dist.	Error on Test. Dist.
SVM with linear kernel	28.8 ± 8.1	72.4 ± 17.0
SVM with Gaussian kernel	5.3 ± 2.6	7.9 ± 4.5

random guessing. Such a phenomenon is also known as *anti-learning*. It is obvious that one could modify the test distribution such that the error of the linear SVM would be even worse. It becomes clear from this simple experiment that classifiers of small capacity are much more sensitive to sample selection bias than classifiers of large capacity. This can also seen directly by comparing the loss with respect to training and test distribution:

$$\text{Training dist.}: \quad \mathbf{E}_{\text{tr}}\left[l(f(X), Y)\right] = \int_X p(x|s = 1) \int_Y l(f(x), y)\, p(y|x, s = 1)\, dy\, dx,$$

$$\text{Test dist.}: \quad \mathbf{E}_{\text{te}}\left[l(f(X), Y)\right] = \int_X p(x) \int_Y l(f(x), y)\, p(y|x)\, dy\, dx,$$

A classifier of large capacity can fit the function (almost) pointwise and therefore only the term $\int_Y l(f(x), y)\, p(y|x, s = 1)\, dy$ matters. If we assume that the Bayes classifiers of training and test distribution agree then minimization of this part will lead in both cases to the same value of f at x. The weighting with $p(x|s = 1)$ or $p(x)$ does not then matter anymore for determining the optimal function. A classifier of small capacity can only fit a limited amount of data and pointwise minimization is not possible. Therefore one has to minimize $\mathbf{E}_{\text{tr}}\left[l(f(X), Y)\right]$ globally. In that case it matters a lot how the errors are weighted and therefore the weighting with $p(x|s = 1)$ instead of $p(x)$ can lead to huge differences in the minimizer. In particular, for classifiers of small capacity it is therefore very important to reweight the loss with $g(x) = \frac{p(x)}{p(x|s=1)}$ given that one has information about the marginal test distribution $p(x)$:

$$\frac{1}{n}\sum_{i=1}^{n} l(f(X_i), Y_i) \quad \longrightarrow \quad \frac{1}{n}\sum_{i=1}^{n} l(f(X_i), Y_i)g(X_i).$$

For classifiers of large capacity the reweighting is (asymptotically) neither improving the results nor does it harm if one has covariate shift as sample selection bias. See Shimodaira [2000]; Zadrozny [2004]; Sugiyama and Müller [2005a], and chapters 6, 7, 8, and 9 in this book for more on reweighting. For the SVM using different kernels one has to distinguish between kernels which lead to Bayes consistency and those which do not. In this respect the statement of Zadrozny [2004] that linear SVMs are asymptotically affected by sample selection bias can be sharpened to that SVMs are asymptotically affected by sample selection bias even if the Bayes classifiers agree if one is not using a kernel which leads to a Bayes consistent classifier.

Up to now we dealt with the special case of covariate shift. In the case of general sample selection bias it is not clear if reweighting is a good strategy. Note that we know from lemma 3.6 the larger $p(s = 1|x) = \frac{p(x|s=1)}{p(x)}p(s = 1)$ the more we are sure that $\text{sign}(\eta_{\text{tr}}(x)) = \text{sign}(\eta_{\text{te}}(x))$. However, the reweighting factor $g(x) = \frac{p(x)}{p(x|s=1)}$ is reciprocal to $p(s = 1|x)$ which means that by reweighting one downweights the regions of $\mathcal{X}$ where one is sure that $\text{sign}(\eta_{\text{tr}}(x)) = \text{sign}(\eta_{\text{te}}(x))$. On the other hand, one increases the weight of regions where one does not know if the signs of η_{tr} and η_{te} agree. It remains a point for future work to resolve this apparent contradiction.

3.6   A Nonparametric Framework for General Sample Selection Bias Using Adaptive Regularization

Basically we have seen in the last sections that without further assumptions on the nature of the sample selection bias there is no way to find the correct sign of $\eta_{\text{te}}(x)$. Using unlabeled data from the test distribution and information about the selection probability we could show that in regions where $|\eta_{\text{tr}}(x)| > \frac{1-p(s=1|x)}{p(s=1|x)}$ we can be sure that $\text{sign}(\eta_{\text{tr}}(x)) = \text{sign}(\eta_{\text{te}}(x))$. In order to make any assertions about the remaining regions we have to make assumptions how the selection bias was generated. The existing approaches for the general case of sample selection bias make explicit parametric assumptions on the relationship between training and test distribution, e.g., the bivariate probit model of Heckman [Heckman, 1979] or other more general models [Dubin and Rivers, 1989]. It is often questionable if these assumptions hold in real data. A natural assumption should be one which is general enough to be true for a large class of datasets. In this remaining part we propose a nonparametric principle to deal with general sample selection bias under the assumption that one has a sample of unlabeled data from the test distribution and eventually knows the selection probability $p(s = 1)$. Both assumptions are fulfilled in the traditional setting of sample selection bias; see section 3.4 for a discussion. The main underlying principle will be a modified cluster assumption. The cluster assumption has been proposed in semisupervised learning and can be formulated as follows.

Cluster assumption Two points which can be connected by a path through high-density regions are likely to have the same label.

In semisupervised learning one usually assumes that labeled and unlabeled data come from the same distribution. In the case of sample selection bias it makes only sense to use the cluster structure of the unlabeled data from the test distribution. Therefore we modify slightly the cluster assumption of SSL

Modified Cluster assumption Two points which can be connected by a path through high-density regions *of the test data* are likely to have the same label.

We think that the modified cluster assumption is quite natural and holds for a large class of datasets.

The other important question is which part of the labels of the training data we should use. In principle, we know by lemma 3.6 that without any assumptions we can only trust the sign of the regression function of the training distribution if $|\eta_{\text{tr}}(x)|$ exceeds a certain threshold. This implies that in the worst case we should not use any information on Y of the training data in regions where $|\eta_{\mathrm{tr}}(x)|$ is below the threshold. On the other hand, if one has random selection or the labels are missing at random, then we have $p(y|x, s = 1) = p(y|x)$ and it would not be reasonable to discard any label information. Both ways can be integrated into the learning framework using different weights in the loss function.

As learning framework we will use regularized empirical risk minimization,

$$f_n = \underset{f \in \mathcal{F}}{\arg\min} \frac{1}{n} \sum_{i=1}^{n} l(f(X_i), Y_i) \, \gamma(X_i) + \mu \, \Omega(f),$$

where $\Omega : \mathcal{F} \to \mathbb{R}_+$ denotes the regularization functional, l the loss function, and $\gamma : \mathcal{X} \to \mathbb{R}_+$ a weighting function. In order to implement the modified cluster assumption we need a regularizer Ω which enforces the cluster structure in the *test* data, that is, it should prefer functions which are almost constant on the clusters and are allowed to change in between. A similar regularization principle is used in SSL, where one uses unlabeled data to build graph-based regularizers which adapt to the cluster structure of training *and* test data; see Bousquet et al. [2004]. We will show that the adaptation to the cluster structure of the test data leads to a modification of an existing learning algorithm for SSL. Our experiments indicate that this modification leads to robustness against sample selection bias.

3.6.1 Adaptive Graph-Based Regularization

Our input space $\mathcal{X}$ will be in the following always a compact subset of the d-dimensional Euclidean space $\mathbb{R}^d$. A regularizer which implements the cluster assumption for SSL where training and test distribution are equal can be built using a graph based on *training* and *test* data; see Bousquet et al. [2004] and Hein [2006].

- Take the sample of test and training data $\{X_i\}_{i=1}^n$ as the set of vertices.
- Edge weight $w(X_i, X_j) = \frac{1}{h^d} k(\|X_i - X_j\| / h)$ if $\|X_i - X_j\| \le h$, otherwise no edge, where $k : \mathbb{R}_+ \to \mathbb{R}_+$ is the kernel function, $h > 0$ is the neighborhood parameter of the resulting graph, and d the dimension of the input space.

The data-dependent graph-based regularization functional is then defined as

$$\tilde{S}_{n,h,\lambda}(f) = \frac{1}{2n^2 \, h^2} \sum_{i,j=1}^{n} \frac{w(X_i, X_j)}{(d(X_i)d(U_j))^\lambda} (f(X_i) - f(X_j))^2,$$

where $d(X_i) = \frac{1}{n} \sum_{j=1}^{n} w(X_i, X_j)$ is the degree function. The parameter $\lambda > 0$ controls the influence of the density as can be seen from the following theorem.

Theorem 3.9 *[Hein, 2006] Let $\{X_i\}_{i=1}^n$ be an i.i.d. sample of a probability measure* P *on a compact set $\mathcal{X} \subset \mathbb{R}^d$. If $f \in C^3(\mathcal{X})$ and $h \to 0$ and $nh^d / \log n \to \infty$, then almost surely*

$$\lim_{n \to \infty} \tilde{S}_{h,n,\lambda}(f) = \frac{C_2}{2C_1^\lambda} \int_{\mathcal{X}} \|\nabla f\|^2 \, p(x)^{2-2\lambda} \, dx,$$

where C_1, C_2 are constants depending on the kernel function k and the dimension d.

This theorem has been strengthened to uniform convergence over the class of Hölder functions on $\mathcal{X}$ and still holds when the data lies on a low-dimensional submanifold M; see Hein [2006]. Since $\|\nabla f\|$ is weighted by the density, this functional is only small if the function varies only very little in high-density regions, whereas variations in low-density regions are hardly penalized. However, in our setting it cannot be applied directly since training and test data are not from the same distribution. In order to implement the cluster structure of the *test* data we need the density of the test data in the limit functional. One can achieve this via reweighting of the regularization functional $\tilde{S}_{n,h,\lambda}(f)$. For simplicity we set $\lambda = 0$ in the following. But the results can be generalized to all values of λ. We have the following setting:

- $\{X_i^{\text{tr}}\}_{i=1}^n$ from the training distribution $p(x|s=1)$,
- $\{X_j^{\text{te}}\}_{j=1}^m$ from the test distribution $p(x)$.
- concatenated sample
$U = \{X_1^{\text{tr}}, \ldots, X_n^{\text{tr}}, X_1^{\text{te}}, \ldots, X_m^{\text{te}}\}, l = n + m.$

Then we define two kernel density estimators based on $\{X_i^{\text{tr}}\}_{i=1}^n$ and $\{X_i^{\text{te}}\}_{i=1}^m$,

- $d_{X^{\text{tr}}}(x) = \frac{1}{n\,h_n^d} \sum_{i=1}^n k\big(\|x - X_i\| / h_n \big),$
- $d_{X^{\text{te}}}(x) = \frac{1}{m\,h_m^d} \sum_{i=1}^m k\big(\|x - Z_i\| / h_m \big),$

where h_m and h_n are the bandwidth of the kernel density estimators. One can use alternatively any other (consistent) density estimator. An estimate[2] of the reweighting function $g(x) = \frac{p(x)}{p(x|s=1)}$ can be computed as $\hat{g}(x) = \frac{d_{X^{\text{te}}}(x)}{d_{X^{\text{tr}}}(x)}$ on the training points. We define

$$\phi(U_i) = \begin{cases} \hat{g}(U_i) & , \quad \text{if} \quad i \leq n, \quad \text{training points} \\ 1 & , \quad i > n, \qquad \text{test points.} \end{cases}$$

Moreover, we define the adaptive regularization functional which implements the modified cluster assumption as

$$S_{l,h}(f) = \frac{1}{2l^2\,h^2} \sum_{i,j=1}^{l} w_{ij}\, \phi(U_i)\, \phi(U_j)\, (f(U_i) - f(U_j))^2,$$

where the weights $w_{ij} = w(U_i, U_j)$ are defined as before with a common scaling function h.

Theorem 3.10 *Let $\mathcal{X} \subset \mathbb{R}^d$ be compact and f, $p(x)$, $p(x|s = 1) \in C^3(\mathcal{X})$. Furthermore, let $p(x)$ and $p(x|s = 1)$ be lower-bounded and $p(x|s = 1)$ be absolutely*

---

2. Estimates of a certain function g will be denoted by $\hat{g}$.

continuous with respect to $p(x)$, then if

$$n \text{ finite, } m \to \infty, \ h_m \to 0 \ \text{such that } mh_m^d \to \infty \ \text{and } l \, h^d \to \infty,$$

or

$$n \to \infty, \ h_n \to 0 \ \text{such that } nh_n^d / \log n \to \infty,$$
$$m \to \infty, \ h_m \to 0 \ \text{such that } mh_m^d / \log m \to \infty,$$
$$\text{and } h = \max\{h_n, h_m\},$$

it holds almost surely,

$$\lim_{l \to \infty} S_{h,l}(f) = \frac{C_2}{2} \int_{\mathcal{X}} \|\nabla f\|^2 \, p(x)^2 \, dx,$$

where C_2 are constants depending on the kernel function k.

Proof: We sketch the proof which is similar to Hein [2006]. First, one shows that $\hat{g}(U_i)$ and $g(U_i)$ are close with high probability. Furthermore the functional $S_{l,h}(f)$ can be decomposed in two one-sample U-statistics and one two-sample U-statistic. Then one uses Bernstein-type large deviation inequalities for U-statistics to show the convergence.

3.6.2   The Learning Problem

We have shown that the adaptive regularization functional $S_{l,h}(f)$ adapts to the cluster structure of the test data as desired. Similar to existing SSL algorithms (see Zhou et al. [2004]) we formulate now the learning problem as a regularized least squares problem:

$$F = \arg\min_{f \in \mathbb{R}^l} \sum_{i=1}^n (f(X_i) - Y_i)^2 \hat{\gamma}(X_i) + \mu \, S_{l,h}(f), \qquad (3.4)$$

where we reweight the loss with different functions $\hat{\gamma}$. In the functional $S_{l,h}(f)$ we use weights of the form

$$w'(U_i, U_j) = \begin{cases} 0 & , \text{ if } \ i, j \leq n, \\ w(U_i, U_j) & , \text{ otherwise.} \end{cases}$$

The solution of this regularized least squares problem can be computed as the solution of the linear system

$$(\hat{\Gamma} + \mu \, \Delta'_l) F = \hat{\Gamma} Y,$$

where $\Delta'_l = D' - W'$ is the graph Laplacian of the graph with weights $w'(U_i, U_j)$ and degree function $d'(U_i) = \sum_{j=1}^l w'(U_i, U_j)$. D' and $\hat{\Gamma}$ denote the diagonal matrices with the functions d', $\hat{\gamma}$ on the diagonal. Note that we have merged the remaining factors of n, l, and h in $S_{l,h}(f)$ into the regularization constant μ.

Three different weighting functions $\hat{\gamma}$ will be used in the loss function in the following.

- *Standard (SL):* $\hat{\gamma}(x) = 1$, standard least squares loss.

- *Reweighting I (RL1):* $\hat{\gamma}(x) = \hat{g}(x)$, if the sample selection type is random or the labels are misssing at random, this reweighting leads to an unbiased estimate of the true loss.

- *Reweighting II (RL2):* Let $\hat{f}$ be a classifier only based on the training data. Then we define for $c > 0$,

$$\hat{\gamma}(X_i) = \begin{cases} \hat{g}(X_i) & , \text{ if } \quad |\hat{f}(X_i)| \geq c \, \frac{\hat{g}(X_i) - p(s=1)}{p(s=1)}, \\ 0 & , \text{ otherwise} \end{cases} \quad .$$

Note that $\frac{\frac{p(x)}{p(x|s=1)} - p(s=1)}{p(s=1)} = \frac{1 - p(s=1|x)}{p(s=1|x)}$. The last weighting function is motivated by lemma 3.6 and only keeps the labels which are not potentially misleading. As a classifier $\hat{f}$ for the training data we use the SVM with a Gaussian kernel and the squared hinge loss since the minimizer of the squared hinge loss is given by the regression function

$$\eta_{\text{tr}} = \arg\min_{f} \mathbf{E}_{P_{\text{tr}}}\left[\max\{0, 1 - Y f(X)\}^2\right].$$

3.6.3   Difference from Semisupervised Learning

The algorithm in (3.4) looks very similar to existing SSL algorithms. However, there is a fundamental difference between SSL and our framework. Namely, in SSL one assumes that training and test data come from the same distribution. A large class of SSL algorithms transfer the labels to the unlabeled points by propagating them along the data, thereby using manifold and cluster structure of the data. Since training and test data come from the same distribution, the cluster structure obviously coincides for training and test data. However, under sample selection bias this assumption need not hold. In general the cluster structure of training and test data will be different. Therefore under sample selection bias only the cluster structure of the *test* data should be used in order to propagate the labels. Therefore we have set in the proposed algorithm the adjacency matrix between the training points to zero. Thereby we ensure that label information only propagates along the test data. We would like to emphasize that the change of the adjacency matrix does not affect the limit of the regularization functional stated in theorem 3.10.

The change of the adjacency matrix mainly makes a difference if the number of training points is larger or at least on the scale of the number of test points. In this case the proposed algorithm can also be seen as a robust extension of SSL in the sense that the algorithm is robust to small differences between test and training distribution and performs as good as standard SSL when training and test distribution are equal. In the extreme case of SSL where one has only a few labeled points but lots of unlabeled ones, the difference between both approaches is negligible, since it is then likely that a labeled point is only connected to unlabeled points. We refer to Chawla and Karakoulas [2005] for further discussion of the relation of SSL and learning under sample selection bias.

3.7   Experiments

We have done experiments on a specific toy dataset, where different types of sample selection bias could be easily simulated. We compare all combinations of the different losses, SL, RL1 and RL2, and standard and reweighted regularization functionals, $\tilde{S}(f)$ and $S(f)$, respectively abbreviated as SR and AR. The combination $SL + SR$ is very similar to existing SSL algorithms; see Zhu et al. [2003a] and Zhou et al. [2004].

In all experiments we use a symmetric kNN-graph with $k = \{5, 10, 20, 40\}$ and Gaussian weights, where the σ of the Gaussian is chosen as the average kNN-distance. The parameters h_n and h_m for the kernel density estimation are set as the average kNN-distance [3] for $k_n = \log(n) + 10$ and $k_m = \log(m) + 10$. For the regularization parameter μ we use $\log_{10} \mu = \{-4, -2, 0, 2, 4\}$. The best parameters are found by cross-validation. In order to be consistent with the loss we use for learning, we use for the cross-validation the same loss, that is, SL, $RL1$, or $RL2$. In all experiments the total number of training and test points is fixed to 1000. All experiments are repeated 20 times. For numerical stability and to limit the influence of outliers we cut off the estimate of $\hat{g}$ used in $RL1$ and $RL2$ at 10 and 0.1. For the weighting function γ of the loss $RL2$ we need to determine the classifier $\hat{f}$ and the constant c. The classifier $\hat{f}$ is an SVM with squared hinge loss where we set the error parameter C to $C = 10$ in all experiments. We use the implementation described in Chapelle [2007]. The parameter c is determined in the following way. We choose the largest c such that at least half of the labels of the positive and negative class are used. Here we have a certain trade-off between keeping labeled data and discarding it in regions where we do not trust the labels.

In all experiments the test distribution is the same. The test class conditional distributions are two two-dimensional Gaussians of isotropic variance $\sigma = 0.6$. The means are at $(-1, 0)$ and $(1, 0)$. The class probabilities are equal, that is, $p(+) = p(-) = 0.5$. The distribution is shown in figure 3.3. We will always explore the two scenarios of unlabeled data discussed in section 3.4.

■ Unlabeled data type 1: As training data we have a sample from $p(y, x | s = 1)$. As unlabeled data we are given an independent sample of the marginal test density $p(x)$.

■ Unlabeled data type 2: We are given a sample of the marginal test density $p(x)$. Some of them are selected to be labeled via $p(s = 1 | x)$ and the labels are drawn

---

3. This choice for h_n and h_m satisfies the condition of theorem 3.10 since the kNN-distance R_k is prop. to $\left(\frac{k}{n}\right)^{\frac{1}{d}}$.

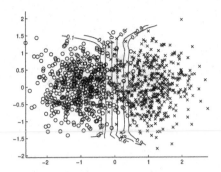

Figure 3.3 A sample of 5000 points of the test distribution with contour lines of $p(+|x)$.

Table 3.2 Results for the random selection shift

Unlabeled 1	SL+SR	RL1+SR	RL2+SR	SL+AR	RL1 +AR	RL2 + AR
Min. test err.	4.1 ± 0.7	4.1 ± 0.8	4.1 ± 0.7	4.1 ± 0.8	4.1 ± 0.8	4.1 ± 0.7
Error from CV	4.4 ± 0.8	4.4 ± 0.8	4.7 ± 0.9	4.5 ± 0.8	4.5 ± 0.8	4.7 ± 1.0
Unlabeled 2	SL+SR	RL1+SR	RL2+SR	SL+AR	RL1 +AR	RL2 + AR
Min. test err.	4.3 ± 1.0	4.3 ± 1.0	4.4 ± 1.1	4.3 ± 0.9	4.3 ± 1.0	4.4 ± 1.1
Error from CV	4.9 ± 1.1	4.8 ± 1.0	4.9 ± 1.1	4.9 ± 1.1	4.9 ± 1.0	5.0 ± 1.1

from $p(y|x, s = 1)$. This will be the training set. The rest of the sample, which was not selected, will be the unlabeled data. It has distribution $p(y, x|s = 0)$. The marginal test density is estimated in this case with all the samples.

We will always report results for both cases. The amount of unlabeled data of type 1 is chosen such that the amount of training and test data is equal for both cases. Moreover, apart from the test error for the parameters chosen by cross-validation on the training set, we also report the minimal test error over all parameters. This is done in order to check if model selection works by cross-validation. We will see in the case of general sample selection bias that this is not the case.

3.7.1 Random Selection

This is the ideal learning scenario. Test and training data come from the same distribution. Here, using the losses SL and $RL1$ and the regularization SR and AR should not make any difference except that with RL and AR we expect more variance since the estimation of $\hat{g}(x) = \frac{d_{X^{\text{te}}}(x)}{d_{X^{\text{tr}}}(x)}$ is noisy. Our experimental results verify this fact. Astonishingly, also using the loss $RL2$ does not lead to a significant reduction of performance despite the fact that we discard up to 50% of the labels. The reason is possibly that this dataset has a cluster structure and therefore our

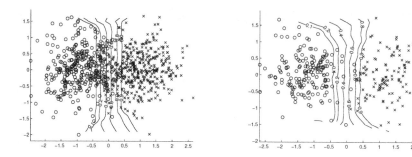

Figure 3.4 Covariate shift. *Left:* The training set of the covariate shift data drawn from $p(y, x|s = 1)$. *Right:* The set of unlabeled points of type 2. Both plots show also the contour lines of $p(y|x, s = 1)$ and $p(y|x, s = 0)$ respectively (the differences come from interpolation in Matlab).

Table 3.3 Results for the covariate shift

Unlabeled 1	SL+SR	RL1+SR	RL2+SR	SL+AR	RL1 +AR	RL2 + AR
Min. est err.	**4.7 ± 0.9**	**4.7 ± 0.8**	5.0 ± 0.9	**4.7 ± 0.9**	**4.7 ± 0.8**	4.9 ± 0.8
Error from CV	**5.3 ± 0.9**	5.4 ± 1.1	5.7 ± 1.0	5.4 ± 0.9	5.4 ± 0.8	5.6 ± 1.1
Unlabeled 2	SL+SR	RL1+SR	RL2+SR	SL+AR	RL1 +AR	RL2 + AR
Min. test err.	**6.1 ± 1.1**	6.2 ± 1.1	6.5 ± 1.2	6.2 ± 1.0	**6.1 ± 1.0**	6.4 ± 1.2
Error from CV	6.8 ± 1.3	6.9 ± 1.4	7.2 ± 1.2	**6.7 ± 1.1**	**6.7 ± 1.1**	7.1 ± 1.2

SSL-type algorithm performs well even with only a small number of labeled points (table 3.2).

3.7.2   Covariate Shift

In this scenario the conditional distributions of training and test data agree: $p(y|x, s = 1) = p(y|x)$. However, the marginal distribution $p(x|s = 1)$ and $p(x)$ differ. The selection probability $p(s = 1|x)$ has the form

$$p(s = 1|x) = \begin{cases} \frac{8}{10} \frac{|x_1|}{1+|x_1|} & \text{, if } \quad x_1 < 0, \\ \frac{5}{10} \frac{|x_1|}{1+|x_1|} & \text{, otherwise.} \end{cases}$$

This form of selection implies that only a small number of points are sampled in the region of the decision boundary. Moreover, we sample more points of the red class than of the blue class; see figure 3.4. This corresponds to a scenario where the training set was generated by only selecting cases where the label is obvious and where one has more samples of one class than the other one, despite in the test case both classes occur equally often.

Table 3.4 Results for general sample selection bias.

Unlabeled 1	SL+SR	RL1+SR	RL2+SR	SL+AR	RL1 +AR	RL2 + AR
Min. Test Err.	5.0 ± 0.8	5.2 ± 0.9	4.9 ± 0.7	5.0 ± 0.8	5.0 ± 0.9	$\mathbf{4.8 \pm 0.8}$
Error from CV	7.3 ± 2.0	7.4 ± 1.7	6.4 ± 3.8	7.6 ± 1.8	7.5 ± 1.6	$\mathbf{5.3 \pm 0.8}$
Unlabeled 2	SL+SR	RL1+SR	RL2+SR	SL+AR	RL1 +AR	RL2 + AR
Min. Test Err.	5.7 ± 1.4	5.8 ± 1.3	5.6 ± 1.0	5.5 ± 1.3	5.5 ± 1.3	$\mathbf{5.2 \pm 0.8}$
Error from CV	9.0 ± 3.0	9.1 ± 3.1	6.3 ± 1.1	9.1 ± 3.2	9.6 ± 3.0	$\mathbf{6.0 \pm 0.9}$

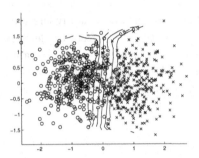 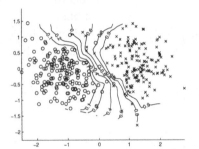

Figure 3.5 General sample selection: *Left:* The training data for the general sample selection problem. *Right:* Unlabeled data of type 2 with labels drawn from $p(y|x, s = 0)$. Both plots show also the contour lines of $p(y|x, s = 1)$ and $p(y|x, s = 0)$ respectively.

The results show that neither one of the combinations is significantly better. As in the case of random selection the combinations with *RL2*-loss are slightly worse, which is due to the reduced amount of labels they use. The loss on unlabeled data of type 2 is slightly higher than for type 2. The reason is that $p(x|s = 0)$ is more concentrated on the decision boundary than $p(x)$ and therefore one has more label noise (table 3.3).

3.7.3   General Sample Selection Bias

In this case both the conditional probability and the marginal density differ between training and test data. The selection probability $p(s = 1|x)$ is given by

$$p(s = 1|x) = \frac{1}{2} \frac{\langle w, x_1 \rangle^2}{\langle w, x_1 \rangle^2 + 2} + \frac{1}{10}$$

and the conditional probability for the selected samples is given by

$$p(y|x, s = 1) = \theta(x) \, p_{\mathrm{mod}}(y|x) + (1 - \theta(x)) \, p(y|x),$$

where $\theta(x) = 0.8 \exp(-\frac{\|x\|^2}{20\sigma_2^2})$ with $\sigma_2 = 0.4$ and $p_{\mathrm{mod}}(y|x)$ is the conditional distribution generated by two Gaussians with means at $(1,1)$ and $(-1,-1)$ and variance $\sigma_2 = 0.4$ as class-conditional probabilities $p(x|+)$ and $p(x|-)$ and equal class probabilities $p(+) = p(-) = 0.5$. Thus we can see the training conditional distribution $p(y|x, s = 1)$ as the test-conditional distribution which is perturbed by another conditional distribution near the origin.

The results show that the use of the $RL2$-loss performs in this case significantly better than all other combinations of loss and regularizers. The adaptive regularizer is slightly better than the standard regularizers for the $RL2$-loss but the difference is not significant. The success of the $RL2$-loss is basically due to the fact that labels are discarded where we are not sure about them. This also helps to select the correct model as we can see from the minimal possible test errors over all parameters. All combinations of loss and regularizer have roughly the same minimal test error. The problem is that one cannot identify the correct model using cross-validation on the training set since the conditional probability of the training data $p(y|x, s = 1)$ and the test data $p(y|x)$ differ. Therefore the $RL2$ loss outperforms the other losses since it discards labels in regions where we are not sure about them (table 3.4, figure 3.5).

3.8   Conclusion

We have discussed the general problem of sample selection bias from a decision-theoretic perspective. We have shown that the information about unlabeled data helps to restrict the difference between training and test distribution. It remains an open question if there exist other ways of characterizing additional information about the learning problem which could restrict the type of sample selection bias.

The problem of general sample selection bias cannot be solved without additional assumptions on the data-generating process. Another open question is the characterization of natural assumptions on how training and test data are related. We have discussed a modified cluster assumption which seems reasonable for a large class of datasets. Another interesting direction would be the integration of causal relationships into a model about sample selection bias.

Acknowledgments

First of all I would like to thank Klaus Robert Müller for introducing me to the problem of sample selection bias. Furthermore, I would like to thank Arthur Gretton, Steffen Bickel, and the organizers and participants of the NIPS workshop "Learning When Test and Training Inputs Have Different Distributions" for helpful and interesting discussions.

4   On Bayesian Transduction: Implications for the Covariate Shift Problem

Lars Kai Hansen

We analyze a nonstationary semisupervised learning problem with different distributions of training and test sets. The main result is an expression for the generalization optimal Bayesian procedure. For semisupervised learning our result implies that all available data, including unlabeled data, should be used in the likelihood, hence in forming the parameter posterior. It is a necessary condition for the utility of unlabeled data that the posterior couples the two parameter sets which control the input and the input-output distributions respectively. In the case of covariate or dataset shift the situation again is contingent on the parameterization. If the input-output conditional and the input distribution share parameters we can in principle track the changes in the input distribution in case of covariate shift. If we assume a drift prior we may also be able to learn from outdated data if the shift is limited.

4.1   Introduction

Supervised learning is the stochastic process of learning a predictive input-output relation from a random finite sample of labeled data, i.e., paired input and output examples. In practice we often encounter more complex scenarios, for example, semisupervised learning, which is learning an input-output relation from a mixed sample of labeled and unlabeled data, covariate shift where we learn from samples for which the input distribution is nonstationary, and dataset drift in which the whole joint input-output distribution is nonstationary.

In this chapter we will develop a general Bayesian approach which is rich enough to be used both for semisupervised learning, covariate shift, and dataset drift.

Often a learning problem has a natural quantitative measure of generalization. If a *loss function* is defined, for example, the natural measure is the *generalization error*, i.e., the *expected loss* on a random sample drawn independently of the training set.

For unsupervised learning, estimation of joint distributions, Bayesian averaging over the posterior is generalization optimal if the prior distribution is correct, as shown in Hansen [2000]. This result was generalized to supervised learning of relations between input x and output y, with a *negative log probability loss* $-\log p(y|x, D)$, in Hansen [2001]. It was found that the generalization optimal predictive distribution is based on Bayesian transduction , i.e., obtained by averaging in a posterior adapted to the specific input location x.

In this chapter we expand the results in two directions. First, we address the question of generalizability of predictors under the *least squares loss*. This is motivated by the many applications and discussions of covariate and dataset shift problems based on this loss function. Secondly, we consider possible forms of nonstationarity in the training data and derive the resulting Bayesian conclusions.

4.2   Generalization Optimal Least Squares Predictions

Consider a smoothly parameterized model A. Predictions in the model are based on a dataset D consisting of two subsamples D_a, D_b of size n_a, n_b respectively. $D_a = \{(x_j, y_j)\}_{j=1}^{n_a}$ is drawn from $p(x, y|\theta_a)$. The second set is assumed drawn either as input data (in the case of semisupervised learning) or as data from a density with shifted parameters $p(x, y|\theta_b)$ (covariate shift).

Thus these data generating "true" densities are assumed to be defined by parameter vectors θ_a, θ_b which themselves are drawn from a density $p(\cdot)$, which we could call "nature". Given this setup, what is the optimal recipe for calculating the prediction $\hat{y} = f(x, D, A)$? To answer this question consider the generalization error for the specific example of least squares learning, i.e., the generalization error is expectation of the squared difference between the label and the prediction,

$$\Gamma(D, \theta, A) = \int (y - f(x, D, A))^2 p(x, y|\theta) dx dy. \tag{4.1}$$

We assume that the datasets D_a, D_b are drawn from distributions in the same family as in (4.1), however, opening for the possibility that they have been drawn with different parameters. The expected value of the generalization error is obtained by further averaging over training sets produced by the θ,

$$\Gamma(\theta, \theta_a, \theta_b, A) = \int \int (y - f(x, D, A))^2 p(x, y|\theta) dx p(D|\theta_a, \theta_b) dD. \tag{4.2}$$

We consider $\theta, \theta_a, \theta_b$ themselves to be random, i.e., we play the game of "guessing a probability distribution" [Haussler and Opper, 1997]. Within this paradigm the generalization error is obtained by the further averaging over the random state of nature

$$\Gamma(A) = \int \Gamma(\theta, \theta_a, \theta_b, A) p(\theta, \theta_a, \theta_b) d\theta d\theta_a d\theta_b \,, \tag{4.3}$$

where we use the notation $p(\theta, \theta_a, \theta_b)$ to denote the joint distribution of the parameters chosen by nature. If the parameters are all the same, the joint distribution is $p(\theta, \theta_a, \theta_b) = \delta(\theta - \theta_a)\delta(\theta - \theta_b)p(\theta)$. If the parameters are drawn independently, we get a prior $p(\theta, \theta_a, \theta_b) = p(\theta_a)p(\theta_b)p(\theta)$, if there is a general, weak, or strong coupling, the joint distribution can be written $p(\theta, \theta_a, \theta_b) = p(\theta_a|\theta)p(\theta_b|\theta)p(\theta)$.

Equation (4.3) represents the typical generalization error for a randomly chosen instance of nature and is a function of the *sizes* of the training sets, the given model structure, and the parameter distribution used by nature.

To find the generalization optimal predictor among the functions $f(x, D)$ that map a dataset D and an input x into a prediction, we form the functional,

$$\mathcal{H}[f(\cdot, \cdot)] = \int (y - f(x, D))^2 p(x, y|\theta)dxdyp(D|\theta_a, \theta_b)dDp(\theta, \theta_a, \theta_b)d\theta d\theta_a d\theta_b. \quad (4.4)$$

The optimal predictor is given by the unique solution to $\frac{\delta \mathcal{H}}{\delta f} = 0$.

$$f(x, D) = \int \int yp(y|x, \theta)dy \frac{p(x|\theta)p(D|\theta_a, \theta_b)p(\theta, \theta_a, \theta_b)}{\int p(x|\theta')p(D|\theta', \theta_a', \theta_b')p(\theta', \theta_a', \theta_b')d\theta' d\theta_a' d\theta_b'} d\theta d\theta_a d\theta_b. \quad (4.5)$$

It is easily verified that this predictive distribution is indeed the global minimum of the generalization error . We also note that if Bayesian averaging is performed with another prior than nature's distribution $p(\theta, \theta_a, \theta_b)$, we can expect a higher generalization error.

4.3 Bayesian Transduction

First, let us consider conventional supervised learning from a single stationary dataset $D = D_a, D_b = \emptyset$. We simplify the prior distribution as $p(\theta, \theta_a, \theta_b) = \delta(\theta - \theta_a)\delta(\theta - \theta_b)p(\theta)$. In this case the optimal predictor reduces to

$$f(x, D) = \int \int yp(y|x, \theta)dy \frac{p(x, D|\theta)p(\theta)}{\int p(x, D|\theta')p(\theta')d\theta'} d\theta. \quad (4.6)$$

This is a simple form of Bayesian transduction in which the predictor combines the information in the training data with the current input point to form a posterior distribution. The test input x vector occurs in the expression with the likelihood term; hence the posterior is to be computed for each input separately.

We can obtain further insight into the role of the input data by being more explicit about the parameters. Let us consider the "fine structure" of the parameterization by dividing the parameters θ into three groups $\theta = (\theta_1, \theta_2, \theta_3)$ so that $p(x, y, \theta) = p(y|x, \theta_1, \theta_2)p(x|\theta_2, \theta_3)$. In this formulation we have parameters that only enter into the conditional (θ_1), parameters that enter into both distributions (θ_2), and parameters that only play a role in the input distribution (θ_3).

If the set of parameters θ_2 is empty, hence, there is no coupling between the input distribution and the conditional distribution in the posterior distribution, our result further simplifies to "conventional" Bayesian modeling:

$$f(x, D) = \int \int y p(y|x, \theta) dy \frac{p(D|\theta)p(\theta)}{\int p(D|\theta')p(\theta')d\theta'} d\theta. \tag{4.7}$$

Note that this widely used Bayesian posterior average for supervised learning is strictly speaking only optimal if θ_2 is empty and the posterior distribution has no coupling between the learned parameters of the conditional and the input density functions.

4.4   Bayesian Semisupervised Learning

In semisupervised learning we have access to both labeled and unlabeled data. Let the dataset consist of two independent sets of unlabeled D_a and labeled data D_b, $D = (D_a, D_b)$, hence $p(D|\theta_a, \theta_b) = p(D_a|\theta_a)p(D_b|\theta_b)$. Since the training set average in (4.6) involves both datasets, we conclude that both sets should contribute on equal terms to the likelihood in (4.5).

Let us consider some relevant scenarios. First, let us assume stationarity, i.e., that the parameters are identical as discussed above, $p(\theta, \theta_a, \theta_b) = \delta(\theta - \theta_a)\delta(\theta - \theta_b)p(\theta)$. In this case we recover a result similar to Hansen [2001],

$$f(x, D_a, D_b) = \int \int y p(y|x, \theta) dy \frac{p(x, D_a, D_b|\theta)p(\theta)}{\int p(x, D_a, D_b|\theta')p(\theta')d\theta'} d\theta. \tag{4.8}$$

To probe a bit deeper into the nature of this result we analyze the parameterization fine structure $p(x, y, \theta) = p(y|x, \theta_1, \theta_2)p(x|\theta_2, \theta_3)$. First, if θ_2 is empty we extend the result from the previous section and conclude that there is no utility of unlabeled data. In this case Bayesian semisupervised learning fails as can be seen from the resulting Bayesian average,

$$f(x, D) = f(x, D_b) = \int \int y p(y|x, \theta) dy \frac{p(D_b|\theta)p(\theta)}{\int p(D_b|\theta')p(\theta')d\theta'} d\theta. \tag{4.9}$$

This no-go situation occurs, for example, in case a supervised learning model is adapted without reference to the input distribution. This could be "conditional mean" type predictors like unregularized linear models, unregularized multilayer perceptrons, or simple Gaussian processes.

We conclude that if the model is realizable and there is a nonempty intersection of the sets of parameters defining the input and conditional distribution, then labeled and unlabeled data should enter the likelihood with full strength. If the intersection between the two parameter sets is empty, on the other hand, the unlabeled data has no utility. The former is in contrast to work by Nigam et al. [2000], which shows that it typically pays off to discount the unlabeled data. The reason is that for misspecified scenarios we can expect frustration between the likelihood contributions from the two datasets. We can not be sure that the parameters that are optimal for the labeled data also are optimal for the unlabeled data. Since the unlabeled likelihood typically is based on many more examples than the labeled likelihood, the former will dominate and skew the predictions.

4.5   Implications for Covariate Shift and Dataset Shift

The covariate and dataset shift situations occur when we consider the datasets D_a and D_b to be drawn from different distributions, i.e., $\theta_a \neq \theta_b$.

Let us first take $\theta = \theta_b$ and a prior which is given by $p(\theta, \theta_a, \theta_b) = \delta(\theta - \theta_b)p(\theta)p(\theta_a)$ corresponding to a dataset D_a drawn independently from (x, y) and D_b. The optimal Bayes predictor reads in this case,

$$f(x, D) = f(x, D_b) = \int \int y p(y|x, \theta) dy \frac{p(x|\theta)p(D_b|\theta)p(\theta)}{\int p(x|\theta')p(D_b|\theta')p(\theta')d\theta'} d\theta. \quad (4.10)$$

Thus we completely forget the initial dataset D_a and there is no tracking and no learning transfer.

As a second and more useful scenario we consider the so-called independent covariate shift situation with a parameter fine structure $\theta = (\theta_1, \theta_2, \theta_3)$, with the further assumption $\theta_{a,1} = \theta_1, \theta_{a,2} = \theta_2$ (no change in the conditional distribution $p(y|x, \theta_1, \theta_2) = p(y|x, \theta_{a,1}, \theta_{a,2})$, but *with* a change in the input distribution $\theta_{a,3} \neq \theta_3$. This leads to a predictor in which we can learn from both D_a, D_b and from the current input x; however, the input distribution learning has contributions only from the test input and from the inputs of the "shifted" dataset D_b.

Finally, as a third scenario we consider a prior that will allow a kind of "tracking". Let $p(\theta, \theta_a, \theta_b) = \delta(\theta_b - \theta)p(\theta_a|\theta)p(\theta)$ with a conditional $p(\theta_a|\theta)$ that captures our expectation on the dependency between the initial dataset and the shifted. In this case the predictor reads

$$f(x, D) = \int \int y p(y|x, \theta) dy \frac{p(x|\theta)p(D_b|\theta)p(D_a|\theta_a)p(\theta_a|\theta)p(\theta)}{\int p(x|\theta')p(D_b|\theta')p(D_a|\theta_a')p(\theta_a'|\theta')p(\theta')d\theta'd\theta_a'} d\theta_a d\theta.$$
$$(4.11)$$

Depending on the size of the shift we can obtain learning transfer through the coupling between the two parameter sets.

4.6   Learning Transfer under Covariate and Dataset Shift: An Example

Let the conditional mean be an affine function of the input data $f(x, w)$ where w is a two-dimensional vector representing a slope and an offset. We will create simulated data with additive normal noise of variance σ^2. Thus the conditional distribution

$p(y|x)$ is given by

$$p(y|x, w, \sigma^2) = \frac{1}{\sqrt{2\pi\sigma^2}} \exp\left(-\frac{(y - f(x, w))^2}{2\sigma^2}\right). \tag{4.12}$$

Further, to be complete let the input distribution be a Gaussian mixture,

$$p(x|\{\mu_k, \sigma_k^2, \pi_k\}) = \sum_{k=1}^{K} \pi_k \frac{1}{\sqrt{2\pi\sigma_k^2}} \exp\left(-\frac{(x - \mu_k)^2}{2\sigma_k^2}\right). \tag{4.13}$$

With these definitions the fine structure is given as $\theta_1 = (w, \sigma^2)$ and $\theta_3 = (\{\mu_k, \sigma_k^2, \pi_k\}_{k=1}^{K})$, while the set θ_2 of parameters that couple the conditional and input distributions is empty.

Let us first consider the semisupervised problem. In this case we have access to the two datasets with labels and without. If we will use a prior $p(\theta_a, \theta_b, \theta) = \delta(\theta - \theta_a)\delta(\theta - \theta_b)p(\theta)$, transfer should be possible, but, because θ_2 is empty the no-go result in (4.9) applies and we cannot learn from the unlabeled data. The same result holds if we invoke priors with hyperparameters, as long as they do not bring in relations between components of θ_1 and θ_3. If that happened, e.g., if we optimized hyperparameters as in MLII, we would effectively produce a nonempty θ_2.

Next, let us consider a scenario inspired by the model used in Sugiyama et al. [2007] to illustrate learning under covariate shift. Datasets for the linear model are based on the nonlinear function $f_0(x) = \frac{\sin(x)}{x}$ with additive normal noise with variance σ^2. We assume σ^2 to be known in this example. Further, the input distribution is assumed nonstationary. In the large ($n_a = 1000$) initial dataset D_a the input distribution is a normal distribution $\mathcal{N}(1.5, 9)$, while in the smaller set ($n_b = 10$) D_b and at time of test, i.e., (x, y), the input distribution is shifted and is given in two separate simulations either as (i) $\mathcal{N}(3, 1)$ or (ii) $\mathcal{N}(4.5, 1)$. We will refer to the two scenarios as small drift (i) and medium drift (ii). The latter input distribution is still overlapping with the preshift distribution justifying the term "medium".

Note that since the model is unrealizable, referring to the fact that our linear model cannot globally represent the nonlinear sinc function $f_0(x)$, what is a covariate shift in the true model is a dataset shift with respect to the linear model.

We consider two different priors. We consider first a "conventional" prior consisting of a weight decay type prior on $w = w_b$ and a uniform prior on w_a:

$$p(w_a, w_b, w) \propto \left(\frac{1}{2\pi\alpha}\right) \exp\left(-\frac{\alpha}{2}w^2\right) \delta(w - w_b). \tag{4.14}$$

Next we introduce a "drift" prior on $w = w_b$ relative to the weights trained on the initial dataset w_a:

$$p(w_a, w_b, w) \propto \left(\frac{1}{2\pi\alpha}\right) \exp\left(-\frac{\alpha}{2}(w_a - w)^2\right) \delta(w - w_b). \tag{4.15}$$

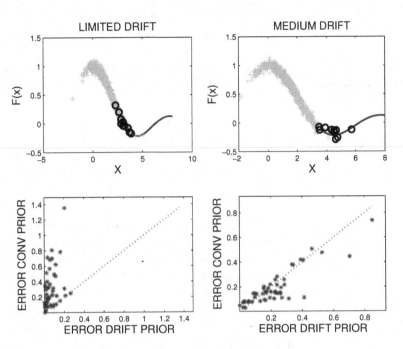

Figure 4.1   Bayesian linear learning of a nonlinear function under limited and "medium" drift of the input distribution. We consider an initial training set D_a with $n_a = 1000$ samples drawn from a normal input distribution $\mathcal{N}(1.5, 9)$. In the limited drift situation shown in the upper left panel, we shift the input distribution for the second training set D_b ($n_b = 10$ data points indicated by circles) and for the test data to a normal $\mathcal{N}(3, 1)$. In the larger drift situation shown in the upper right panel, we shift the input distribution for the second training set D_b and for the test data to $\mathcal{N}(4.5, 1)$. For either of the two covariate shift cases we train two models, one with a weight decay-type prior on the weights after shift w, and a model with a drift prior linking the weights before and after the covariate shift as normal distribution with a hyperparameter α. The hyperparameters for both weight decay prior and drift prior are integrated numerically assuming a uniform hyperparameter prior. In the two lower panels we show the normalized test error scatter plots for 50 realizations of the simulations. In the left lower panel (data with limited covariate shift) we see that the errors are all improved for the drift prior and we thus experience a significant learning transfer, while in the right plot (data with a larger drift) we find that the conventional prior is more appropriate.

For both priors we will assign a uniform hyperprior on α and we will integrate over the hyperparameter numerically.

In the simulations we created 50 realizations of the each of the four combinations of covariate shift ("small", "medium") and priors ("conventional", "drift"). The predictions by the two priors were in each realization evaluated on a large test dataset drawn from the same distribution as D_b. All test errors were normalized by the output variance in the corresponding test set.

Results of the simulations are presented in figure 4.1. For the case of a limited covariate shift the drift prior provides a consistent and at times very large improvement relative to the conventional prior. However, for the larger drift we find that the conventional prior is either equal to or an improvement over the drift prior.

4.7   Conclusion

We have analyzed Bayesian supervised learning with extensions to semisupervised learning, and learning with covariate or dataset shift.

The main result is an expression for the generalization optimal Bayesian procedure. The resulting "Bayesian transduction" average is optimal for a realizable model. For semisupervised learning this implies that all available data, including unlabeled data, should be used in the likelihood, hence in forming the parameter posterior. We noted an important caveat, namely that a prerequisite for using unlabeled data is that there is a coupling in the posterior between the parameters that control the input distribution model and the input-output relation. If, for example, we use a straightforward unregularized classifier we should not expect any benefit from additional unlabeled data.

In the case of covariate or dataset shift the situation again is contingent on the parameterization. If we have shared parameters between the input-output conditional distribution and the input distribution we can in principle track the changes in the input distribution in case of covariate shift. If we assume a drift prior we may also be able to learn from outdated data if the shift is limited. We also noted in the simple example that what by definition was a covariate shift in the complex model could appear as a dataset shift for a simpler model.

Acknowledgments

I thank the organizers of the NIPS∗06 workshop "Learning When Test and Training Inputs Have Different Distributions" and the editors of this book for their patient help in preparing this chapter. My work is funded by the Danish Research Councils and by the Lundbeck foundation.

5   On the Training/Test Distributions Gap: A Data Representation Learning Framework

Shai Ben-David

We discuss some dataset shift learning problems from a formal, statistical point of view. We offer definitions for "multitask learning," "inductive transfer," and "domain adaptation" and discuss the parameters along which such learning scenarios may be taxonomized. We then focus on one concrete setting of domain adaptation and demonstrate how error bounds can be derived for that setting. Our bounds can be reliably estimated from finite samples of training data, and do not rely on any assumptions concerning similarity between the domain from which the labeled training data is sampled and the target (or test) data. However, these bounds are relative to the performance of some optimal classifier, rather than providing any absolute performance guarantee.

5.1   Introduction

We consider a setting where a learner has access to labeled training data generated according to some *training data* distribution (or several different data distributions), and wishes to learn a classifier which performs well with respect to a different, "target" (or "test"), data distribution.

Such learning scenarios are usually discussed under the titles "domain adaptation," "inductive transfer," and "multitask learning." We propose formal definitions for these learning problems. These definitions may further partition along different input availability settings. Namely, what kind of target distribution data is available to the learner: Labeled? Unlabeled? Distribution description? Constraints on possible such distributions?, etc.

Clearly, the success of any such learning depends on the knowledge the learner has about the test data or on its relationship to the training data. Common approaches to this problem rely on postulating some prior assumptions in that respect. We propose a different approach. Rather than aiming for *absolute* error bounds that are (inevitably) conditioned upon such prior assumptions, we make no prior assumptions about the test domain, and derive error bounds which are *relative* to the best possible performance in the relevant setting.

We focus on scenarios where the learner can access samples generated by the test data distribution, alas, without the labels of these data points (this is on top of having access to labeled examples generated by the training data distribution).

In such scenarios, data shift learning paradigms can be divided along another aspect – the distinction between what we call *conservative* and *adaptive* learners . A conservative algorithm is one that makes its choice of predictor function based only on the labeled sample from the training domain. Such a learner uses the unlabeled target sample only as a tool for evaluating the quality of the chosen predictor. In contrast, adaptive learners incorporate the unlabeled target sample as an integral part of the learning process. We focus our analysis on conservative learners, and argue, in section 5.5, that, as long as the learner has access to only unlabeled samples from the target distribution, no reliable adaptive learning can take place (unless further assumptions concerning that distribution are made). This claim remains valid even in the *covariate shift* setting, where one assumes that the conditional distribution of label values, given the unlabeled data, is unchanged between the training and target distributions.

We introduce some parameters, depending on the learning algorithm, the distribution of labeled training data and the distribution of unlabeled test data, that determine the generalization error of conservative learning in our framework. A key component in our discussion is the introduction of a special measure for the similarity between probability distributions. We show that, for the purpose of domain adaptation, it is useful to define that similarity as the error that the relevant learning algorithm will make when applied to distinguish between the training and target unlabeled data distributions.

We prove convergence rates for the (quality of) approximation of these relevant parameters from finite samples of labeled training data and unlabeled test data, and derive some basic theoretical performance guarantees for classifiers in terms of these parameters.

5.2   Formal Framework and Notation

In this chapter, a learning task is modeled by a probability distribution P over labeled examples. Namely, for some domain set, $\mathcal{X}$, and a set of labels $\mathcal{Y}$ (which, for concreteness, we take to be $\{0, 1\}$), P is a distribution over $\mathcal{X} \times \mathcal{Y}$. We shall also consider probability distributions over the space, $\mathcal{X}$, of unlabeled examples. Given a task, P, as above, we use D_P to denote the probability distribution over the domain set (the data marginal distribution), $\mathcal{X}$, obtained by projecting P to $\mathcal{X}$ (by erasing the labels). Namely, for a subset $A \subseteq \mathcal{X}$, $D_P(A) = P(\{(x, y) : x \in A\})$ the probability of drawing $x \in A$ regardless of the label it is paired with.

By a *sample* for a task, P, we mean a multiset of labeled points, $S = ((x_1, \ell_1), \ldots, (x_m, \ell_m))$, picked i.i.d. according to the distribution P. An *unlabeled* sample of P is a multiset of points from $\mathcal{X}$ picked i.i.d. according to the unlabeled distribution D_P.

For some parts of our discussion, we shall need to get into some further detail and consider also the measure space over which our distributions (or 'tasks') are defined. A measure space is a pair, $(\mathcal{X}, \mathcal{B})$, where $\mathcal{X}$ is any domain space, as above, and $\mathcal{B}$ is a σ-algebra of subsets of $\mathcal{X}$. We shall assume that all the probability distributions considered are defined over some measure space (that will remain implicit for most of our discussion). Given a domain space, $(\mathcal{X}, \mathcal{B})$, and a finite label space, $\mathcal{Y}$, a task P over it is assumed to be defined over the space $(\mathcal{X} \times \mathcal{Y}, \{b \times l : b \in \mathcal{B} : \text{and } l \subseteq \mathcal{Y}\})$. As mentioned above, we shall focus on the case that $\mathcal{Y} = \{0, 1\}$ and shall make no explicit reference to $\mathcal{Y}$ in our notation.

A *multitask* is an array of tasks, $P_1, \ldots, P_n$, all defined over the same space. For most of our discussion, we shall focus on the case of an array of size 2, where we have just two tasks, a *training task* that we shall denote by P_{tr}, and a *target task* that we shall denote by P_{te}.

The learner wishes to construct a predictor $h : \mathcal{X} \to \{0, 1\}$ for the target task. Namely, the learner wishes to minimize the error of its predictor on the target task distribution. That error is defined as the expectation, w.r.t. the distribution P_{te}, of the 0/1 loss of h. That is, $Er^{P_{te}}(h) = Ex_{(x,\ell) \sim P_{te}} L(h, (x, \ell))$, where $L(h, (x, \ell)) = 0$ if $h(x) = \ell$ and $L(h, (x, \ell)) = 1$ if $h(x) \neq \ell$.

5.3   A Basic Taxonomy of Tasks and Paradigms

Learning for the case of multiple tasks has been considered in various settings. We attempt to provide a basic taxonomy for such problems by considering several determining aspects. The first is the distinction between *symmetric* and *asymmetric* settings. In the symmetric case, the learner has the same type of information for all the relevant learning tasks, and wishes to use the existence of multiple tasks to improve the learning in all of them. This is the scenario that is considered by Baxter's seminal work [Baxter, 2000]. In such settings (e.g., in Baxter [2000]), the learner is interested in improving the *average* quality of prediction, over the full array of tasks (compared to learning *each* of them separately), or in improving the learning quality over each of the tasks [Ben-David and Schuller, 2003]. We call this scenario *multitask learning* . In the asymmetric setting, there is some designated *target task*, and the learner aims to improve the quality of learning on that particular task (again, compared to learning it without access to the additional tasks in the array). We call this type of task *inductive transfer* . Such settings may further partition according to the type of target-task information available to the learner. We propose using the term *domain adaptation* for situations in which the learner has access to only *unlabeled* target samples.

Symmetric Setting – Multitask Learning We say that $P_1, \ldots, P_n$ allows *multitask learning* (MTL) if, for any sequence of learning algorithms, $A_1, \ldots, A_n$, one for each of the tasks, there exists a learning algorithm $\widehat{A}$ that takes an array of samples, one from each task, as input, and outputs an array of predictors, one for each task, such that for any large enough m, if, for all i, S_i is an m-size sample of the task P_i, then, with high probability (over the choice of the S_i's), for any $k \leq n$, $E_k(\widehat{A}(S_1, \ldots, S_n)) < E(A_k(S_k))$ (where E_k is the expectation of the error of $\widehat{A}$ when predicting on the kth task, over the input random samples).

That is, $\widehat{A}$ utilizes samples from the different tasks to improve the individual task predictions based on single-task training data.

Possible variant: Weak MTL. Rather than having $\widehat{A}$ beat the single-task algorithms on every task, require only that the *average* of these errors, over the array of tasks, is better than the average one would get by learning each task separately.

Asymmetric Setting – Domain Adaptation We say that $P_1, \ldots, P_{n-1}$ allows *domain adaptation* to a task T_n if there exists a learning algorithm $\widehat{A}$ that takes an array of samples $S_1, \ldots, S_{n-1}$, one from each task, as input, and outputs a predictor for T_n such that for every large enough m, if, for all $i < n$, S_i is an m-size sample of the task P_i, then, with high probability (over the choice of the S_i's), $Er_{(\widehat{A}(S_1, \ldots, S_{n-1}))}(P_n) < \min\{Er_1(P_n), Er_0(P_n)\}$, where $Er_i(P_n)$ is the error of the constant label-i predictor on the task P_n, and $Er_{(\widehat{A}(S_1, \ldots, S_{n-1}))}(P_n)$ is the error on T_n of $\widehat{A}$, trained on $S_1, \ldots, S_{n-1}$. That is, using training samples for the tasks P_i, $i < n$, one can come up with a nontrivial predictor for P_n, without having access to training data from that task ("nontrivial" in the sense that it has lower error than any of the two constant-value predictors).

Variations: One can readily define several variations of these types of task, e.g., allowing for the use of unlabeled target data as part of the input to $\widehat{A}$ in any of the above, or demanding that, having access to large enough samples, the error of $\widehat{A}$ can be made arbitrarily small.

Conservative vs. Adaptive Prediction An orthogonal dimension along which relevant approaches may be classified is the algorithmic paradigms they employ. Do they address the data shift explicitly or do they ignore the data shift in the learning process and address it only for the evaluation of the resulting predictor?

We distinguish between two possible learning paradigms. In the first, the learner chooses the predictor that works best with respect to the training task(s), and wishes to evaluate how good that predictor will be when employed on the target task. We call this "conservative prediction." In the second setting, we consider learning strategies that allow the predictor they pick for the target task to differ from the predictor they would use for the training task. We call this "adaptive prediction."

5.4   Error Bounds for Conservative Domain Adaptation Prediction

In the conservative prediction setting, one wishes to upper-bound the error of a predictor on the target (or "goal") task by its error on the training task. Clearly, such a bound depends on the similarity between the training distribution and the goal distribution. Any performance guarantee of this type should therefore involve a measure of that task similarity. A common measure for the dissimilarity between two probability distributions is the L_1 distance (also called the *total variance* or *statistical distance*). It is defined as

$$d_{L_1}(P, Q) = 2 \sup_{A \in \mathcal{B}} |P(A) - Q(A)|.$$

Recall that $\mathcal{B}$ denotes the set of all P-measurable domain subsets.

Based on this L_1 distance between the two (unlabeled) data distributions, one can readily get a rather straightforward bound on the error on the goal distribution in terms of the error of a hypothesis on the training distribution (in the covariate shift setting):

Lemma 5.1 *Under the covariate shift assumption, for every predictor, $h : x \to \{0, 1\}$,*

$$Er^G(h) \leq Er^T(h) + \frac{d_{L_1}(D_T, D_G)}{2}.$$

Proof: Note that, due to the covariate shift assumption, for every point $x \in \mathcal{X}$, $G(1|x) = T(1|x)$. Let us denote this quantity by $\ell(x, 1)$ (the probability, under either G or T, that the label of x is 1) and let $\ell(x, 0) = 1 - \ell(x, 1)$ (namely, the probability that the label of x is 0). The only possible source of the error of a predictor h to be greater for G than for T is that G puts more weight on points on which h has a relatively large error. Namely,

$$Er^G(h) - Er^T(h) \leq D_G\{x : \ell(x, h(x)) > Er^T(h)\} - D_T\{x : \ell(x, h(x)) > Er^T(h)\}$$

Now, note that by the definition of d_{L_1}, the right hand side of this inequality is at most $1/2 d_{L_1}(D_T, D_G)$.

The above bound has two major weaknesses. First, it may be overly pessimistic. A second concern is that, based on the data available to the learner in the setting we discuss, there is no way to estimate the crucial similarity parameter $d_{L_1}(D_T, D_G)$ reliably.

We address these issues by developing an alternative error bound. The new bound is based on a different measure of similarity between distributions.

5.4.1   A Special Measure of Between-Distributions Distance

To measure the similarity between two probability distributions, we shall use the $d_{\mathcal{A}}$ measure, introduced in Kifer et al. [2004] and He et al. [2006]. The $d_{\mathcal{A}}$ measure is parameterized by a collection $\mathcal{A}$ of subsets of the domain over which the probability distributions are defined. Intuitively speaking, $\mathcal{A}$ is the collection of "subsets of interest" with respect to the properties of the distributions that one wishes to analyze. In our case, when we analyze a domain adaptation learning algorithm, that collection is determined by the learning algorithm that is used to generate the classification predictors (more precisely, by the set of potential predictors that that algorithm may output). The motivation behind the introduction of that measure come from real life scenarios in which one cares only about certain distribution changes. For example, in Kifer et al. [2004] we discuss detecting changes in the generating distribution of streaming real valued data, in that context one cares only about changes that effect the probabilities of real intervals.

Definition 5.2 *Let $\mathcal{X}$ be some domain set and let $\mathcal{B}$ be a σ-algebra of subsets of $\mathcal{X}$. Let $\mathcal{A} \subseteq \mathcal{B}$. For probability distributions P, Q over $(\mathcal{X}, \mathcal{B})$,*

$$d_{\mathcal{A}}(P, Q) = 2 \sup_{A \in \mathcal{A}} |P(A) - Q(A)| .$$

Note that the only difference between this measure and the L_1 distance is that in the $d_{\mathcal{A}}$ distance, we restrict our attention to some fixed collection $\mathcal{A}$ of subsets, rather than considering the full σ-algebra of measurable sets. This difference becomes meaningful when $\mathcal{A}$ is "small" compared to the full collection of measurable sets. Below, we demonstrate the benefits gained when that smallness is reflected by the VC dimension .

Lemma 5.3 *For any pair of probability distributions, P, Q, over some domain measure space $(\mathcal{X}, \mathcal{B})$, and for every family of sets $\mathcal{A} \subseteq \mathcal{B}$,*

$$d_{\mathcal{A}}(P, Q) \leq d_{L_1}(P, Q) .$$

Example 5.4 *Let $\mathcal{X}$ be some Euclidean space, $\mathbb{R}^d$ and let $\mathcal{B} = \mathcal{L}(\mathbb{R}^d)$ be the collection of Lebesgue measurable subsets of $\mathbb{R}^d$. Let P be the uniform distribution over $D_{100}^{odd} = \{(x_1, \ldots, x_d) \in [0,1]^d : \Sigma_{i=1}^d (\text{the 100th decimal digit of } d_i) \text{ is odd}\}$ and let Q be the uniform distribution over its complement, $([0,1]^d \setminus D_{100}^{odd})$. It is easy to see that $D_{L_1}(P, Q) = 2$ (note that, for any P, Q, it is always the case that $D_{L_1}(P, Q) \leq 2$). Just the same, if we let $\mathcal{A}$ be the set of all linear half-spaces in $\mathbb{R}^d$, then $d_{\mathcal{A}}(P, Q) = 0$.*

Note that one could easily modify the above example so that the two distributions will be absolutely continuous with respect to each other; let $0 \leq \lambda \leq 1$, the distributions $P^{\prime} = \lambda U + (1 - \lambda P$ and $Q^{\prime} = \lambda U + (1 - \lambda Q$ (where U is the uniform distribution over $[0,1]^d$), satisfy $d_{\mathcal{A}}(P', Q') = 0$ and $D_{L_1}(P', Q') = 2 - 2\lambda$

Kifer et al. [2004] use a uniform convergence argument to show that, if $\mathcal{A}$ has a finite VC dimension , then it is possible to reliably estimate the $\mathcal{A}$-distance from finite samples. We state here the relevant result from that work:

Lemma 5.5 *Let $\mathcal{A}$ be a class of subsets of some domain set $\mathfrak{X}$ and let $d < \infty$ be the VC dimension of $\mathcal{A}$. Let P, Q be any probability distributions over $\mathfrak{X}$ and $\epsilon \in (0,1)$. Then, for any sample size, m, for i.i.d. m samples, S, S', drawn by P, Q respectively,*

$$\Pr\left[|d_{\mathcal{A}}(P,Q) - d_{\mathcal{A}}(S,S')| \geq \epsilon \right] < (2m)^d 4 e^{-m\epsilon^2/4},$$

where $\Pr[\cdot]$ is over random draws of m-size independent samples from the distributions P and Q, and we identify a finite sample S with the probability distribution that assigns each point a weight equal to its relative frequency in S.

Note that the above claim is in sharp contrast to the d_{L_1} case, as the following claim demonstrates.

Claim 5.6 *Let U be the uniform distribution over the unit interval with the Lebesgue algebra of measurable subsets, $([0,1]^d, \mathcal{L}([0,1]^d))$. For any statistical test T and any number m, there exists a probability distribution, P, over the same domain space, such that $d_{L_1}(U,P) = 1$ and yet, given a pair of m-size samples, S_1, S_2 as input, the test T cannot distinguish between the case that both samples were both drawn i.i.d. from U and the case that S_1 was drawn i.i.d. from U and S_2 was drawn i.i.d. from P.*

Alternatively, one could define the $D_{\mathcal{A}}$ measure from a learning perspective. Intuitively speaking, viewing $\mathcal{A}$ as a set of functions from $\mathfrak{X}$ to $\{0,1\}$ (or, label predictors), we ask how well can a function from $\mathcal{A}$ separate examples generated by the two distributions. It turns out that the prediction error on such a task can be used to define the $d_{\mathcal{A}}$ distance.

Definition 5.7 (Alternative, Equivalent Definition of $d_{\mathcal{A}}$) *For $\mathfrak{X}$, $\mathcal{A}$, P, and Q as above, consider the task of finding a predictor, $h : \mathfrak{X} \rightarrow \{0,1\}$ that distinguishes points generated by P from points generated by Q. That is, consider the mixture distribution $(P,Q) = \frac{1}{2}[P \times \{1\} + Q \times \{0\}]$ over $\mathfrak{X} \times \{0,1\}$ (i.e., with probability $1/2$, x is drawn from P and has label $\ell(x) = 1$, and with probability $1/2$, x is drawn from Q and has label 0); define the error of such a predictor as $Err^{(P,Q)}(h) = \Pr_{(P,Q)}[h(x) \neq \ell(x)]$. Given a set $A \in \mathcal{A}$, let h_A be the characteristic function of A (that is, $h(x) = 1$ iff $x \in A$). We can rewrite the definition of $[d_{\mathcal{A}}$ as*

$$d_{\mathcal{A}}(P,Q) = 1 - 2 \inf_{h_A | A \in \mathcal{A}} Er^{(P,Q)}(h_A).$$

It is straightforward to see that the two definitions of D above are equivalent.

5.4.2   Relative Error Bounds

We wish to bound the error of a predictor w.r.t. P_{te} in terms of its error w.r.t. P_{tr}. Since we must rely on finite samples (rather than having access to the actual distributions, P_{tr} and P_{te}), and since we wish to use that bound for selecting the best predictor, we must restrict our attention to some restricted class of predicting functions. Let H denote such a class. As mentioned above, even under the covariate shift assumption, it may still be the case that predictors that perform well with respect to P_{tr} fail badly w.r.t. P_{te}. Can the similarity between P_{tr} and P_{te} bound that gap in the quality of predictors over the two tasks? Lemma 5.1 shows that the answer is positive once the two probability distributions are close in the L_1 sense. However, as demonstrated above, such a requirement is severely restrictive and its validity cannot be assessed on the basis of the information available to the learner in the model we consider. Can similarity in terms of d_A, for some A with a finite VC dimension suffice to imply such a bound? The following example shows that it does not.

Example 5.8 *Let X be the real unit interval $[0, 1]$, and let A, as well as H, be the set of all linear half-spaces over X (that is, the set of all threshold classifiers). Let $f : [0, 1] \to \{0, 1\}$ be defined by $f(x) = 1$ if the 100th digit of X (in its decimal expansion, without a tail of 9s), and $f(x) = 0$ otherwise. Now let P_{tr} be the uniform distribution over $f^{-1}(1)$ and let P_{te} be the uniform distribution over $f^{-1}(0)$. Now, $d_H(P_{tr}, P_{te}) = 0$, and yet, the constant predictor $h(x) \equiv 1$ has zero error w.r.t. P_{tr} but has error 1 w.r.t.P_{te}.*

As long as no data about the distribution of labels w.r.t. P_{te} is available, and no assumption about it is made (apart from the covariate shift assumption), we suggest that, rather than aiming toward *absolute* error bounds, one should settle for *relative* bounds, namely, bounds with respect to the best possible performance under the given circumstances. More concretely,

Definition 5.9 *Given a domain space X, a class of binary predictors, H over it (a hypothesis class), and probability distributions P_{tr} and P_{te} as above, let*

$$\lambda_{H,P_{tr},P_{te}} = \inf_{h \in H} (Er^{P_{te}}(h) + Er^{P_{te}}(h))$$

Notation: We identify a binary function, $h : X \to \{0, 1\}$, with the subset $h^{-1}(1))$ of X. We denote by $\Delta(H)$ the class of symmetric differences of functions from H. Namely, $\Delta(H) = \{h \Delta h' : h, \ h' \in H\}$.

We are now ready to present our main error bound .

Theorem 5.10 *Let P_{tr} and P_{te} be probability distributions over $X \times \{0, 1\}$ for some space (X, B), and let H be a class of measurable binary functions over that space. For any $h \in H$,*

$$|Er^{P_{te}}(h) - Er^{P_{tr}}(h)| \leq \lambda_{H,P_{tr},P_{te}} + \frac{1}{2} d_{\Delta(H)}(D_{P_{tr}}, D_{P_{te}}),$$

where $D_{P_{te}}$ and $D_{P_{tr}}$ are the projections on X of P_{te} and P_{tr} respectively.

Proof: Let $h^* = \text{argmin}_{h \in H} \left(Er^{P_{tr}}(h) + Er^{P_{te}}(h) \right)$, and let $\lambda_{P_{tr}}$ and $\lambda_{P_{te}}$ be the errors of h^* with respect to P_{tr} and P_{te} respectively. Notice that $\lambda_{H,P_{tr},P_{te}} = \lambda_{P_{tr}} + \lambda_{P_{te}}$.

$$
\begin{aligned}
Er^{P_{te}}(h) \;&\leq\; \lambda_{P_{te}} + \Pr_{D_{P_{te}}}[h \Delta h^*] \\
&\leq\; \lambda_{P_{te}} + \Pr_{D_{P_{tr}}}[h \Delta h^*] + \left(\Pr_{D_{P_{te}}}[h \Delta h^*] - \Pr_{D_{P_{tr}}}[h \Delta h^*] \right) \\
&\leq\; \lambda_{P_{te}} + \Pr_{D_{P_{tr}}}[h \Delta h^*] + \frac{1}{2} d_{\Delta(H)}(D_{P_{tr}}, D_{P_{te}}) \\
&\leq\; \lambda_G + \lambda_{P_{tr}} + Er^{P_{tr}}(h) + \frac{1}{2} d_{\Delta(H)}(D_{P_{te}}, D_{P_{tr}}) \\
&\leq\; \lambda + Er^{P_{tr}}(h) + \frac{1}{2} d_{\Delta(H)}(D_{P_{te}}, D_{P_{tr}})
\end{aligned}
$$

Probably the only step that requires explanation is the inequality $\Pr_{D_{P_{tr}}}[h \Delta h^*] \leq \lambda_{P_{tr}} + Er^{P_{tr}}(h)$ used for moving from the third line above to the fourth. This inequality holds since, for every point $x \in h \Delta h^*$, the error probability of h on x and the error probability of h^* on x sum to 1. The theorem now follows by noting that the above argument is symmetric—the roles of P_{tr} and P_{te} are interchangeable

Corollary 5.11 *Let P_{tr} and P_{te} and H, be as above. If H has a finite VC dimension , d, then for every $m, m' \in \mathbb{N}$. If a random labeled sample, S_{tr}, of size m is i.i.d by P_{tr} and random unlabeled samples, U_{tr}, U_{te}, each of size m', are generated i.i.d. by $D_{P_{tr}}$ and $D_{P_{te}}$ respectively, then, with probability at least $1 - \delta$ (over the choice of the samples), for every $h \in H$:*

1.

$$
Er^{P_{te}}(h) \leq Er^{P_{tr}}(h) + \lambda_{P_{tr}, P_{te}, H} + \frac{1}{2} d_{\Delta(H)}(U_{tr}, U_{te}) + 4 \sqrt{\frac{d \log(2m') + \log(\frac{4}{\delta})}{m'}}
$$

Where, for finite samples, S, the same notation is used to denote both the sample itself and the uniform probability distribution over its elements.

2.

$$
\begin{aligned}
Er^{P_{tr}}(h) \leq\; &Er^{S_{tr}}(h) + \frac{4}{m} \left(d \log \frac{2em}{d} + \log \frac{4}{\delta} \right) + \lambda_{P_{tr}, P_{te}, H} \\
&+ \frac{1}{2} d_{\Delta(H)}(U_{tr}, U_{te}) + 4 \sqrt{\frac{d \log(2m') + \log(\frac{4}{\delta})}{m'}}
\end{aligned}
$$

Proof: The corollary follows from theorem 5.10 by replacing $Er^{P_{tr}}$ by its VC-based empirical upper bound, and upper-bounding $d_{\Delta(H)}(D_{P_{tr}}, D_{P_{te}})$ in terms of its empirical value on samples, through lemma [Kifer et al., 2004].

Note, that while part 2 of corollary 5.11 sounds more practical than part 1 and than theorem 5.10 (since all the parameters involved in the bound are derived from available training data), the latter formulations are more general. Theorem 5.10 allows flexibility in estimating the true error of hypotheses, and in choosing the preferred predictor. For example, theorem 5.10 and part 1 of corollary 5.11

apply also to algorithms employing regularization methods (such as margin or description complexity penalty terms) rather than empirical risk minimization. Likewise, theorem 5.10 is applicable also in cases where the method used to assess the distance between the training and goal task distribution is different than picking random unlabeled samples and computing their empirical distance.

5.4.3 Distinguishing Features of Our Bounds

Let us summarize the main aspects in which the bounds presented above may differ from other theoretical analysis of domain adaptation.

- Maybe the most significant merit of this bound is that it can be *reliably estimated* using the data available to the learner. A learner can run any learning algorithm on the training data (the labeled training task sample), estimate the error of the outcome predictor for the training task (using any common error estimation technique), and then, using the unlabeled sample from the goal task, apply the bound of theorem 5.10 to obtain a (guaranteed) upper bound on the error of that predictor on the goal task. Such a bound may be used by a learner to determine whether the application of a more elaborate paradigm (like adaptive prediction) is required.

- Another distinctive feature of our bounds is that they do not rely on any assumptions concerning the relationship between the training data domain and the goal (or test) data domain. Obviously, this feature makes our bounds more general. However, the other side of the coin is that this generality has a cost in terms of the tightness of the bounds. Whenever prior knowledge about the relationship between the two learning domains is available, it is conceivable that that prior knowledge can be utilized to get better bounds. Furthermore, such prior domain knowledge may allow the application of *adaptive prediction* — choosing predictors that have better performance on the goal domain than the predictors chosen just based on their training domain performance (as is the case with the conservative prediction that we analyzed above).

- Finally, it should be noted that our bounds are *relative* bounds, in the sense that rather than providing absolute upper bounds for the learned predictors error, they bound only the difference between that error and the error of some baseline predictor - the sum of the training and test errors of the best predictor in the hypothesis class, H (this is what $\lambda_{T,G,H}$ denotes). This relaxation of the guarantee is an inevitable consequence of not making any prior task assumptions (as discussed in the previous point). In a way, this is similar to the distinction between the agnostic and PAC (probably approximately correct) models of learning. The first makes no prior assumptions about the label generating distribution, but settles for generalization bounds that are relative to those of the best predictor in some reference hypothesis class. The latter, the PAC model, assumes that the hypothesis class contains a perfect (i.e., zero error) predictor, and, under that assumption, can expect absolute numeric bounds on the error of the learner's predictor.

5.5 Adaptive Predictors

Conservative predictors seem quite limited. Rather than performing a learning process over the target domain examples (in a way that utilizes training domain data), they just perform learning over the training domain and apply the resulting predictor to the target task. Strategies that allow the predictor they pick for the target task to differ from the predictor they would use for the training task seem to carry greater promise. However, in the context of domain adaptation, when no target domain-labeled data is available, the reliability of such paradigms is not guaranteed.

It should be realized that to allow reliable success of such paradigms, rather strong assumptions concerning the learning tasks should be made. In particular, assuming *covariate shift* (namely, that the conditional distribution of label values, given the unlabeled data, is unchanged between the training and target distributions) is far from being sufficient to guarantee domain adaptation. In example 5.8 above, we described a pair of tasks for which there exists a perfect label predictor for the training distribution that has error probability 1 on a goal probability, in spite of both tasks being defined on the same domain and sharing the same conditional label distribution ($\Pr[label|x]$). In that example, availability of unlabeled samples of the target task does not help to overcome the training/test discrepancy.

Some recent work on learning under the covariate shift assumption suggests overcoming this problem by estimating the data density ratio between the training and target distributions by using sample-based empirical values (see, e.g., Sugiyama et al. [2007] and Huang et al. [2007]). However, it should be noted that, without restricting the family of possible distributions, no finite sample can yield a reliable approximation of the actual distribution. This is sharply demonstrated by example 5.4, above. Even in settings where the support of the data distribution is finite, in order to obtain reliable empirical estimates of the target distribution one needs sample sizes that approach the cardinality of that support (see Batu et al. [2000]), which seem way too much for all practical applications.

5.5.1 Some Solutions

We shall briefly list below some common approaches providing settings that allow reliable adaptive inductive transfer learning algorithms. These solutions are all based on assuming some prior knowledge about the learning tasks.

Restriction of the Family of Potential Target Distributions Ben-David and Schuller [2003] consider a framework in which there is some known family of distribution transformations, such that the target task is obtained by applying one of these transformations to the training task. They show that in cases where that family of transformations has a finite VC dimension, reliable adaptive learning can be guaranteed (in fact, that paper considers the multitask setting, and shows that under such conditions the learnability of each of the tasks improves as a result of having access to training samples from other tasks).

Existence of "Good" Domain Embedding Ben-David et al. [2007] consider the domain adaptation setting where the learner has access to an unlabeled target task sample (but no access to labeled samples from the target task). They show that if the learner can come up with data embedding for both the training and target domains, such that the images of the unlabeled distributions (of the training and target tasks) are similar, and such that under that embedding learnability of the training task is possible, then that embedding can be used to achieve reliable adaptive learning of the target task. The key component in their argument can be viewed as an "embedding version" of Theorem 5.10 above.

It is interesting to note that by using such an embedding the learner sacrifices the covariate shift assumption (in cases where that assumption holds for the original task domains) in order to gain similarity between the unlabeled distributions.

III Algorithms for Covariate Shift

6   Geometry of Covariate Shift with Applications to Active Learning

Takafumi Kanamori
Hidetoshi Shimodaira

We study learning algorithms under the covariate shift in which training and test data are drawn from different distributions. A naive estimator used under the covariate shift, such as the maximum likelihood estimator (MLE), will yield serious estimation bias when the assumed statistical model is misspecified. For the purpose of correcting this estimation bias, we introduce the maximum weighted log-likelihood estimator (MWLE) with an information criterion to determine an optimal weight function for samples. In the latter half of the chapter, we investigate active learning in which the covariate shift is used to improve prediction. In the learning process of active learning, the planner of an experiment can choose the covariate distribution. Thus, the covariate shift naturally occurs. By incorporating the MWLE into active learning, one can reduce estimation bias and obtain a consistent estimator even under model misspecification. Moreover, we illustrate the reason why active learning is often better than the ordinary learning scheme from the viewpoint of information geometry. The geometrical concept makes it clear how the modification of estimators improves ordinary learning methods.

6.1   Introduction

We study learning algorithms under the *covariate shift*covariate shift in which training and test data are drawn from different distributions. Also in chapter 7, chapter 8, and chapter 9, learning algorithms under similar situations are deeply investigated. The covariate shift is seen in various fields. In sample surveys, the distribution of training data is determined by a sampling scheme, while that of test data is governed by the population. Under the covariate shift, a naive estimator, such as the maximum likelihood estimator (MLE), will yield serious estimation bias when the statistical model is misspecified. To adjust the estimation bias, we introduce the maximum weighted log-likelihood estimator (MWLE). In the MWLE, a large part of data with less importance in the test distribution is downweighted. The price we pay for the unbiased estimation of the MWLE is its larger variance than the MLE. We derived an information criterion to determine moderate weights on training data. Applying the criterion, we can take into account the trade-off between the bias and variance to achieve high prediction accuracy.

In the latter half of the paper, we introduce active learning in which the covariate shift is exploited to improve prediction. The active learning method is closely connected with the optimal experimental design or the quantum estimation theory. In the learning process of active learning, the planners of experiments can determine the input distribution appropriately. Thus, the covariate shift naturally occurs. By incorporating the MWLE into active learning to make the estimator consistent, one can reduce the estimation bias even under model misspecification. In our setup, we can specify the optimal input distribution for active learning. The optimal one depends on the test distribution, which is generally unknown. We propose an estimation procedure for the optimal input distribution based on labeled and unlabeled dataset. The prediction accuracy is improved by using the input distribution intentionally altered from that of the test data.

We illustrate the reason that active learning is often better than the ordinary learning scheme. The information-geometrical view provides intuitive understanding of active learning. We show that the shift of the input distribution corresponds to the parallel shift of the statistical model, and that the curvature of the statistical model has the key role in explaining the advantage of active learning. The geometrical concept makes clear how the modification of estimator improves the ordinary learning methods.

6.2   Statistical Inference under Covariate Shift

6.2.1   Covariate Shift and Estimation Bias

Let $x \in \mathcal{X}$ be the input pattern or the covariate, and $y \in \mathbb{R}$ be the target value. In predictive inference with the regression analysis, we are interested in estimating the conditional density $q(y|x)$ of y given x, using a parametric model. Let $p(y|x, \theta)$ be the model of the conditional density which is parameterized by $\theta = (\theta^1, \ldots, \theta^k)' \in \Theta \subset \mathbb{R}^k$. Having observed i.i.d. samples of size n, denoted by $(X, Y) = \{(x_i, y_i) : i = 1, \ldots, n\}$, we obtain a predictive density $p(y|x, \hat{\theta})$ by giving an estimate $\hat{\theta} = \hat{\theta}(X, Y)$. In this section, we discuss improvement of the maximum likelihood estimate (MLE) under both (i) *covariate shift* in distribution and (ii) *misspecification* of the model as explained below.

Let $p_{\text{te}}(x)$ be the density of x for evaluation of the predictive performance, while $p_{\text{tr}}(x)$ be the density of x in the observation. We consider the loss function

$$\text{loss}_0(\theta) := \mathbf{E}_{\text{tr}}\left[\ell(y|x, \theta)\right], \quad \text{loss}_1(\theta) := \mathbf{E}_{\text{te}}\left[\ell(y|x, \theta)\right],$$

where $\ell(x, y|\theta) = -\ln p(y|x, \theta)$, and $\mathbf{E}_{tr}[\cdot]$ or $\mathbf{E}_{te}[\cdot]$ denotes the expectation by $q(y|x)p_{tr}(x)$ or $q(y|x)p_{te}(x)$, respectively. We employ $\text{loss}_1(\hat{\theta})$ for evaluation of $\hat{\theta}$, rather than the usual $\text{loss}_0(\hat{\theta})$. The situation $p_{tr}(x) \neq p_{te}(x)$ will be called covariate shift in distribution, which is one of the premises of this chapter.

This situation is not so odd as it might look at first. In fact, it is seen in various fields as follows. In sample surveys, $p_{tr}(x)$ is determined by the sampling scheme, while $p_{te}(x)$ is determined by the population. In regression analysis, covariate shift often happens because of the limitation of resources, or the design of experiments. In machine learning literature, "active learning" is the typical situation where we control $p_{tr}(x)$ for more accurate prediction [Abe and Mamitsuka, 1998; Cohn, 1994; Fukumizu, 1996; Sugiyama and Ogawa, 2000; Kanamori and Shimodaira, 2003; Kanamori, 2002, 2007; MacKay, 1992b; Seung et al., 1992]

We could say that the distribution of x in future observations is different from that of the past observations; x is not necessarily distributed as $p_{te}(x)$ in future, but we can give imaginary $p_{te}(x)$ to specify the region of x where the prediction accuracy should be controlled. Note that $p_{tr}(x)$ and/or $p_{te}(x)$ are often estimated from data, but we assume they are known or estimated reasonably in advance.

The second premise is misspecification of the model. Let $\hat{\theta}_0$ be the MLE of θ, and θ_0^* be the asymptotic limit of $\hat{\theta}_0$ as $n \to \infty$. Under certain regularity conditions, MLE is consistent and $p(y|x, \theta_0^*) = q(y|x)$ provided that the model is correctly specified. In practice, however, $p(y|x, \theta_0^*)$ deviates more or less from $q(y|x)$. Misspecification is the situation such that $q(y|x)$ may not be realized by the model $p(y|x, \theta)$ for any value of θ.

Under both the covariate shift and the misspecification, MLE does not necessarily provide a good inference. We will show that MLE is improved by giving a weight function w of the input in the log-likelihood function. The weighted log-likelihood function is defined as

$$-\sum_{i=1}^{n} w(x_i)\ell(y_i|x_i, \theta), \tag{6.1}$$

and the maximum weighted log-likelihood estimate (MWLE), denoted by $\hat{\theta}_w$, is given as the maximizer of (6.1) over Θ. It will be seen that the weight function $w(x) = p_{te}(x)/p_{tr}(x)$ is the optimal choice for sufficiently large n in terms of the expected loss with respect to $p_{te}(x)$. We denote the MWLE with this weight function by $\hat{\theta}_1$. Under some conditions, the MWLE $\hat{\theta}_1$ is a consistent estimator of θ_1^* which minimizes $\text{loss}_1(\theta)$. Figure 6.1 illustrates the bias of the MLE $\hat{\theta}_0$ and the consistency of the MWLE $\hat{\theta}_1$.

6.2.2   Illustrative Examples in Regression

Here we consider the normal regression to predict the response $y \in \mathbb{R}$ using a polynomial function of $x \in \mathcal{X} = \mathbb{R}$. We assume the true $q(y|x)$ is also given by

$$y = -x + x^3 + \varepsilon, \quad \varepsilon \sim \mathcal{N}(0, 0.3^2). \tag{6.2}$$

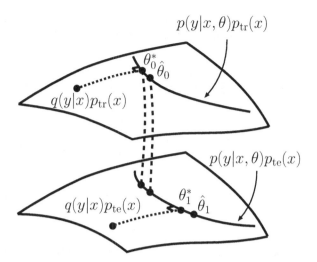

Figure 6.1 Under the condition of covariate shift and misspecification, the MLE $\hat{\theta}_0$ can be heavily biased and inconsistent. On the other hand the MWLE $\hat{\theta}_1$ is a consistent estimator for θ_1^*.

The density $p_{\mathrm{tr}}(x)$ of the input x is

$$x \sim \mathcal{N}(\mu_0, \tau_0^2), \tag{6.3}$$

where $\mu_0 = 0.5$, $\tau_0^2 = 0.5^2$. A dataset (X, Y) of size $n = 100$ is generated from $q(y|x)p_{\mathrm{tr}}(x)$, and plotted by circles in figure 6.2(a). The MLE $\hat{\theta}_0$ is obtained by the ordinary least squares (OLS) for the normal regression; we consider a model of the form

$$y = \theta_0 + \theta_1 x + \varepsilon, \quad \varepsilon \sim \mathcal{N}(0, \sigma^2), \tag{6.4}$$

and the regression line fitted by OLS is drawn as a solid line in figure 6.2(a).

On the other hand, MWLE $\hat{\theta}_w$ is obtained by weighted least squares (WLS) with weights $w(x_i)$ for the normal regression. We again consider the model (6.4) and the regression line fitted by WLS with $w(x) = p_{\mathrm{te}}(x)/p_{\mathrm{tr}}(x)$ is drawn as a dotted line in figure 6.2(a). Here, the density $p_{\mathrm{te}}(x)$ for imaginary "future" observations or that for the whole population in sample surveys is specified in advance by

$$x \sim \mathcal{N}(\mu_1, \tau_1^2), \tag{6.5}$$

where $\mu_1 = 0.0$, $\tau_1^2 = 0.3^2$. The ratio of $p_{\mathrm{te}}(x)$ to $p_{\mathrm{tr}}(x)$ is

$$\frac{p_{\mathrm{te}}(x)}{p_{\mathrm{tr}}(x)} = \frac{\exp(-(x-\mu_1)^2/2\tau_1^2)/\tau_1}{\exp(-(x-\mu_0)^2/2\tau_0^2)/\tau_0} \propto \exp\left(-\frac{(x-\bar{\mu})^2}{2\bar{\tau}^2}\right), \tag{6.6}$$

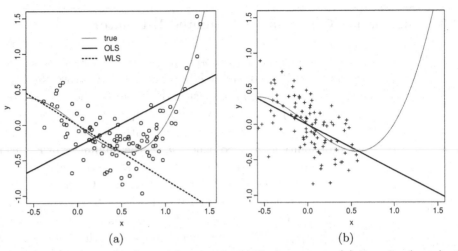

(a)   (b)

Figure 6.2   Fitting of polynomial regression with degree one. **(a)** Samples (x_i, y_i) of size $n = 100$ are generated from $q(y|x)p_{\mathrm{tr}}(x)$ and plotted as circles, where the underlying true curve is indicated by the thin dotted line. The solid line is obtained by OLS, and the dotted line is WLS with weight $p_{\mathrm{te}}(x)/p_{\mathrm{tr}}(x)$. **(b)** Samples of $n = 100$ are generated from $q(y|x)p_{\mathrm{te}}(x)$, and the regression line is obtained by OLS.

where $\bar{\tau}^2 = (\tau_1^{-2} - \tau_0^{-2})^{-1} = 0.38^2$, and $\bar{\mu} = \bar{\tau}^2(\tau_1^{-2}\mu_1 - \tau_0^{-2}\mu_0) = -0.28$.

The estimated regression line of WLS is very different from that of OLS. The question is: which is better than the other? It is known that OLS is the best linear unbiased estimate and makes a small mean squared error of prediction in terms of $q(y|x)p_{\mathrm{tr}}(x)$ which generated the data. On the other hand, WLS with weight (6.5) makes a small prediction error in terms of $q(y|x)p_{\mathrm{te}}(x)$ which will generate future observations, and thus WLS is better than OLS here. To confirm this, a dataset of size $n = 100$ is generated from $q(y|x)p_{\mathrm{te}}(x)$. The regression line fitted by OLS is shown in figure 6.2(b) which is considered to have small prediction error for the "future" data. The regression line of WLS fitted to the past data in figure 6.2(a) is quite similar to the line of OLS fitted to the future data in figure 6.2(b). In practice, only the past data is available. The WLS with past data gives almost the equivalent result to the future OLS.

The underlying true curve is the cubic polynomial, and thus the regression line of the model (6.5) cannot be fitted to it nicely over all the region of x. However, the true curve is almost linear in the region of $\mu_1 \pm 2\tau_1$, and the nice fit of the WLS in this region is obtained by throwing away the observed samples outside this region.

This type of estimation is not new in statistics. Actually, $\hat{\theta}_1$ is regarded as a generalization of the pseudo maximum likelihood estimation in sample surveys [Pfeffermann et al., 1998; Skinner et al., 1989]; the log-likelihood is weighted inversely proportional to $p_{\mathrm{tr}}(x)$, the probability of selecting unit x, while $p_{\mathrm{te}}(x)$ is equal probability for all possible values of x.

6.3   Information Criterion for Weighted Estimator

In spite of the asymptotic optimality of $w(x) = p_{\text{te}}(x)/p_{\text{tr}}(x)$ mentioned above, another choice of the weight function can improve the expected loss for moderate sample size by compromising the bias and the variance of $\hat{\theta}_w$. In this section we develop a practical method for this improvement.

From the law of large numbers with regularity conditions, we have $\hat{\theta}_w \to \theta_w^*$ in probability as $n \to \infty$, where θ_w^* is the minimizer of $\mathbf{E}_{\text{tr}}\left[w(x)\ell(x, y|\theta)\right]$ over $\theta \in \Theta$. Hereafter, we restrict our attention to proper $w(x)$ such that $\mathbf{E}_{\text{tr}}\left[w(x)\ell(x, y|\theta)\right]$ exists for all $\theta \in \Theta$ and that the Hessian of $\mathbf{E}_{\text{tr}}\left[w(x)\ell(x, y|\theta)\right]$ is nonsingular at θ_w^*, which is uniquely determined and interior to Θ.

In general, we have $\theta_w^* \neq \theta_1^*$ under misspecification except for the weight $w(x) \propto p_{\text{te}}(x)/p_{\text{tr}}(x)$. From the definition of θ_1^*, therefore, $\text{loss}_1(\theta_w^*) > \text{loss}_1(\theta_1^*)$. This immediately implies the asymptotic optimality of the weight $w(x) = p_{\text{te}}(x)/p_{\text{tr}}(x)$, because $\hat{\theta}_w \to \theta_w^*$ and $\hat{\theta}_1 \to \theta_1^*$ and thus $\text{loss}_1(\hat{\theta}_w) > \text{loss}_1(\hat{\theta}_1)$ for sufficiently large n.

The MWLE, $\hat{\theta}_1$, has consistency in a sense that it converges to the optimal parameter value θ_1^*. However, $\hat{\theta}_0$ is more efficient than $\hat{\theta}_1$ in terms of the asymptotic variance. This will be significant for moderate sample size, where n is large enough for the asymptotic expansions to be allowed, but not enough for the optimality of $\hat{\theta}_1$ to hold.

The performance of MWLE for a specified $w(x)$ is given by $\mathbf{E}_{\text{tr},n}\left[\text{loss}_1(\hat{\theta}_w)\right]$, where $\mathbf{E}_{\text{tr},n}\left[\cdot\right]$ denotes the expectation with respect to (X, Y) which follows $\prod_{i=1}^{n} q(y_i|x_i)p_{\text{tr}}(x_i)$. While we cannot calculate the value of the expected loss in practice, because $q(y|x)$ is unknown, we provide a variant of the information criterion as an estimate of $\mathbf{E}_{\text{tr},n}\left[\text{loss}_1(\hat{\theta}_w)\right]$.

Theorem 6.1 (Shimodaira [2000]) *Let the information criterion for MWLE $\hat{\theta}_w$ be*

$$\text{IC}_w := -2\sum_{i=1}^{n} \frac{p_{\text{te}}(x_i)}{p_{\text{tr}}(x_i)} \log p(y_i|x_i, \hat{\theta}_w) + 2\mathbf{tr}\left(K_0(w)H_0(w)^{-1}\right), \qquad (6.7)$$

where

$$K_0(w) = \mathbf{E}_{\text{tr}}\left[w(x)\frac{p_{\text{te}}(x)}{p_{\text{tr}}(x)}\frac{\partial \ell(y|x, \theta_w^*)}{\partial \theta}\frac{\partial \ell(y|x, \theta_w^*)}{\partial \theta'}\right], \quad H_0(w) = \mathbf{E}_{\text{tr}}\left[w(x)\frac{\partial^2 \ell(y|x, \theta_w^*)}{\partial\theta\partial\theta'}\right].$$

The matrices K_0 and H_0 can be replaced by their consistent estimates. Then, $\text{IC}_w/2n$ is an estimate of the expected loss unbiased up to $O(n^{-1})$ term:

$$\mathbf{E}_{\text{tr},n}\left[\text{IC}_w/2n\right] = \mathbf{E}_{\text{tr},n}\left[\text{loss}_1(\hat{\theta}_w)\right] + o(n^{-1}). \qquad (6.8)$$

It is easily seen that the information criterion IC_w is an extension of AIC or TIC [Akaike, 1974; Takeuchi, 1976].

As an illustrative example of (6.7), we compute IC_w for a Gaussian linear regression model with known variance $\sigma^2 = 1$, that is,

$$-\log p(y|x, \theta) = \frac{1}{2}(y - \langle x, \theta \rangle)^2 + \mathrm{const},$$

where $x, \theta \in \mathbb{R}^k$. Let $\varepsilon_i = y_i - \langle x_i, \hat{\theta}_w \rangle$, then IC_w is given as

$$\mathrm{IC}_w = \sum_{i=1}^{n} \frac{p_{\mathrm{te}}(x_i)}{p_{\mathrm{tr}}(x_i)} \varepsilon_i^2 + 2\mathbf{tr}\left(\hat{K}_0(w)\hat{H}_0(w)^{-1} \right),$$

$$\hat{K}_0(w) = \frac{1}{n} \sum_{i=1}^{n} w(x_i) \frac{p_{\mathrm{te}}(x_i)}{p_{\mathrm{tr}}(x_i)} \varepsilon_i^2 x_i x_i^\top, \quad \hat{H}_0(w) = \frac{1}{n} \sum_{i=1}^{n} w(x_i) x_i x_i^\top.$$

Given the model $p(y|x, \theta)$ and the data (X, Y), we choose a weight function $w(x)$ which attains the minimum of IC_w over a certain class of weights. This is selection of the weight rather than model selection. We shall pick a better one from the two extreme cases of $w(x) \equiv 1$ and $w(x) = p_{\mathrm{te}}(x)/p_{\mathrm{tr}}(x)$, or consider a class of weights by connecting the two extremes continuously:

$$w(x) = \left(\frac{p_{\mathrm{te}}(x)}{p_{\mathrm{tr}}(x)} \right)^\lambda, \quad \lambda \in [0, 1], \tag{6.9}$$

where $\lambda = 0$ corresponds to $\hat{\theta}_0$ and $\lambda = 1$ corresponds to $\hat{\theta}_1$. Figure 6.3(a) shows the plot of the information criterion and its two components. By increasing λ from 0 to 1, the first term of IC_w decreases while the second term increases. We numerically find $\hat{\lambda} = 0.56$ so that the two terms balance. The regression curves obtained by this method are shown in figure 6.3(b). When we have several candidate forms of $p(y|x, \theta)$, the model and the weight are selected simultaneously by minimizing IC_w.

6.4 Active Learning and Covariate Shift

In active learning, one can determine the input distribution, $p_{\mathrm{tr}}(x)$, and then the probability of training samples is $q(y|x)p_{\mathrm{tr}}(x)$. The predictive performance is assessed by the distribution $q(y|x)p_{\mathrm{te}}(x)$. This setting naturally causes covariate shift. In this section, we assume that $p_{\mathrm{te}}(x)$ is known. This assumption will be relaxed in section 6.5.

We study the preferable input distribution for the estimation of $q(y|x)$. Suppose that the input distribution is chosen from the set of probabilities $\{p_\xi(x) \mid \xi \in \Xi \subset \mathbb{R}^h\}$. As shown in section 6.2.1, when the input distribution is $p_\xi(x)$, the MWLE with the weight $w(x) = p_{\mathrm{te}}(x)/p_\xi(x)$ provides the asymptotically unbiased estimates of θ_1^*. For the sample distribution $q(y|x)p_\xi(x)$ and the MWLE estimate with the weight $w(x) = p_{\mathrm{te}}(x)/p_\xi(x)$, the expected loss is asymptotically equal to

$$\mathbf{E}_{\xi,n}\left[\mathrm{loss}_1(\hat{\theta}_w) \right] = \mathrm{loss}_1(\theta_1^*) + \frac{1}{2n}\mathbf{tr}\left(K(p_\xi)H^{-1} \right) + o(n^{-1}), \tag{6.10}$$

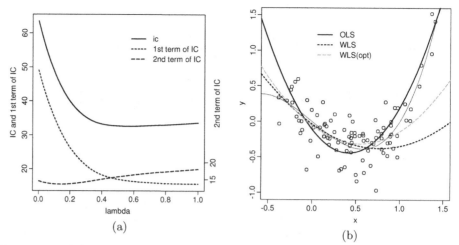

Figure 6.3 **(a)** Curve of IC_w vs. $\lambda \in [0, 1]$ for the model of (6.4). The weight function (6.9) connecting from $w(x) \equiv 1$ (i.e. $\lambda = 0$) to $w(x) = p_{\text{te}}(x)/p_{\text{tr}}(x)$ (i.e. $\lambda = 1$) was used. Also shown are the first term of IC_w in dotted lines, and the second term of IC_w in broken lines. **(b)** The estimated regression curves. The WLS curve with the optimal $\hat{\lambda}$, as well as those for OLS ($\lambda = 0$) and WLS ($\lambda = 1$), are drawn.

where we have used $\mathbf{E}_{\xi,n}[\cdot]$ to denote the expectation by the probability distribution $\prod_{i=1}^{n} q(y_i|x_i)p_\xi(x_i)$, and the matrices $K(p_\xi)$ and H are given as

$$K(p_\xi) := K_0(p_{\text{te}}/p_\xi) = \mathbf{E}_{\text{te}}\left[\frac{p_{\text{te}}(x)}{p_\xi(x)}\frac{\partial \ell(y|x,\theta_1^*)}{\partial \theta'}\frac{\partial \ell(y|x,\theta_1^*)}{\partial \theta'}\right],$$

$$H := H_0(p_{\text{te}}/p_\xi) = \mathbf{E}_{\text{te}}\left[\frac{\partial^2 \ell(y|x,\theta_1^*)}{\partial \theta \partial \theta'}\right].$$

Thus, the preferable distribution, $p_{\hat{\xi}}$, is the minimizer of the sample approximation of $\mathbf{tr}\left(K(p_\xi)H^{-1}\right)$ over $\xi \in \Xi$.

We show an algorithm for active learning in figure 6.4. This algorithm works under the above-mentioned assumptions, that is, p_{te} is known. In step 1, the preferable distribution $p_{\hat{\xi}}(x)$ is estimated as the minimizer of the second term of the expected loss (6.10). Here, the MLE over the samples (X_0, Y_0) is available for estimation of $\mathbf{tr}\left(K(p_\xi)H^{-1}\right)$. For example, when we assume the Gaussian linear regression model with known variance $\sigma^2 = 1$, that is,

$$\ell(y|x,\theta) = \frac{1}{2}(y - \langle x,\theta\rangle)^2 + \text{const},$$

an estimator of $\mathbf{tr}\left(K(p_\xi)H^{-1}\right)$ is $\mathbf{tr}\left(\hat{K}(p_\xi)\hat{H}^{-1}\right)$. Here the matrices are defined as

$$\hat{K}(p_\xi) = \frac{1}{s}\sum_{i=1}^{s}\frac{p_{\text{te}}(x_i)}{p_\xi(x_i)}\varepsilon_i^2 x_i x_i^\top, \quad \hat{H} = \frac{1}{s}\sum_{i=1}^{s} x_i x_i^\top.$$

As the result, the preferable distribution $p_{\hat{\xi}}(x)$ is the minimum solution of

---

Input: Training samples $(X_0, Y_0) = \{(x_i, y_i)|i = 1, \ldots, s\}$ independently obtained from $q(y|x)p_{te}(x)$. Total number of training samples, n.

1. Estimate the preferable input distribution $p_{\hat{\xi}}(x)$ based on (X_0, Y_0).

2. Obtain $n - s$ samples $(X_1, Y_1) = \{(x_i, y_i)|i = s+1, \ldots, n\}$ from $q(y|x)p_{\hat{\xi}}(x)$.

3. Compute the MWLE $\hat{\theta}$ from the samples $(X, Y) = \{(x_i, y_i)|i = 1, \ldots, n\}$. The information criterion IC_w is available for adjusting the weight of the form of $(p_{te}(x)/p_{\hat{\xi}}(x))^{\lambda}$ for $\lambda \in [0, 1]$.

Figure 6.4   Algorithm for active learning.

$\mathbf{tr}\left(\hat{K}(p_{\xi})\hat{H}^{-1}\right)$. In step 3, the MWLE is applied, where the weight is 1 on the samples (x_i, y_i), $i = 1, \ldots s$, and $p_{te}(x_i)/p_{\hat{\xi}}(x_i)$ on the latter samples (x_j, y_j), $j = s + 1 \ldots n$, that is, the weighted log-likelihood is

$$\sum_{i=1}^{s} \ell(y_i|x_i, \theta) + \sum_{i=s+1}^{n} \frac{p_{te}(x_i)}{p_{\hat{\xi}}(x_i)} \ell(y_i|x_i, \theta).$$

The information criterion IC_w is available to adjust the weight for the variance reduction.

Note that the samples (X, Y) are not independently distributed, that is, the former part (X_0, Y_0) and the latter part (X_1, Y_1) are correlated. As a result, IC_w is not asymptotically unbiased for the expected loss in the context of active learning. We can derive the asymptotically unbiased information criterion for the expected loss by taking the correlation into account. The information criterion IC_w in (6.7), however, may work well to reduce the variance of final estimate $\hat{\theta}$. We show simple numerical experiments below.

Active learning for normal regression is studied. The statistical model $p(y|x, \theta)$ with the parameter $\theta = (\theta_0, \theta_1, \theta_2, \theta_3)$ is defined by

$$y = \theta_0 + \theta_1 x + \theta_2 x^2 + \varepsilon, \quad \varepsilon \sim \mathcal{N}(0, \theta_3),$$

and the test probability distribution $q(y|x)p_{te}(x)$ is determined by

$$y = 1 - x + x^2 + \delta x^3 + \varepsilon, \quad \varepsilon \sim \mathcal{N}(0, 0.3^2),$$
$$x \sim \mathcal{N}(0.2, 0.4^2),$$

where δ determines the deviation from the model. The input probability $p_{\xi}(x)$ is defined as

$$x \sim \mathcal{N}(0, \xi^2).$$

We compare the following three learning methods.

ols: the distribution of all input samples is $p_{te}(x)$, and the ordinary least squares is applied for the parameter estimation.

act: active learning without IC_w, that is, the weight of the MWLE is given as $p_{\mathrm{te}}(x)/p_{\hat{\xi}}(x)$.

actIC: active learning with IC_w, that is, the weight of the MWLE is given as $(p_{\mathrm{te}}(x)/p_{\hat{\xi}}(x))^{\lambda}$, and the λ is determined by IC_w.

The total sample size is $n = 100$. For **act** and **actIC**, the number of samples in the former part is $s = 30$. The experiments are repeated 1000 times with different random seed for samples. Results are shown in figure 6.5. The abscissa axis denotes the model deviation which is measured by the Kullback-Leibler divergence between $q(y|x)$ and $p(y|x, \theta_1^*)$ under $x \sim p_{\mathrm{te}}(x)$, that is, $\mathbf{E}_{\mathrm{te}}\left[\log \frac{q(y|x)}{p(y|x,\theta_1^*)}\right]$. Note that the expected loss (6.10) is written as

$$\mathbf{E}_{\xi,n}\left[\mathbf{E}_{\mathrm{te}}\left[\log \frac{q(y|x)}{p(y|x,\hat{\theta}_w)}\right]\right] = \mathbf{E}_{\mathrm{te}}\left[\log \frac{q(y|x)}{p(y|x,\theta_1^*)}\right] + \frac{1}{2n}\mathbf{tr}\left(K(p_\xi)H^{-1}\right) + o(n^{-1}),$$

thus the Kullback-Leibler divergence measures model deviation more directly than the parameter δ.

Figure 6.5(a) shows the difference of the expected loss between **ols** and **actIC**. When the test probability is very close to the model, **ols** is better than **actIC**. On the other hand, if the model deviation is more than about 0.005, **ols** becomes worse. This indicates the effectiveness of active learning. Figure 6.5(b) shows the difference of the expected loss between **act** and **actIC**. When the test probability is close to the model, **actIC** is better than **act**. This is because the appropriate value of λ is determined by IC_w. For the model deviation larger than about 0.01, **act** becomes better than **actIC**, while the difference is small in comparison with figure 6.5(a). The values of λ estimated by IC_w are plotted in figure 6.5(c). For the small deviation, λ is close to zero. This result is reasonable, because the **ols** is the best estimate for $\delta = 0$. On the other hand, when the model deviation becomes larger, λ approaches 1, and as a result, the estimation bias reduces. As explained, IC_w with active learning works relatively well, though IC_w is not an asymptotically unbiased estimate of the expected loss due to the correlation among the samples.

6.5   Pool-Based Active Leaning

In this section, we introduce the pool-based active learning algorithm. Suppose that samples $(X, Y) = \{(x_i, y_i)|i = 1, \ldots, n\}$ and inputs $\tilde{X} = \{\tilde{x}_1, \ldots, \tilde{x}_N\}$ are independently observed from the probability distribution $q(y|x)p_{\mathrm{te}}(x)$ and $p_{\mathrm{te}}(x)$, respectively. N is often much larger than n. For example in Zhu et al. [2003b], N is about 1000 and n is at most 50 for document categorization problems.

In pool-based active learning, one can select m points among $\tilde{X}$, say $\check{X} = \{\tilde{x}_{i_1}, \ldots, \tilde{x}_{i_m}\} \subset \tilde{X}$. Usually m is of similar size as n. Through the additional observations, response values on $\check{X}$ are given according to $q(y|x)$, and the training

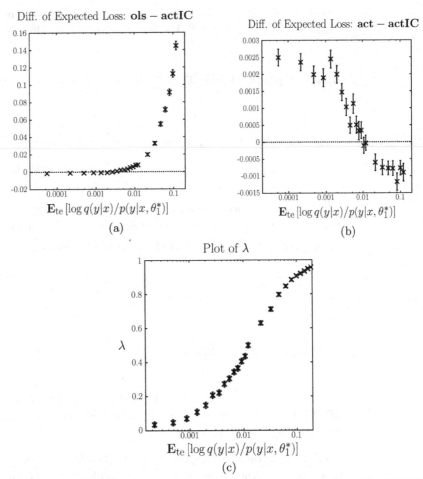

Figure 6.5 **(a)** Difference of the expected loss between **ols** and **actIC**. **(b)** Difference of the expected loss between **act** and **actIC**. **(c)** Plot of $\hat{\lambda}$ estimated by IC_w to the model deviation $\mathbf{E}_{te}\left[\log \frac{q(y|x)}{p(y|x,\theta_1^*)}\right]$.

samples $(\check{X}, \check{Y}) = \{(\tilde{x}_{i_1}, \tilde{y}_{i_1}), \ldots, (\tilde{x}_{i_m}, \tilde{y}_{i_m})\}$ are obtained. Based on the total samples (X, Y), $\tilde{X}$ and $(\check{X}, \check{Y})$, we estimate the conditional probability $q(y|x)$.

6.5.1 Optimal Input Distribution

According to Kanamori [2007], we introduce the most preferable input distribution $p_{\mathrm{tr}}(x)$ for active learning. First, let us define the function $A(x)$ by

$$A(x) = \int q(y|x) \frac{\partial \ell(y|x, \theta_1^*)}{\partial \theta'} H^{-1} \frac{\partial \ell(y|x, \theta_1^*)}{\partial \theta} dy, \tag{6.11}$$

where the integrand is of quadratic form. The inequality $A(x) \geq 0$ is assured because the matrix H is positive definite. When the expectation of $\mathbf{E}_{\mathrm{te}}\left[\sqrt{A(x)}\right]$ exists, the second term in the right hand of (6.10) is written as

$$\mathbf{tr}\left(K(p_{\mathrm{tr}})H^{-1}\right) = \left(\mathbf{E}_{\mathrm{te}}\left[\sqrt{A(x)}\right]\right)^2 \left\{1 + \int \frac{(r(x) - p_{\mathrm{tr}}(x))^2}{p_{\mathrm{tr}}(x)} dx\right\},$$

where $r(x)$ is defined by

$$r(x) = \frac{p_{\mathrm{te}}(x)\sqrt{A(x)}}{\mathbf{E}_{\mathrm{te}}\left[\sqrt{A(x)}\right]}. \tag{6.12}$$

As a result, the active learning with the input distribution $p_{\mathrm{tr}}(x) = r(x)$ and the MWLE involving $w(x) = p_{\mathrm{te}}(x)/p_{\mathrm{tr}}(x)$ is asymptotically optimal in the sense of the expected loss up to the order of $O(n^{-1})$.

As an illustrative example, let $q(y|x)$ be the conditional probability defined as $y = g(x) + \varepsilon$, where $\varepsilon \sim \mathcal{N}(0, \sigma^2)$, and $p(y|x, \theta)$ be the Gaussian linear regression model, i.e., $\ell = \frac{1}{2\sigma^2}(y - \langle x, \theta \rangle)^2$ up to constant with know variance. Then, the function $A(x)$ is

$$A(x) = x^{\top} H^{-1} x \left(1 + \frac{(g(x) - \langle x, \theta_1^* \rangle)^2}{\sigma^2}\right), \quad H = \mathbf{E}_{\mathrm{te}}\left[xx^{\top}\right].$$

Figure 6.6 displays the optimal distribution $r(x)$ under the following setup. The model $p(y|x, \theta)$ is the Gaussian linear regression model,

$$p(y|x, \theta) = \frac{1}{\sqrt{2\pi}} \exp\left\{-\frac{1}{2}(y - \theta_0 - \theta_1 x)^2\right\},$$

and $p_{\mathrm{te}}(x)$ is the uniform distribution on the interval $[-1, 1]$. The true conditional probability $q(y|x)$ is given as

$$q(y|x) = \frac{1}{\sqrt{2\pi}} \exp\left\{-\frac{1}{2}(y - \delta x^2)^2\right\},$$

where we examined the cases of $\delta = 0$ and $\delta = 1.0$. On the other hand, the preferable

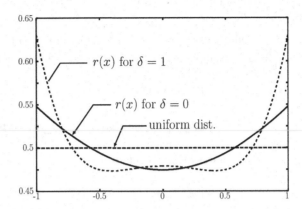

Figure 6.6 Plots of optimal input distributions. The value of δ controls the degree of the misspecification from the statistical model.

input distribution in terms of D-optimal criterion [Fedorov, 1972] is given as

$$P_{\text{tr}}\{x = 1\} = P_{\text{tr}}\{x = -1\} = \frac{1}{2}.$$

Under the misspecification of the model, however, the active learning with D-optimal input distribution does not work well as shown in the simulation studies in section 6.5.3.

6.5.2   Learning Algorithm

In order to apply active learning using optimal input distribution $r(x)$, we need to estimate the function $A(x)$ based on the observation. From the form of (6.11), we find that the regression function of the samples defined as

$$\left\{\left(x_i, \ \frac{\partial \ell(y_i|x_i, \tilde{\theta})}{\partial \theta'} \widehat{H}^{-1} \frac{\partial \ell(y_i|x_i, \tilde{\theta})}{\partial \theta}\right) \ \middle| \ i = 1, \ldots, m\right\} \tag{6.13}$$

provides an approximation of $A(x)$. Here $\widehat{H}$ is a naive estimator of H such as

$$\widehat{H} = \frac{1}{m} \sum_{i=1}^{m} \frac{\partial^2 \ell(y_i|x_i, \tilde{\theta})}{\partial \theta \partial \theta'},$$

and $\tilde{\theta}$ is the MLE given by (X, Y). For the Gaussian linear regression model with known variance $\sigma^2 = 1$, the samples (6.13) are given as

$$\left\{(x_i, \ \varepsilon_i^2 x_i^\top \hat{H}^{-1} x_i) \ \middle| \ i = 1, \ldots, m, \right\}, \tag{6.14}$$

where $\hat{H} = \frac{1}{m} \sum_{i=1}^{m} x_i x_i^\top$ and $\varepsilon_i = y_i - \langle x_i, \tilde{\theta} \rangle$. Simple learning methods such as *rpart* [Breiman et al., 1984] are available for the estimation of $A(x)$.

Input. Samples : (X, Y), Input samples : $\tilde{X}$, Number of input samples picked up from $\tilde{X} : m$.

1. Compute the MLE $\tilde{\theta}$ and the estimator $\hat{A}(x)$ from samples (X, Y) and $\tilde{X}$.

2. Input samples, $\check{X}$, are resampled according to $\hat{r}(x)$, and then obtain the additional observation, $(\check{X}, \check{Y})$.

3. Compute the MWLE based on total samples as follows:

$$\hat{\theta} = \arg\max_{\theta} \left\{ \sum_{i=1}^{n} \log p(y_i | x_i, \theta) + \sum_{s=1}^{m} w_s \log p(\check{y}_{i_s} | \check{x}_{i_s}, \theta) \right\},$$

where the weight, w_s is defined as

$$w_s = \frac{1}{N} \frac{\sum_{j=1}^{N} \sqrt{\hat{A}(\tilde{x}_j)}}{\sqrt{\hat{A}(\tilde{x}_{i_s})}}.$$

4. Output the estimated parameter $\hat{\theta}$.

Figure 6.7 Pool-based active learning.

The optimal input distribution is approximated by the probability function $\hat{r}(x)$ over the $\tilde{X}$ such as

$$\hat{r}(x = \tilde{x}_i) = \frac{\sqrt{\hat{A}(\tilde{x}_i)}}{\sum_{j=1}^{N} \sqrt{\hat{A}(\tilde{x}_j)}}, \qquad i = 1, \ldots, N, \tag{6.15}$$

where $\hat{A}(x)$ is an estimator of $A(x)$.

Provided the estimates of the optimal input distribution, pool-based active learning is constructed as shown in figure 6.7. In the pool-based active learning, the optimal input distribution is replaced by an estimated one. Hence, if the estimation of the optimal input distribution is not accurate, the active learning algorithm may not work well. Next, we compare the proposed learning method with the other existing methods.

6.5.3 Simulation Studies

A numerical experiment is shown to examine the proposed method. The dimension of x is ten, and the dth element of x is denoted by x_d for $d = 1, \ldots, 10$. The samples (X, Y) are independently generated according to the model,

$$y = \sum_{d=1}^{10} x_d + \delta\, x_1^2 + \varepsilon, \quad \varepsilon \sim \mathcal{N}(0, 1).$$

The value of δ takes from 0.0 to 0.05 to control the degree of misspecification. Let $p_{\text{te}}(x)$ be the probability density of the normal distribution $\mathcal{N}(0, 5^2 \mathbf{I}_{10})$, where $\mathbf{I}_k$ is $k \times k$ identity matrix. The samples $\tilde{X}$ are also generated from $p_{\text{te}}(x)$. The statistical

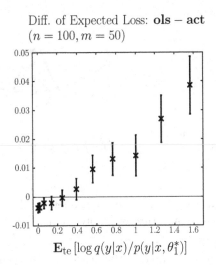

Figure 6.8 The difference of the expected loss between ols and act is depicted.

model of regression functions is defined by

$$S = \left\{ p(y|x, \theta) = \frac{1}{\sqrt{2\pi}} \exp \left\{ -\frac{1}{2}(y - g(x|\theta))^2 \right\} \mid \theta \in \mathbb{R}^{11} \right\},$$

where $g(x|\theta)$ is the linear model, $g(x|\theta) = \theta_0 + \sum_{d=1}^{10} \theta_d x_d$.

We compare the following two learning methods:

ols: the sampling distribution on $\tilde{X}$ is the uniform distribution. The MLE is applied for the parameter estimation.

act: the sampling distribution on $\tilde{X}$ is $\hat{r}(x)$ in (6.15). The MWLE is used for the parameter estimation.

The number of samples is set to $n = 100$ and $N = 1000$, and the number of additional samples is $m = 50$. To evaluate the average performance of estimators, the expected loss is approximately computed over the replicated 1000 sets of samples with different random seeds.

Figure 6.8 indicates the difference of the expected loss between **ols** and **act**. Positive value of the plot denotes that **act** is superior to **ols**. When the model is misspecified, **act** outperforms **ols**. In the numerical experiment, we find that the approximation of the function $A(x)$ does not degrade the performance of the active learning.

6.6 Information Geometry of Active Learning

Information geometry [Amari, 1985; Amari and Nagaoka, 2000] is useful for intuitive understanding of statistical inference. Here, we introduce a geometrical view of

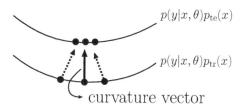

curvature vector

Figure 6.9 The shift of the statistical model to the opposite direction of the mean curvature vector leads the shrinkage in the dispersion of estimated parameter.

active learning. In information geometry, a statistical model such as $p(y|x, \theta)p(x)$ is regarded as a manifold parameterized by $\theta \in \Theta \subset \mathbb{R}^d$, and its geometrical structure such as curvature is deeply connected to the property of statistical inference under the model.

In the setup of active learning, we assume that $q(y|x)$ is included in the statistical model, that is, there exists $\theta_1^* \in \Theta$ such as $q(y|x) = p(y|x, \theta_1^*)$. This assumption can be relaxed to some extent, that is, if the true probability is written as $q(y|x) = p(y|x, \theta_1^*) + \varepsilon \cdot u(x)$ for small ε, the argument below holds with some modifications.

In active learning, the model of training samples and that of test samples are different in general, while in standard statistical inference, $p_{\text{tr}} = p_{\text{te}}$ holds. That is, samples for parameter estimation are drawn from $q(y|x)p_{\text{tr}}(x)$ and the prediction accuracy is assessed under the probability density $q(y|x)p_{\text{te}}(x)$. This situation is regarded as the change of training distribution from p_{te} to p_{tr}. Thus, we need to consider two statistical manifolds, $p(y|x, \theta)p_{\text{te}}(x)$ and $p(y|x, \theta)p_{\text{tr}}(x)$. Statistical inference by active learning with input distribution $p_{\text{tr}}(x)$ corresponds to shifting the statistical model from $p(y|x, \theta)p_{\text{te}}(x)$ to $p(y|x, \theta)p_{\text{tr}}(x)$.

Figure 6.9 illustrates the intuitive reason why active learning improves the standard estimator. When the direction of the model shift from $p_{\text{te}}(x)$ to $p_{\text{tr}}(x)$ is opposite to the curvature vector, the model shift leads the shrinkage of the variance of estimates as shown in figure 6.9. That is, the relation between the curvature vector and the direction of the model shift is crucial to understand the improvement by active learning.

From the asymptotic expansion (6.10), the difference of the expected loss between the MLE with samples from $p_{\text{te}}(x)$ and active learning with samples from $p_{\text{tr}}(x)$ is asymptotically measured by

$$\Delta = \mathbf{tr}\left(H^{-1}K(p_{\text{te}})\right) - \mathbf{tr}\left(H^{-1}K(p_{\text{tr}})\right).$$

A large positive value of Δ is preferable when active learning is applied. We will show that the quantity Δ is represented by the inner product of the direction of the model shift and the curvature vector of the statistical model such as (6.17) in the argument below. That representation provides an intuitive understanding of the advantage of active learning.

We show a simple example. Let the statistical model $p(y|x, \theta)$ be

$$p(y|x, \theta) = \frac{1}{\sqrt{2\pi\theta}} \exp\left\{ -\frac{1}{2\theta}(y - f(x))^2 \right\}, \quad \theta > 0. \tag{6.16}$$

Intuitively it is clear that active learning will not improve the accuracy of estimation under the above model, because the distribution of $y - f(x)$ does not depend on the covariate. When the MWLE is applied to estimate the variance parameter θ, the weight $p_{\text{te}}(x_i)/p_{\text{tr}}(x_i)$ is assigned on each sample $y_i - f(x_i)$. However, it is easy to see that the uniform weight provides the most accurate estimator of the variance. Thus, the MWLE always degrades the estimation accuracy. The geometrical understanding will be shown below.

First, we prepare some notations for information geometry. See Kanamori [2007] for a rigorous definition of notations. Let $\mathcal{P}$ be the set of all joint probability densities of x and y, and the statistical model $\mathcal{S}$ is defined by

$$\mathcal{S} = \{p(x)p(y|x, \theta) \mid p(x) \in \mathcal{P}_{\text{x}}, \ \theta \in \Theta\} \subset \mathcal{P},$$

where $\mathcal{P}_{\text{x}}$ is the set of all input probability densities. The tangent space at $q \in \mathcal{S}$ is denoted as T_q. Roughly speaking, the tangent vector $v \in T_q$ is a function satisfying $\int v(x, y)q(x, y)dxdy = 0$. The inner product of $a, b \in T_q$ is defined as

$$\langle a, b \rangle_q = \int a(x, y)b(x, y)q(x, y)dxdy.$$

For the density $q = p(x)p(y|x, \theta) \in \mathcal{S}$, the θ-score functions, $\frac{\partial \ell(y|x, \theta)}{\partial \theta_i}, i = 1, \ldots, d$, represent tangent vectors of T_q along changes in the parameter of interest. For $p_{\text{tr}}(x), p_{\text{te}}(x) \in \mathcal{P}_{\text{x}}$, let the tangent vector v_{tr} at $p_{\text{tr}}(x)p(y|x, \theta) \in \mathcal{S}$ be

$$v_{\text{tr}} := \frac{d}{dt} \log\left((1 - t)\, p_{\text{tr}}(x)p(y|x, \theta) + t\, p_{\text{te}}(x)p(y|x, \theta)\right)\Big|_{t=0} = \frac{p_{\text{te}}(x) - p_{\text{tr}}(x)}{p_{\text{tr}}(x)}.$$

Note that the expectation of $\frac{\partial \ell(y|x, \theta)}{\partial \theta_i}$ and v_{tr} over $p_{\text{tr}}(x)p(y|x, \theta)$ vanishes because the infinitesimal shift along these tangent vector preserves the total mass of $p_{\text{tr}}(x)p(y|x, \theta)$.

We consider parallel transports between tangent spaces. Let T_{tr} and T_{te} be the tangent space at $p_{\text{tr}}(x)p(y|x, \theta_1^*)$ and $p_{\text{te}}(x)p(y|x, \theta_1^*)$, respectively. The parallel transport of $a \in T_{\text{te}}$ to T_{tr} is defined as

$$\Pi_{\text{te} \to \text{tr}}^{(m)} a(x, y) = \frac{p_{\text{te}}(x)}{p_{\text{tr}}(x)} a(x, y),$$

which is called m-parallel transport. This geometrical structure coincides with that induced from the Kullback-Leibler divergence on $\mathcal{S}$ according to the theory of information geometry [Amari and Nagaoka, 2000].

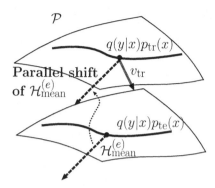

Figure 6.10 Geometrical interpretation of active learning. The angle between the parallel transported mean curvature vector $\Pi_{\text{te}\to\text{tr}}^{(m)}\mathcal{H}_{\text{mean}}^{(e)}$ and v_{tr} corresponds to the difference of the MLE and active learning in the sense of the expected loss.

The embedding curvature at $p_{\text{te}}(x)p(y|x,\theta_1^*)$ is given as

$$\mathcal{H}_{ij}^{(e)} = -\frac{\partial^2 \ell(y|x,\theta_1^*)}{\partial\theta_i\partial\theta_j} + \sum_{k=1}^{d} \Gamma_{ij}^{(e)k} \frac{\partial\ell(y|x,\theta_1^*)}{\partial\theta_k},$$

where $\Gamma_{ij}^{(e)k}, i,j,k = 1,\ldots,d$ are connection coefficients determined by the equalities $\mathbf{E}_{\text{te}}\left[\mathcal{H}_{ij}^{(e)}\frac{\partial\ell(y|x,\theta_1^*)}{\partial\theta_k}\right] = 0$ for all $k = 1,\ldots,d$. The embedding curvature is a normal vector of tangent space T_{te}. The mean curvature vector $\mathcal{H}_{\text{mean}}^{(e)}$ is given as

$$\mathcal{H}_{\text{mean}}^{(e)} = \sum_{i,j=1}^{d} H_{ij}^{-1}\mathcal{H}_{ij}^{(e)},$$

where the matrix H is defined in section 6.4. In the context of Riemannian geometry, the mean curvature vector denotes the direction in which the volume of the submanifold decreases locally. In statistical inference, the volume of the submanifold corresponds to the expected loss.

The geometrical meaning of Δ is given by the formula

$$\Delta = \left\langle v_{\text{tr}}, \Pi_{\text{te}\to\text{tr}}^{(m)}\mathcal{H}_{\text{mean}}^{(e)} \right\rangle_{\text{tr}}, \tag{6.17}$$

where $\langle\cdot,\cdot\rangle_{\text{tr}}$ is the inner product over T_{tr}. That is, active learning has an advantage over conventional learning methods, if the direction of the model shift, v_{tr}, is matched with the mean curvature vector. The geometrical meaning of Δ is depicted in figure 6.10. Here, m-parallel transport is formally applied to the mean curvature vector, while $\mathcal{H}_{\text{mean}}^{(e)}$ is not the tangent vector. To justify the argument, we need to extend the tangent vector to the tangent bundle.

The model shift, v_{tr}, depends only on input x. On the other hand, $\Pi_{\text{te}\to\text{tr}}^{(m)}\mathcal{H}_{\text{mean}}^{(e)}$ does depend on both x and y. Note that what we can do in active learning is only shift the model along with the input distribution. When the mean curvature vector does not depend on the input variable, the shift of the model along with v_{tr} does not affect the estimation accuracy, because the curvature does not change in that direction.

We revisit the example in which the statistical model is given as (6.16). The mean curvature vector for the model is written as

$$\mathcal{H}_{\text{mean}}^{(e)} = \frac{1}{H_{11}} \left\{ \frac{1}{2\theta^2} - \frac{(y - f(x))^2}{\theta^3} \right\} - \frac{1}{H_{11}} \Gamma_{11}^{(e)1} \frac{\partial \ell(y|x, \theta)}{\partial \theta},$$

and the gain of active learning is

$$\Delta = -\frac{1}{2H_{11}\theta^2} \int \frac{(p_{\text{te}}(x) - p_{\text{tr}}(x))^2}{p_{\text{tr}}(x)} dx \ \leq \ 0.$$

That is, the direction of model shift is always at an obtuse angle to the parallel shifted mean curvature vector.

6.7   Conclusions

We introduced the maximum weighted log-likelihood estimator for the estimation under the covariate shift and the model misspecification. There exist other kinds of weighting estimators in the literature of the robust parametric estimation [Green, 1984; Hampel et al., 1986; Lindsay, 1994; Basu and Lindsay, 1994; Field and Smith, 1994; Windham, 1995]. In robust statistics, the samples which are not concordant with the model will be regarded as "outliers" and downweighted to reduce the impact on the parameter estimation. The specification of the weight function is thus the focal point of the argument. Although the covariate shift is a mechanism different from the outliers, there exists a connection between the MWLE and the robust estimation [Shimodaira, 2000]. A variant of AIC for MWLE under covariate shift is also proposed. The MWLE can be improved by using the information criterion which adjusts the weight function in the MWLE.

Next, we introduced active learning as a statistical inference under covariate shift. The MWLE is effectively applied for active learning. We pointed out that the information criterion will be helpful to improve the prediction accuracy of active learning. We also explained the pool-based active learning with optimal input distribution. This algorithm works even under the unknown input distribution $p_{\text{te}}(x)$. The view of information geometry made clear the effectiveness of active learning.

The covariate shift is common in practical data analysis. For example, measurement error is regarded as a kind of covariate shift. An interesting future work is to investigate the statistical inference under the measurement error from the viewpoint of the covariate shift. It is also an important future work to extend active learning to nonparametric estimation such as kernel methods.

7 A Conditional Expectation Approach to Model Selection and Active Learning under Covariate Shift

Masashi Sugiyama
Neil Rubens
Klaus-Robert Müller

In the previous chapter, Kanamori and Shimodaira provided generalization error estimators which can be used for model selection and active learning. The accuracy of these estimators is theoretically guaranteed in terms of the expectation over realizations of training input-output samples. In practice, we are only given a single realization of training samples. Therefore, ideally, we want to have an estimator of the generalization error that is accurate in each single trial. However, we may not be able to avoid taking the expectation over the training output noise since it is not generally possible to know the realized value of noise. On the other hand, the location of the training input points is accessible by nature. Motivated by this fact, we propose to estimate the generalization error without taking the expectation over training input points. That is, we evaluate the unbiasedness of the generalization error in terms of the conditional expectation of training output noise given training input points.

7.1 Conditional Expectation Analysis of Generalization Error

In order to illustrate a possible advantage of the conditional expectation approach, let us consider a simple model selection scenario where we have only one training sample (x, y) (see figure 7.1). The solid curves in figure 7.1(a) depict $G_{M_1}(y|x)$, the generalization error for a model M_1 as a function of the (noisy) training output value y given a training input point x. The three solid curves correspond to the cases where the realization of the training input point x is x', x'', and x''', respectively. The value of the generalization error for the model M_1 in the full

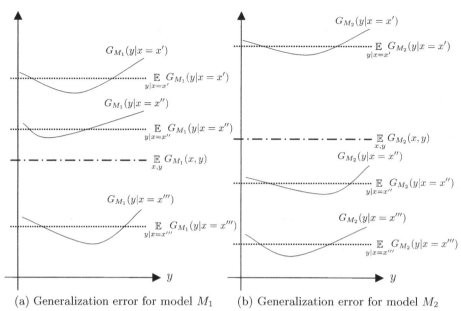

(a) Generalization error for model M_1 (b) Generalization error for model M_2

Figure 7.1 Schematic illustrations of the conditional expectation and full expectation of the generalization error.

expectation approach is depicted by the dash-dotted line, where the expectation is taken over both the training input point x and the training output value y (this corresponds to the mean of the three solid curves). The values of the generalization error in the conditional expectation approach are depicted by the dotted lines, where the expectation is taken only over the training output value y, conditioned on $x = x', x'', x'''$, respectively (this corresponds to the mean value of each solid curve). The graph in figure 7.1(b) depicts the generalization errors for a model M_2 in the same manner.

In the full expectation framework, the model M_1 is judged to be better than M_2 regardless of the realization of the training input point since the dash-dotted line in figure 7.1(a) is lower than that in figure 7.1(b). However, M_2 is actually better than M_1 if x'' or x''' is realized as x. In the conditional expectation framework, the goodness of the model is adaptively evaluated depending on the realization of the training input point x. This illustrates that the conditional expectation framework *can* indeed provide a better model choice than the full expectation framework.

In this chapter, we address the problems of model selection and active learning in the conditional expectation framework. The rest of this chapter is organized as follows. After the problem formulation in section 7.2, we introduce a model selection criterion (section 7.3) and an active learning criterion (section 7.4) in the conditional expectation framework and show that they are more advantageous than the full expectation methods in the context of approximate linear regression. Then, in section 7.5, we discuss how model selection and active learning can be combined. Finally, we give concluding remarks and future prospects in section 7.6.

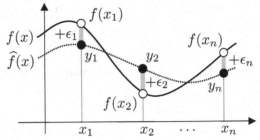

Figure 7.2 Regression problem of learning $f(x)$ from $\{(x_i, y_i)\}_{i=1}^n$. $\{\epsilon_i\}_{i=1}^n$ are i.i.d. noise with mean zero and variance σ^2, and $\widehat{f}(x)$ is a learned function.

7.2 Linear Regression under Covariate Shift

In this section, we formulate a linear regression problem with covariate shift.

7.2.1 Statistical Formulation of Linear Regression

Let us consider a regression problem of estimating an unknown input-output dependency from training samples. Let $\{(x_i, y_i)\}_{i=1}^n$ be the training samples, where $x_i \in \mathcal{X} \subset \mathbb{R}^d$ is an i.i.d. training input point following a probability distribution $P_{\mathrm{tr}}(x)$ and $y_i \in \mathcal{Y} \subset \mathbb{R}$ is a corresponding training output value following a conditional probability distribution $P(y|x = x_i)$. We denote the conditional mean of $P(y|x)$ by $f(x)$ and assume that the conditional variance is σ^2, which is independent of x. Then $P(y|x)$ may be regarded as consisting of the true output $f(x)$ and the noise ϵ with mean 0 and variance σ^2 (see figure 7.2).

Let us employ a linear regression model for learning $f(x)$.

$$\widehat{f}(x; \boldsymbol{\alpha}) = \sum_{\ell=1}^t \alpha_\ell \varphi_\ell(x), \tag{7.1}$$

where $\{\alpha_\ell\}_{\ell=1}^t$ are parameters to be learned and $\{\varphi_\ell(x)\}_{\ell=1}^t$ are fixed basis functions. A model $\widehat{f}(x; \boldsymbol{\alpha})$ is said to be *correctly specified* if there exists a parameter $\boldsymbol{\alpha}^*$ such that

$$\widehat{f}(x; \boldsymbol{\alpha}^*) = f(x). \tag{7.2}$$

Otherwise the model is said to be *misspecified*. In the following, we do not assume that the model is correct.

Let us consider a test sample, which is not given to the user in the training phase, but will be given in a future test phase. We denote the test sample by $(x^{\mathrm{te}}, y^{\mathrm{te}})$, where $x^{\mathrm{te}} \in \mathcal{X}$ is a test input point and $y^{\mathrm{te}} \in \mathcal{Y}$ is a corresponding test output value. The goal of regression is to determine the value of the parameter $\boldsymbol{\alpha}$ so that the generalization error G (the test error expected over test samples) is minimized:

$$G \equiv \mathbf{E}_{x^{\text{te}}, y^{\text{te}}} \left[(\widehat{f}(x^{\text{te}}; \boldsymbol{\alpha}) - y^{\text{te}})^2 \right], \tag{7.3}$$

where $\mathbf{E}_{x^{\text{te}}, y^{\text{te}}} [\cdot]$ denotes the expectation over $(x^{\text{te}}, y^{\text{te}})$.

7.2.2   Covariate Shift

In standard supervised learning theories, the test sample $(x^{\text{te}}, y^{\text{te}})$ is assumed to follow the joint distribution $P(y|x)P_{\text{tr}}(x)$, which is the same as the training samples [e.g., Wahba, 1990; Bishop, 1995; Vapnik, 1998; Duda et al., 2001; Hastie et al., 2001; Schölkopf and Smola, 2002]. On the other hand, here, we consider the *covariate shift* situation, i.e., the conditional distribution $P(y|x)$ remains unchanged, but the test input point x^{te} follows a different probability distribution $P_{\text{te}}(x)$.

Let $p_{\text{tr}}(x)$ and $p_{\text{te}}(x)$ be the probability density functions corresponding to the input distributions $P_{\text{tr}}(x)$ and $P_{\text{te}}(x)$, respectively. We assume that $p_{\text{tr}}(x)$ and $p_{\text{te}}(x)$ are strictly positive over the entire domain $\mathcal{X}$.

7.2.3   Functional Analytic View of Linear Regression

Technically, we assume that the target function $f(x)$ and the basis functions $\{\varphi_\ell(x)\}_{\ell=1}^t$ are included in a functional Hilbert space $\mathcal{F}$, where the inner product and the norm in $\mathcal{F}$ are defined by

$$\langle f, g \rangle_{\mathcal{F}} = \int_{\mathcal{X}} (f(x) - g(x))^2 \, p_{\text{te}}(x) dx, \tag{7.4}$$

$$\|f\|_{\mathcal{F}} = \sqrt{\langle f, f \rangle_{\mathcal{F}}}. \tag{7.5}$$

Then the generalization error G (7.3) is expressed in terms of $\mathcal{F}$ as

$$G = \left\| \widehat{f} - f \right\|_{\mathcal{F}}^2 + \sigma^2. \tag{7.6}$$

Given our linear regression model (7.1), the learning target function $f(x)$ can be decomposed as

$$f(x) = g(x) + \delta r(x), \tag{7.7}$$

where $g(x)$ is the optimal approximation in the model (7.1):

$$g(x; \boldsymbol{\alpha}^*) = \sum_{\ell=1}^t \alpha_\ell^* \varphi_\ell(x). \tag{7.8}$$

$\boldsymbol{\alpha}^*$ is the unknown optimal parameter under G:

$$\boldsymbol{\alpha}^* \equiv \underset{\boldsymbol{\alpha}}{\text{argmin}} \, G. \tag{7.9}$$

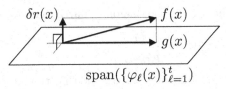

Figure 7.3 Decomposition of $f(x)$ in a functional Hilbert space $\mathcal{F}$.

$r(x)$ is the residual function orthogonal to $\{\varphi_\ell(x)\}_{\ell=1}^t$ in $\mathcal{F}$, i.e.,

$$\langle r, \varphi_\ell \rangle_\mathcal{F} = 0 \quad \text{for } \ell = 1, 2, \dots, t. \tag{7.10}$$

Without loss of generality, we normalize $r(x)$ as

$$\|r\|_\mathcal{F} = 1. \tag{7.11}$$

Thus the function $r(x)$ governs the nature of the model error and δ (≥ 0) is the magnitude of the error.

Geometrically, in the functional Hilbert space $\mathcal{F}$, $g(x)$ is the orthogonal projection of $f(x)$ onto the subspace spanned by $\{\varphi_\ell(x)\}_{\ell=1}^t$ and $\delta r(x)$ is the residual (see figure 7.3).

Let U be a $t \times t$ matrix with the (ℓ, ℓ')th element:

$$U_{\ell,\ell'} = \langle \varphi_\ell, \varphi_{\ell'} \rangle_\mathcal{F}. \tag{7.12}$$

In the following theoretical analysis, we assume that U is accessible.

7.2.4   Parameter Learning

We learn the parameter $\boldsymbol{\alpha}$ in our linear regression model (7.1) by a linear learning method, i.e., a learned parameter $\widehat{\boldsymbol{\alpha}}$ is given by the following form:

$$\widehat{\boldsymbol{\alpha}} = L\boldsymbol{y}, \tag{7.13}$$

where L is a $t \times n$ matrix called the *learning matrix* and

$$\boldsymbol{y} = (y_1, y_2, \dots, y_n)^\top. \tag{7.14}$$

We assume that L does not depend on the noise in $\boldsymbol{y}$.

Adaptive importance weighted least squares (AIWLS) introduced in chapter 6 is an example of linear learning methods:

$$\widehat{\boldsymbol{\alpha}}_{\text{AIWLS}} \equiv \underset{\boldsymbol{\alpha}}{\operatorname{argmin}} \left[\sum_{i=1}^n \left(\frac{p_{\text{te}}(x_i)}{p_{\text{tr}}(x_i)} \right)^\lambda (\widehat{f}(x_i; \boldsymbol{\alpha}) - y_i)^2 \right], \tag{7.15}$$

where $0 \leq \lambda \leq 1$. We call λ a *flattening parameter* since it flattens the importance weights. The corresponding learning matrix L_{AIWLS} is given by

$$L_{\text{AIWLS}} = (X^\top W^\lambda X)^{-1} X^\top W^\lambda, \tag{7.16}$$

where W is the diagonal matrix with the diagonal element being the *importance*:

$$W_{i,i} = \frac{p_{\text{te}}(x_i)}{p_{\text{tr}}(x_i)}. \tag{7.17}$$

In the following, we assume that the importance is known. If it is unknown, we may estimate it by proper methods such as *kernel mean matching* (KMM, see chapter 8), *kernel logistic regression* (see chapter 9), the *Kullback-Leibler importance estimation procedure* [KLIEP, see Sugiyama et al., 2008].

7.3   Model Selection

In this section, we address the problem of model selection in the conditional expectation framework. Here, the term "model" refers to the number t and the type $\{\varphi_\ell(x)\}_{\ell=1}^t$ of basis functions. Some tuning parameters contained in the learning matrix L, e.g., the flattening parameter λ in AIWLS (7.15), are also included in the model.

The goal of model selection is to choose the best model M^* from a model set $\mathcal{M}$ such that the generalization error G is minimized.

$$M^* \equiv \underset{M \in \mathcal{M}}{\text{argmin}}\, G(M). \tag{7.18}$$

The true generalization error G is inaccessible since it contains the unknown target function $f(x)$ (see (7.6))—in practice, we replace G by its estimator $\widehat{G}$. Therefore, the main goal of model selection research is to obtain an accurate estimator of the generalization error.

In this section, we introduce a generalization error estimator called the *importance-weighted subspace information criterion* (IWSIC) [Sugiyama and Müller, 2005a]. IWSIC is an extension of SIC, which is a generalization error estimator derived within the conditional expectation framework [Sugiyama and Ogawa, 2001, 2002; Sugiyama and Müller, 2002]. IWSIC is shown to possess proper unbiasedness even under covariate shift. For simplicity, we consider fixed basis functions $\{\varphi_\ell(x)\}_{\ell=1}^t$ and focus on choosing the flattening parameter λ in AIWLS (7.15). However, IWSIC can be generally used for choosing basis functions and moreover the learning matrix L.

7.3.1   IWSIC

The generalization error G (7.3) is expressed as

$$G = \left\|\widehat{f}\right\|_{\mathcal{F}}^2 - 2\left\langle \widehat{f}, g + \delta r \right\rangle_{\mathcal{F}} + \|f\|_{\mathcal{F}}^2 + \sigma^2$$
$$= \langle U\boldsymbol{\alpha}, \boldsymbol{\alpha}\rangle - 2\langle U\boldsymbol{\alpha}, \boldsymbol{\alpha}^*\rangle + C + \sigma^2, \tag{7.19}$$

where C is constant:

$$C \equiv \|f\|_{\mathcal{F}}^2 . \tag{7.20}$$

In (7.19), the first term $\langle U\boldsymbol{\alpha}, \boldsymbol{\alpha}\rangle$ is accessible and the third term C and the fourth term σ^2 are constants independent of the model. For this reason, we focus on estimating the second term $\langle U\boldsymbol{\alpha}, \boldsymbol{\alpha}^*\rangle$. Let

$$G' \equiv \langle U\boldsymbol{\alpha}, \boldsymbol{\alpha}\rangle - 2\langle U\boldsymbol{\alpha}, \boldsymbol{\alpha}^*\rangle = G - C - \sigma^2, \tag{7.21}$$

which is an essential part of G.

A basic idea of IWSIC is to replace the unknown $\boldsymbol{\alpha}^*$ by its linear estimator $\widetilde{\boldsymbol{\alpha}}$:

$$\widetilde{\boldsymbol{\alpha}} \equiv \widetilde{L}\boldsymbol{y}, \tag{7.22}$$

where

$$\widetilde{L} \equiv (X^\top W X)^{-1} X^\top W. \tag{7.23}$$

Note that $\widetilde{\boldsymbol{\alpha}}$ is an unbiased estimator of $\boldsymbol{\alpha}^*$ if the model is correct (i.e., $\delta = 0$); otherwise it is asymptotically unbiased in general.

However, simply replacing $\boldsymbol{\alpha}^*$ by $\widetilde{\boldsymbol{\alpha}}$ induces a bias in generalization error estimation since the same sample $\boldsymbol{y}$ is used for obtaining $\widehat{\boldsymbol{\alpha}}$ and $\widetilde{\boldsymbol{\alpha}}$—here, we are addressing the bias in terms of the conditional expectation over training output values $\{y_i\}_{i=1}^n$ given training input points $\{x_i\}_{i=1}^n$. The bias can be expressed as

$$\mathbf{E}_{\boldsymbol{y}}\left[\langle U\boldsymbol{\alpha}, \widetilde{\boldsymbol{\alpha}}\rangle - \langle U\boldsymbol{\alpha}, \boldsymbol{\alpha}^*\rangle\right] = \mathbf{E}_{\boldsymbol{y}}\left[\left\langle U\boldsymbol{\alpha}, \widetilde{L}(\boldsymbol{y} - \boldsymbol{z})\right\rangle\right], \tag{7.24}$$

where $\mathbf{E}_{\boldsymbol{y}}\left[\cdot\right]$ denotes the expectation over $\boldsymbol{y}$ (or equivalently $\{\epsilon_i\}_{i=1}^n$) and

$$\boldsymbol{z} \equiv (f(x_1), f(x_2), \ldots, f(x_n))^\top. \tag{7.25}$$

Based on (7.24), we define

$$\text{preIWSIC} \equiv \langle U\boldsymbol{\alpha}, \boldsymbol{\alpha}\rangle - 2\langle U\boldsymbol{\alpha}, \widetilde{\boldsymbol{\alpha}}\rangle + 2\mathbf{E}_{\boldsymbol{y}}\left[\left\langle U\boldsymbol{\alpha}, \widetilde{L}(\boldsymbol{y} - \boldsymbol{z})\right\rangle\right]. \tag{7.26}$$

If we can compute (or approximate) the third term in preIWSIC (7.26), the entire criterion becomes accessible and therefore it can be used for model selection.

If the learning matrix L is determined based on AIWLS (7.15), we have

$$\mathbf{E}_{\boldsymbol{y}}\left[\left\langle U\widehat{\boldsymbol{\alpha}}, \widetilde{L}(\boldsymbol{y} - \boldsymbol{z})\right\rangle\right] = \sigma^2 \text{tr}\left(U L \widetilde{L}^\top\right). \tag{7.27}$$

Let us replace the unknown noise variance σ^2 by an ordinary estimator $\widehat{\sigma}^2$:

$$\widehat{\sigma}^2 \equiv \frac{\left\|X(X^\top X)^{-1}X^\top \boldsymbol{y} - \boldsymbol{y}\right\|^2}{n - t}, \tag{7.28}$$

which is known to be unbiased if $\delta = 0$. Summarizing the above approximations, we have IWSIC:

$$\text{IWSIC} \equiv \langle U\widehat{\alpha}, \widehat{\alpha} \rangle - 2 \langle U\widehat{\alpha}, \widetilde{\alpha} \rangle + 2\widehat{\sigma}^2 \mathbf{tr}\left(UL\widetilde{L}^\top \right). \tag{7.29}$$

IWSIC satisfies

$$\mathbf{E}_y \left[\text{IWSIC} - G' \right] = O_p(\delta n^{-\frac{1}{2}}), \tag{7.30}$$

where O_p denotes the asymptotic order in probability. This means that IWSIC is an exact unbiased estimator of the essential generalization error G' if the model is correct (i.e., $\delta = 0$); generally, IWSIC is asymptotically unbiased with asymptotic order $n^{-\frac{1}{2}}$. In addition to the unbiasedness, IWSIC is shown to be useful for comparing the generalization error of two different models [Sugiyama and Müller, 2005a].

Equation (7.30) further shows that the bias of IWSIC is proportional to the model error δ. Thus IWSIC is more accurate if the target model has a smaller model error. This is practically a useful property in model selection because of the following reason. The goal of model selection is to choose the best model from a model set $\mathcal{M}$. The set $\mathcal{M}$ may contain various models, including good ones and poor ones. In practice, it may not be difficult to distinguish very poor models from good ones; just using a rough estimator of the generalization error would be enough for this purpose. Therefore, what is really important in model selection is how to choose a very good model from a set of good models. Usually good models have small model errors and IWSIC is accurate for such models. For this reason, IWSIC is most useful when choosing a very good model from a set of good models.

A variance reduction method of SIC is discussed in Sugiyama et al. [2004], which could be used for further improving the model selection performance of IWSIC. IWSIC can also be extended to the situation where the learning transformation L is nonlinear [Sugiyama, 2007].

In the above discussion, the matrix U (see (7.12)) and the importance $\{p_{\text{te}}(x_i)/p_{\text{tr}}(x_i)\}_{i=1}^n$ (see (7.17)) are assumed known. Even when they are estimated from data, the unbiasedness of IWSIC is still approximately maintained [Sugiyama and Müller, 2005a].

7.3.2 Relation to Other Model Selection Methods

IWSIC is shown to possess proper unbiasedness within the conditional expectation framework. Here, we qualitatively compare IWSIC with other model selection methods.

Importance-Weighted AIC The modified AIC given in chapter 6, which we refer to as *important-weighted AIC* (IWAIC) here, is unbiased in terms of the full expectation over the training set.

For the linear regression model (7.1) with the linear learning method (7.13), IWAIC is expressed as follows (we properly shifted and rescaled it for better comparison):

$$\text{IWAIC} = \left\langle \widehat{U}\widehat{\boldsymbol{\alpha}}, \widehat{\boldsymbol{\alpha}} \right\rangle - 2\left\langle \widehat{U}\widehat{\boldsymbol{\alpha}}, \widetilde{\boldsymbol{\alpha}} \right\rangle + 2\mathbf{tr}\left(\widehat{U}L\widehat{\Sigma}\widetilde{L}^{\top} \right), \tag{7.31}$$

where

$$\widehat{U} \equiv \frac{1}{n}X^{\top}WX, \tag{7.32}$$

and $\widehat{\Sigma}$ is the diagonal matrix with the ith diagonal element

$$\widehat{\Sigma}_{i,i} \equiv (y_i - \widehat{f}(x_i; \widehat{\boldsymbol{\alpha}}))^2. \tag{7.33}$$

The appearances of IWAIC and IWSIC are similar but different in two aspects.

(i) The matrix U in IWSIC is replaced by its empirical estimate $\widehat{U}$ in IWAIC.

(ii) Instead of $\widehat{\Sigma}$ in IWAIC, $\widehat{\sigma}^2\mathbf{I}$ is used in IWSIC, where $\mathbf{I}$ denotes the identity matrix.

IWAIC satisfies

$$\mathbf{E}_{X,\boldsymbol{y}}\left[\text{IWAIC} - G'\right] = o(n^{-1}), \tag{7.34}$$

where $\mathbf{E}_{X,\boldsymbol{y}}\left[\cdot\right]$ denotes the expectation over $\{(x_i, y_i)\}_{i=1}^{n}$. This shows that IWAIC has a smaller asymptotic bias in the full expectation analysis. On the other hand, if only the conditional expectation of training output values $\boldsymbol{y}$ given training input points X is taken, IWAIC satisfies

$$\mathbf{E}_{\boldsymbol{y}}\left[\text{IWAIC} - G'\right] = O_p(n^{-\frac{1}{2}}), \tag{7.35}$$

which is the same asymptotic order as IWSIC (see (7.30)). However, a crucial difference is that the bias of IWAIC is not proportional to the model error δ. In approximately linear regression where the model error is $\delta = o(1)$ with respect to n, the bias of IWSIC is

$$\mathbf{E}_{\boldsymbol{y}}\left[\text{IWSIC} - G'\right] = o_p(n^{-\frac{1}{2}}), \tag{7.36}$$

which is smaller than IWAIC. Thus IWSIC is more accurate than IWAIC in approximate linear regression.

Note that the range of IWAIC is not limited to linear regression; it can be applied to any statistically regular models [Watanabe, 2001] and any smooth loss functions.

Importance-Weighted CV   *Cross-validation* (CV) is another popular method for model selection [Stone, 1974; Wahba, 1990], which gives an estimate of the generalization error G. Under covariate shift, a variant of CV called *importance-weighted CV* (IWCV) has proper unbiasedness [Sugiyama et al., 2007]. In IWCV, the training set $\mathcal{T} = \{(x_i, y_i)\}_{i=1}^{n}$ is randomly divided into k disjoint subsets $\{\mathcal{T}_i\}_{i=1}^{k}$ with (approximately) same size. The *k-fold IWCV* estimate of the generalization error G is given by

$$k\text{IWCV} \equiv \frac{1}{k}\sum_{r=1}^{k}\frac{1}{|\mathcal{T}_r|}\sum_{(x,y)\in\mathcal{T}_r}(\widehat{f}(x;\widehat{\boldsymbol{\alpha}}_{\mathcal{T}_r})-y)^2, \tag{7.37}$$

where $\widehat{f}(x;\widehat{\boldsymbol{\alpha}}_{\mathcal{T}_r})$ is a function learned from $\{\mathcal{T}_i\}_{i\neq r}$. That is, $\mathcal{T}_r$ is not used for learning, but is used for computing the validation error. When $k=n$, kIWCV is particularly called *leave-one-out IWCV* (LOOIWCV):

$$\text{LOOIWCV} \equiv \frac{1}{n}\sum_{r=1}^{n}(\widehat{f}(x_r;\widehat{\boldsymbol{\alpha}}_r)-y_r)^2, \tag{7.38}$$

where $\widehat{f}(x;\widehat{\boldsymbol{\alpha}}_r)$ is a function learned from $\{(x_i,y_i)\}_{i\neq r}$.

LOOIWCV is almost unbiased in the full expectation framework.

$$\mathbf{E}_{X,\boldsymbol{y}}\left[\text{LOOIWCV}\right] = G^{(n-1)} \approx G^{(n)}, \tag{7.39}$$

where $G^{(n)}$ is the expected generalization error over all the training set with size n:

$$G^{(n)} = \mathbf{E}_{X,\boldsymbol{y}}\left[G\right]. \tag{7.40}$$

Thus LOOIWCV with n training samples is an exact unbiased estimator of the expected generalization error with $n-1$ training samples. However, in the conditional expectation framework, its unbiasedness is only asymptotic:

$$\mathbf{E}_{\boldsymbol{y}}\left[\text{LOOIWCV}\right] = \mathbf{E}_{\boldsymbol{y}}\left[G\right] + O_p(n^{-\frac{1}{2}}). \tag{7.41}$$

This means that LOOIWCV has the same asymptotic order as IWSIC (see (7.30)). However, the bias of IWSIC is proportional to the model error δ, so IWSIC has a smaller bias than LOOIWCV in approximately linear regression.

Note that the unbiasedness of IWCV is valid for any loss function, any model, and any parameter learning method; even nonparametric learning methods are allowed.

7.3.3   Numerical Examples

Here, we illustrate how IWSIC works through numerical experiments.

Let the input dimension be $d=1$ and the target function $f(x)$ be

$$f(x) = \text{sinc}(x). \tag{7.42}$$

We use the following linear regression model for learning:

$$\widehat{f}(x) = \alpha_0 + \alpha_1 x. \tag{7.43}$$

We determine the parameters α_0 and α_1 by AIWLS (7.15). Let the training input distribution be Gaussian with mean 1 and standard deviation $1/2$, and let the test input distribution be Gaussian with mean 2 and standard deviation $1/4$. Let

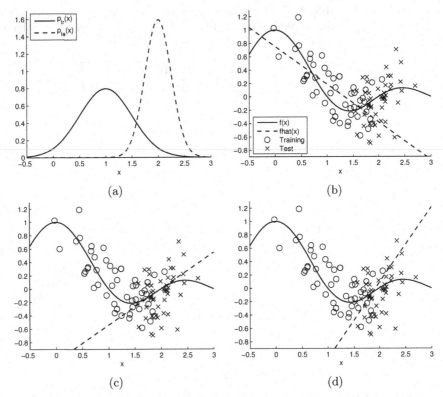

Figure 7.4 **(a)** Training and test input densities. **(b)**, **(c)**, and **(d)** Learning target function and functions learned by AIWLS with $\lambda = 0, 0.5, 1$.

the conditional distribution $P(y|x)$ be Gaussian with mean $\mathrm{sinc}(x)$ and standard deviation $1/2$, and let the number of training samples be

$$n = 50, 100, 200. \tag{7.44}$$

The above setting is summarized in figure 7.4(a).

In addition to the training samples, we draw 1000 test unlabeled samples and estimate the importance by KLIEP [Sugiyama et al., 2008] using these data samples. Figure 7.4(b)-(d) depicts examples of functions learned by AIWLS with flattening parameter $\lambda = 0, 0.5, 1$. Our model selection task here is to choose the flattening parameter λ in AIWLS from

$$\lambda = 0, 0.1, 0.2, \dots, 1. \tag{7.45}$$

We use IWSIC, IWAIC, and IWCV for the selection of λ. The simulation is repeated $30,000$ times for each n. The obtained generalization error by each model selection method is summarized in table 7.1, showing that IWSIC is significantly better than other approaches, particularly when n is small.

Table 7.1 Means and standard deviations of generalization error. All values in the table are multiplied by 10^2. The best method and comparable ones by the t-test at the significance level 5% are marked by "∘".

n	IWSIC	IWAIC	IWCV
50	∘12.01±10.86	13.50±13.54	12.22±11.85
100	∘8.57±3.92	9.01±4.56	∘8.63±4.01
200	∘7.34±1.85	7.54±2.16	∘7.37±1.95

7.4 Active Learning

In this section, we address the problem of active learning in the conditional expectation framework. The goal of (batch) active learning is to choose training input points $\{x_i\}_{i=1}^n$ such that the generalization error G is minimized. However, directly optimizing $\{x_i\}_{i=1}^n$ may be computationally hard since n input points of d dimensions needs to be simultaneously optimized. Here, we avoid this difficulty by optimizing the training input density $p_{\mathrm{tr}}(x)$ from which we draw training input points:

$$p_{\mathrm{tr}}^* \equiv \underset{p_{\mathrm{tr}}}{\mathrm{argmin}}\, G(p_{\mathrm{tr}}). \tag{7.46}$$

The true generalization error G is inaccessible since it contains the unknown target function $f(x)$. Therefore, the main goal of active learning research is to obtain an accurate estimator of the generalization error, which is actually the same as model selection. However, generalization error estimation in active learning is generally harder than model selection since the generalization error has to be estimated *before* observing training output values $\{y_i\}_{i=1}^n$.

We assume that the test input density $p_{\mathrm{te}}(x)$ is known and the parameter $\boldsymbol{\alpha}$ is learned by IWLS, i.e.,

$$\widehat{\boldsymbol{\alpha}}_{\mathrm{IWLS}} \equiv \underset{\boldsymbol{\alpha}}{\mathrm{argmin}} \left[\sum_{i=1}^n \frac{p_{\mathrm{te}}(x_i)}{p_{\mathrm{tr}}(x_i)} (\widehat{f}(x_i; \boldsymbol{\alpha}) - y_i)^2 \right]. \tag{7.47}$$

The corresponding learning matrix L_{IWLS} is given by

$$L_{\mathrm{IWLS}} = (X^\top W X)^{-1} X^\top W. \tag{7.48}$$

In this section, we introduce an active learning method called *ALICE* (active learning using importance-weighted least squares learning based on conditional expectation of the generalization error) [Sugiyama, 2006]. ALICE is an extension of the traditional *variance-only* method [Fedorov, 1972; Cohn et al., 1996; Fukumizu, 2000] to approximately correct models (see section 7.4.2 for details).

7.4.1 ALICE

The conditional expectation of the generalization error G over training output values $\{y_i\}_{i=1}^n$ given training input points $\{x_i\}_{i=1}^n$ can be decomposed as

$$\mathbf{E}_{\boldsymbol{y}}\left[G\right] = B + V + \delta^2 + \sigma^2, \tag{7.49}$$

where

$$B \equiv \left\|g - \mathbf{E}_{\boldsymbol{y}}\left[\widehat{f}\right]\right\|_{\mathcal{F}}^2, \tag{7.50}$$

$$V \equiv \mathbf{E}_{\boldsymbol{y}}\left[\left\|\widehat{f} - \mathbf{E}_{\boldsymbol{y}}\left[\widehat{f}\right]\right\|_{\mathcal{F}}^2\right] = \sigma^2\mathbf{tr}\left(U L_{\mathrm{IWLS}} L_{\mathrm{IWLS}}^\top\right). \tag{7.51}$$

B is the squared conditional bias and V is the conditional variance of the learned function. δ^2 and σ^2 are constants. Let

$$G'' \equiv G - \delta^2 - \sigma^2, \tag{7.52}$$

which is an essential part of the generalization error G. Note that it is different from G' (cf. (7.21)).

The bias term B depends on the unknown target function $f(x)$. Therefore, it is generally not possible to estimate the bias term B before observing $\{y_i\}_{i=1}^n$ since we have no information on the target function $f(x)$. On the other hand, the variance term V only depends on the learned function, and (7.51) implies that V can be computed without $\{y_i\}_{i=1}^n$ up to the scaling factor σ^2, which is an unknown noise variance. The basic idea of variance-only active learning methods is to guarantee that B can be safely ignored and focus on evaluating V/σ^2; when IWLS (7.47) is used for parameter learning, we can show that

$$B = O_p(\delta^2 n^{-1}), \tag{7.53}$$
$$V = O_p(n^{-1}). \tag{7.54}$$

Based on these, ALICE is defined as

$$\mathrm{ALICE} \equiv \mathbf{tr}\left(U L_{\mathrm{IWLS}} L_{\mathrm{IWLS}}^\top\right). \tag{7.55}$$

The use of ALICE can be justified in approximate linear regression, i.e., if the model error is $\delta = o(1)$ with respect to n, ALICE satisfies

$$\sigma^2\mathrm{ALICE} - G'' = o_p(n^{-1}). \tag{7.56}$$

7.4.2 Relation to Other Active Learning Methods

ALICE is shown to be a sound active learning criterion in approximately linear regression. Here, we qualitatively compare ALICE with other active learning methods.

Traditional Variance-Only Method with Ordinary Least Squares A traditional approach to variance-only active learning employs *ordinary least squares* (OLS) for parameter learning, i.e.,

$$\widehat{\boldsymbol{\alpha}}_{\mathrm{OLS}} \equiv \operatorname*{argmin}_{\boldsymbol{\alpha}} \left[\sum_{i=1}^{n} (\widehat{f}(x_i; \boldsymbol{\alpha}) - y_i)^2 \right]. \tag{7.57}$$

The corresponding learning matrix L_{OLS} is given by

$$L_{\mathrm{OLS}} = (X^\top X)^{-1} X^\top. \tag{7.58}$$

Based on OLS, an active learning criterion, which we refer to as the *variance-only criterion with least-squares* (VOLS) here, is given as follows [Fedorov, 1972; Cohn et al., 1996; Fukumizu, 2000]:

$$\mathrm{VOLS} = \mathbf{tr}\left(U L_{\mathrm{OLS}} L_{\mathrm{OLS}}^\top \right). \tag{7.59}$$

The use of VOLS is justified also in approximate linear regression, i.e., if the model error is $\delta = o(n^{-\frac{1}{2}})$, VOLS satisfies the following property [Sugiyama, 2006]:

$$\sigma^2 \mathrm{VOLS} - G'' = o_p(n^{-1}). \tag{7.60}$$

However, the condition on the model error δ is stronger than for ALICE.

Full Expectation Variance-Only Method Within the full expectation framework, Kanamori and Shimodaira [2003] proved that the expected generalization error is asymptotically expressed as follows (see also chapter 6):

$$\mathbf{E}_{X,\boldsymbol{y}}\left[G'' \right] = \frac{1}{n} \mathbf{tr}\left(U^{-1} H \right) + O(n^{-\frac{3}{2}}), \tag{7.61}$$

where H is the n-dimensional square matrix defined by

$$H = S + \sigma^2 T. \tag{7.62}$$

S and T are the t-dimensional square matrices with the (ℓ, ℓ')th elements

$$S_{\ell,\ell'} = \int_{\mathcal{X}} \varphi_\ell(x) \varphi_{\ell'}(x) (\delta r(x))^2 \frac{(p_{\mathrm{te}}(x))^2}{p_{\mathrm{tr}}(x)} dx, \tag{7.63}$$

$$T_{\ell,\ell'} = \int_{\mathcal{X}} \varphi_\ell(x) \varphi_{\ell'}(x) \frac{(p_{\mathrm{te}}(x))^2}{p_{\mathrm{tr}}(x)} dx. \tag{7.64}$$

Note that $\frac{1}{n} \mathbf{tr}\left(U^{-1} S \right)$ corresponds to the squared bias while $\frac{\sigma^2}{n} \mathbf{tr}\left(U^{-1} T \right)$ corresponds to the variance. T is accessible by assumption, but S is not (due to $\delta r(x)$).

Based on this decomposition, a variance-only active learning criterion, which we refer to as the *full expectation variance-only* (FEVO) method, is given as follows [Wiens, 2000]:

$$\mathrm{FEVO} = \frac{1}{n} \mathbf{tr}\left(U^{-1} T \right). \tag{7.65}$$

Sugiyama [2006] proved that the use of FEVO is also justified in approximate linear regression, i.e., if the model error is $\delta = o(1)$ with respect to n, FEVO satisfies

$$\sigma^2 \text{FEVO} - G'' = o(n^{-1}). \tag{7.66}$$

This implies that the asymptotic order of FEVO is the same as ALICE. Furthermore, ALICE and FEVO are actually equivalent asymptotically, i.e.,

$$\text{ALICE} - \text{FEVO} = O_p(n^{-\frac{3}{2}}). \tag{7.67}$$

However, they are different in the order of $O_p(n^{-1})$. To investigate this difference more precisely, let us measure the goodness of a generalization error estimator $\widehat{G}$ by

$$\mathbf{E}_y\left[(\widehat{G} - G'')^2\right]. \tag{7.68}$$

If $\delta = o(n^{-\frac{1}{4}})$ and terms of $o_p(n^{-3})$ are ignored, we have

$$\mathbf{E}_y\left[(\sigma^2 \text{ALICE} - G'')^2\right] \leq \mathbf{E}_y\left[(\sigma^2 \text{FEVO} - G'')^2\right]. \tag{7.69}$$

Thus, for approximate linear regression with $\delta = o(n^{-\frac{1}{4}})$, ALICE is a more accurate estimator of the generalization error than FEVO in the above sense.

FEVO does not depend on the realization of training input points $\{x_i\}_{i=1}^n$ (though it does depend on the training input density $p_{\text{tr}}(x)$). Thanks to this property, the optimal training input density $\widehat{p}_{\text{tr}}(x)$ can be obtained in a closed form as follows [Wiens, 2000]:

$$\widehat{p}_{\text{tr}}(x) = \frac{\widehat{h}(x)}{\int_{\mathcal{X}} \widehat{h}(x)dx}, \tag{7.70}$$

where

$$\widehat{h}(x) = p_{\text{te}}(x)\left(\sum_{\ell,\ell'=1}^t [U^{-1}]_{\ell,\ell'}\varphi_\ell(x)\varphi_{\ell'}(x)\right)^{\frac{1}{2}}. \tag{7.71}$$

Full Expectation Bias-Variance Method   Another idea of approximating H in (7.61) is a two-stage sampling scheme introduced in chapter 6: in the first stage, $\widetilde{n}$ ($\leq n$) training input points $\{\widetilde{x}_i\}_{i=1}^{\widetilde{n}}$ are created independently following the test input distribution with density $p_{\text{te}}(x)$, and the corresponding training output values $\{\widetilde{y}_i\}_{i=1}^{\widetilde{n}}$ are gathered. Then a consistent estimator $\widetilde{H}$ of the unknown matrix H in (7.61) can be obtained based on $\{(\widetilde{x}_i, \widetilde{y}_i)\}_{i=1}^{\widetilde{n}}$ as

$$\widetilde{H}_{\ell,\ell'} = \frac{1}{\widetilde{n}}\sum_{i=1}^{\widetilde{n}} \frac{p_{\text{te}}(\widetilde{x}_i)}{p_{\text{tr}}(\widetilde{x}_i)}(\widetilde{y}_i - \widehat{f}(\widetilde{x}_i; \widetilde{\alpha}_{\text{OLS}}))^2 \varphi_\ell(\widetilde{x}_i)\varphi_{\ell'}(\widetilde{x}_i), \tag{7.72}$$

where $\widetilde{\alpha}_{\text{OLS}}$ is obtained from $\{(\widetilde{x}_i, \widetilde{y}_i)\}_{i=1}^{\widetilde{n}}$ by OLS (7.57). This corresponds to estimating the bias term S and the noise variance σ^2 from $\{(\widetilde{x}_i, \widetilde{y}_i)\}_{i=1}^{\widetilde{n}}$. U^{-1} is also replaced by a consistent estimator $\widetilde{U}^{-1}$:

$$\widetilde{U}_{\ell,\ell'} = \frac{1}{\widetilde{n}} \sum_{i=1}^{\widetilde{n}} \varphi_\ell(\widetilde{x}_i)\varphi_{\ell'}(\widetilde{x}_i). \tag{7.73}$$

Based on these approximations, an active learning criterion, which we refer to as the *full expectation bias-variance* (FEBV) method here, is given as

$$\text{FEBV} = \frac{1}{n}\mathbf{tr}\left(\widetilde{U}^{-1}\widetilde{H}\right). \tag{7.74}$$

In the second stage, this criterion is used for optimizing the location of the remaining $n - \widetilde{n}$ training input points. Kanamori and Shimodaira [2003] proved that the use of FEBV can be justified for misspecified models, i.e., for $\delta = O(1)$ with respect to n, FEBV satisfies

$$\sigma^2\text{FEBV} - G'' = o(n^{-1}). \tag{7.75}$$

The order of δ required above is weaker than that required in ALICE or FEVO. Therefore, FEBV theoretically has a wider range of applications. However, this strong theoretical property is not necessarily useful in practice since learning with totally misspecified models (i.e., $\delta = O(1)$) may not work well due to large model errors. Furthermore, due to the two-stage sampling scheme, FEBV allows us to choose only $n - \widetilde{n}$ training input points. This can be very restrictive when the total number n is not so large.

Note that the range of FEBV is not restricted to linear regression; it can be applied to any statistically regular models [Watanabe, 2001] and any smooth loss functions.

7.4.3   Numerical Examples

Here, we illustrate how ALICE works through numerical experiments.

Let the input dimension be $d = 1$ and the target function $f(x)$ be

$$f(x) = 1 - x + x^2 + \delta r(x), \tag{7.76}$$

where

$$r(x) = \delta\frac{z^3 - 3z}{\sqrt{6}} \quad \text{with} \quad z = \frac{x - 0.2}{0.4}. \tag{7.77}$$

We use the following linear regression model for learning:

$$\widehat{f}(x) = \alpha_0 + \alpha_1 x + \alpha_2 x^2. \tag{7.78}$$

Note that for this regression model, the residual function $r(x)$ fulfills (7.10) and (7.11). Let us consider the following three cases.

$$\delta = 0, 0.005, 0.05, \tag{7.79}$$

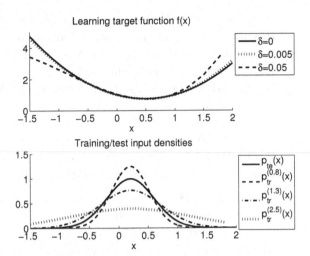

Figure 7.5   Target function and training/test input densities. $p_{\mathrm{tr}}^{(c)}(x)$ denotes the training input density with width parameter c.

Table 7.2   The mean and standard deviation of the generalization error $G - \sigma^2$ obtained by each method for the toy dataset. The best method and comparable ones by the t-test at the significance level 5% are marked by "○". The value of VOLS for $\delta = 0.05$ is extremely large but it is not a typo. All values in the table are multiplied by 10^3.

δ	ALICE	FEVO	FEVO*	FEBV	VOLS	Passive
0	2.08±1.95	2.40±2.15	2.32±2.02	3.09±3.03	○1.31±1.70	3.11±2.78
0.005	○2.10±1.96	2.43±2.15	2.35±2.02	3.13±3.00	2.53±2.23	3.14±2.78
0.05	○4.61±2.12	4.89±2.26	4.84±2.14	5.95±3.58	124±7.4	6.01±3.43

which correspond to "*correctly specified*," "*approximately correct*," and "*misspecified*" cases, respectively.

Let the test input distribution be Gaussian with mean 0.2 and standard deviation 0.4, which is assumed to be known in this illustrative simulation. Let us gather 100 training samples by active learning. Our task here is to choose the training input distribution from a set of Gaussians with mean 0.2 and standard deviation $0.4c$, where

$$c = 0.8, 0.9, 1.0, \ldots, 2.5. \tag{7.80}$$

We add i.i.d. Gaussian noise with mean zero and standard deviation 0.3 to the training output values. The above setting is summarized in figure 7.5. We repeat this simulation 1000 times for each δ.

In table 7.2, the mean and standard deviation of the generalization error obtained by each method are described. FEVO* denotes the case where the closed-form solution of FEVO (see (7.70)) is used.

When $\delta = 0$, VOLS works significantly better than other methods. Actually, in this case, training input densities that approximately minimize the generalization error were successfully found by ALICE, FEVO, FEBV, and VOLS. This implies that the difference in the obtained error is caused not by the quality of the active learning criteria but by the difference between IWLS and OLS since IWLS generally has larger variance than OLS [Shimodaira, 2000]. Therefore, when $\delta = 0$, OLS would be more accurate than IWLS since both IWLS and OLS are unbiased. Although ALICE, FEVO, and FEBV are outperformed by VOLS, they still work better than Passive (training input density is equal to the test input density). Note that ALICE is significantly better than FEVO, FEBV, and Passive by the t-test.

When $\delta = 0.005$, ALICE gives significantly smaller errors than other methods. All the methods except VOLS work similarly to the case with $\delta = 0$, while VOLS tends to perform poorly. This result is surprising since the learning target functions with $\delta = 0$ and $\delta = 0.005$ are visually almost the same, as illustrated in the top graph of figure 7.5. Therefore, intuitively, the result when $\delta = 0.005$ should not be much different from the result when $\delta = 0$. However, this slight difference appears to make VOLS unreliable. Other methods are shown to be robust against model misspecification.

When $\delta = 0.05$, ALICE again works significantly better than others. FEVO still works reasonably well. The performance of FEBV is slightly degraded, although it is still better than Passive. VOLS gives extremely large errors.

The above results are summarized as follows. For all three cases ($\delta = 0, 0.005, 0.05$), ALICE, FEVO, and FEBV work reasonably well and consistently outperform Passive. Among them, ALICE appears to be better than FEVO and FEBV for all three cases. VOLS works excellently for correctly specified models, although it tends to perform poorly once the correctness of the model is violated. Therefore, ALICE is shown to be robust against model misspecification and therefore works well.

7.5 Active Learning with Model Selection

The problems of model selection and active learning share a common goal—minimizing the generalization error (see (7.18) and (7.46)). However, they have been studied separately as two independent problems so far. If models and training input points are optimized at the same time, the generalization performance could be further improved. We call the problem of simultaneously optimizing training input points and models *active learning with model selection*:

$$\min_{M, p_{\text{tr}}} G(M, p_{\text{tr}}). \tag{7.81}$$

This is the problem we address in this section.

7.5.1 Direct Approach and Active Learning/Model Selection Dilemma

A naive and direct solution to (7.81) would be to simultaneously optimize M and p_{tr}. However, this direct approach may not be possible by simply combining an existing active learning method and an existing model selection method in a batch manner due to the *active learning/model selection dilemma*: when choosing the model M with existing model selection methods, the training input points (or the training input density) must have been fixed and the corresponding training output values must have been gathered [Akaike, 1974; Rissanen, 1978; Schwarz, 1978; Craven and Wahba, 1979; Shimodaira, 2000; Sugiyama and Müller, 2005a]. On the other hand, when selecting the training input density with existing active learning methods, the model must have been fixed [Fedorov, 1972; MacKay, 1992b; Cohn et al., 1996; Fukumizu, 2000; Wiens, 2000; Kanamori and Shimodaira, 2003; Sugiyama, 2006]. For example, IWSIC (7.29) cannot be computed without fixing the training input density (and without training output values) and ALICE (7.55) cannot be computed without fixing the model.

If there exist training input points which are optimal for all model candidates, it is possible to solve both active learning and model selection without regard to the dilemma: choose the training input points for some model by some active learning method (e.g., ALICE), gather corresponding training output values, and perform model selection using some method (e.g., IWSIC). It is shown that such common optimal training input points exist for correctly specified trigonometric polynomial models [Sugiyama and Ogawa, 2003]. However, such common optimal training input points may not exist in general and thus the range of application of this approach is limited.

7.5.2 Sequential Approach

A standard approach to coping with the active learning/model selection dilemma for arbitrary models would be the *sequential approach* [MacKay, 1992a], i.e., in an iterative manner, a model is chosen by a model selection method and the next input point (or a small portion) is optimized for the chosen model by an active learning method (see figure 7.6(a) on page 127).

In the sequential approach, the chosen model $M^{(i)}$ varies through the online learning process (see the dashed line in figure 7.6(b)), where $M^{(i)}$ denotes the model chosen at the ith step. We refer to this phenomenon as the *model drift*. The model drift phenomenon could be a weakness of the sequential approach since the location of optimal training input points depends *strongly* on the target model in active learning; a good training input point for one model could be poor for another model. Depending on the transition of the chosen models, the sequential approach can work very well. For example, when the transition of the model is the solid line in figure 7.6(b), most of the training input points are chosen for the finally selected model $M^{(n)}$ and the sequential approach has an excellent performance. However, when the transition of the model is the dotted line in figure 7.6(b), the performance becomes poor since most of the training input points are chosen for other models. Note that we *cannot* control the transition of the model properly since we do not know a priori which model will be chosen in the end. Therefore, the performance of the sequential approach is unstable.

Another issue that needs to be taken into account in the sequential approach is that the training input points are not i.i.d. in general—the choice of the $(i+1)$th training input point x_{i+1} depends on the previously gathered samples $\{(x_j, y_j)\}_{j=1}^i$. Since standard model selection methods and active learning methods require the i.i.d. assumption for establishing their statistical properties such as unbiasedness and consistency, they may not be directly employed in the sequential approach [Bach, 2007].

IWSIC (7.29) and ALICE (7.55) also suffer from the violation of the i.i.d. condition and lose their unbiasedness and consistency. However, this problem can be easily settled by slightly modifying the criteria. Suppose we draw u input points from $p_{\mathrm{tr}}^{(i)}(x)$ in each iteration (let $n = uv$, where v is the number of iterations). If u tends to be infinity, simply redefining the diagonal matrix W as follows makes IWSIC and ALICE still asymptotically unbiased and consistent:

$$W_{k,k} = \frac{p_{\mathrm{te}}(x_k)}{p_{\mathrm{tr}}^{(i)}(x_k)}, \tag{7.82}$$

where $k = (i-1)u + j$, $i = 1, 2, \ldots, v$, and $j = 1, 2, \ldots, u$. This would be another advantage of the conditional expectation approach.

7.5.3　Batch Approach

An alternative approach to active learning with model selection is to choose all the training input points for an initially chosen model $M^{(0)}$. We refer to this approach as the *batch approach* (see figure 7.7(a) on page 127). Due to the batch nature, this approach does not suffer from the model drift (cf. figure 7.6(b)); the batch approach can be optimal in terms of active learning if an initially chosen model $M^{(0)}$ agrees with the finally chosen model $M^{(n)}$ (see the solid line in figure 7.7(b)).

The performance of this batch approach heavily depends on the initial model $M^{(0)}$. In order to choose the initial model appropriately, we may need a generalization error estimator that can be computed before observing training output values—for example, ALICE (7.55). However, this does not work well since ALICE only evaluates the variance of the estimator; thus using ALICE for choosing the initial model $M^{(0)}$ merely results in always selecting the simplest model in the candidates. Note that this problem is not specific to ALICE, but is common to most generalization error estimators since it is generally not possible to estimate the bias before observing training output values. For this reason, in practice, we may have to choose the initial model $M^{(0)}$ *randomly*. If we have some prior preference of models, $P(M)$, we may draw the initial model according to it.

Due to the randomness of the initial model choice, the performance of the batch approach may be unstable (see the dotted line in figure 7.7(b)).

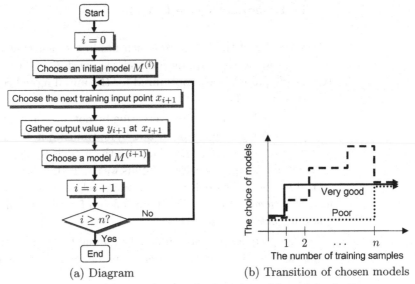

(a) Diagram   (b) Transition of chosen models

Figure 7.6   Sequential approach to active learning with model selection.

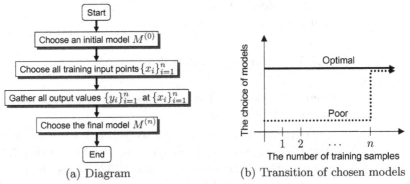

(a) Diagram   (b) Transition of chosen models

Figure 7.7   Batch approach to active learning with model selection.

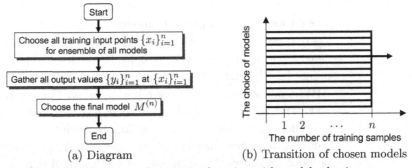

(a) Diagram   (b) Transition of chosen models

Figure 7.8   Ensemble approach to active learning with model selection.

7.5.4   Ensemble Active Learning

The weakness of the batch approach lies in the fact that the training input points chosen by an active learning method are *overfitted* to the initially chosen model—the training input points optimized for the initial model could be poor if a different model is chosen later.

We may reduce the risk of overfitting by not optimizing the training input density *specifically* for a single model, but by optimizing it for *all* model candidates (see figure 7.8 on page 127). This allows all the models to contribute to the optimization of the training input density and thus we can hedge the risk of overfitting to a single (possibly inferior) model. Since this approach could be viewed as applying a popular idea of *ensemble learning* to the problem of active learning, this method is called *ensemble active learning* (EAL).

This idea could be realized by determining the training input density so that the *expected* generalization error over *all* model candidates is minimized:

$$\min_{p_{\mathrm{tr}}} \sum_M \mathrm{ALICE}_M(p_{\mathrm{tr}}) P(M), \tag{7.83}$$

where ALICE_M denotes ALICE for a model M and $P(M)$ is the prior preference of the model M. If no prior information on goodness of the models is available, the uniform prior may be simply used.

7.5.5   Numerical Examples

Here, we illustrate how the ensemble active learning method behaves through numerical experiments.

We use the same toy example as section 7.4.3; the difference is the learning target function and parameter learning methods. In section 7.4.3, the target function is changed through δ (see (7.76)) and IWLS is used; here we fix the target function at $\delta = 0.05$ and use AIWLS (7.15) for parameter learning. We choose the flattening parameter λ in AIWLS by IWSIC (7.29) from

$$\lambda = 0, 0.5, 1. \tag{7.84}$$

The choice of λ corresponds to model selection in this scenario.

First, we investigate the dependency between the goodness of the training input density (i.e., c) and the model (i.e., λ). For each λ and each c, we draw training input points $\{x_i\}_{i=1}^{100}$ and gather output values $\{y_i\}_{i=1}^{100}$. Then we learn the parameter by AIWLS and compute the generalization error. The mean generalization error over 1000 trials as a function of c for each λ is depicted in figure 7.9(a). This graph underlines that the best training input density c could strongly depend on the model λ, implying that a training input density that is good for one model could be poor for others. For example, when the training input density is optimized for the model $\lambda = 0$, $c = 1.1$ would be an excellent choice. However, $c = 1.1$ is not

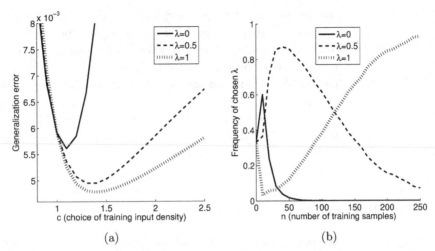

Figure 7.9 (a) Mean generalization error $G-\sigma^2$ over 1000 trials as a function of training input density c for each λ (when $n=100$). (b) Frequency of chosen λ over 1000 trials as a function of the number of training samples.

Table 7.3 Means and standard deviations of generalization error for the toy dataset. All values in the table are multiplied by 10^3. The best method and comparable ones by the t-test at the significance level 5% are marked by "∘".

n	Passive	Sequential	Batch	Ensemble
100	5.92±3.28	5.57±2.75	5.65±2.92	∘5.12±2.50
150	4.77±2.18	4.43±1.77	4.64±1.91	∘4.11±1.55
200	4.21±1.75	3.89±1.40	4.19±1.60	∘3.68±1.19
250	3.78±1.32	3.47±1.02	3.91±1.42	∘3.35±0.92

so suitable for other models $\lambda = 0.5, 1$. This figure illustrates a possible weakness of the batch method: when an initially chosen model is significantly different from the finally chosen model, the training input points optimized for the initial model could be less useful for the final model and the performance is degraded.

Next, we investigate the behavior of the sequential approach. In our implementation, ten training input points are chosen at each iteration. Figure 7.9(b) depicts the transition of the frequency of chosen λ in the sequential learning process over 1000 trials. It shows that the choice of models varies over the learning process; a smaller λ (which has smaller variance thus low complexity) is favored in the beginning, but a larger λ (which has larger variance thus higher complexity) tends to be chosen as the number of training samples increases. Figure 7.9(b) illustrates a possible weakness of the sequential method: the target model drifts during the sequential learning process and the training input points designed in an early stage could be poor for the finally chosen model.

Finally, we investigate the generalization performance of each method when the number of training samples to gather is $n = 100, 150, 200, 250$. Table 7.3 describes the means and standard deviations of the generalization error obtained by the sequential, batch, and ensemble methods; as a baseline, we also included the result of passive learning (or equivalently $c = 1$). The table shows that all three methods tend to outperform passive learning. However, the improvement of the sequential method is not so significant, which would be caused by the model drift phenomenon (see figure 7.9). The batch method also does not provide significant improvement due to the overfitting to the randomly chosen initial model (see figure 7.9(a)). On the other hand, the proposed ensemble method does not suffer from these problems and works significantly better than other methods.

7.6   Conclusions

We introduced a conditional expectation approach to model selection and active learning under covariate shift and proved that it is more accurate than the full expectation approach in approximate linear regression. Furthermore, a method to combine active learning and model selection was introduced that was nicely showing its experimental validity.

Future work will consider nonlinear extensions to the proposed methods and study their use for classification. From the practical application viewpoint, we will employ covariate shift compensation techniques for brain-computer interface (BCI) following the lines of Sugiyama et al. [2007] and use the novel active learning strategies for improving experimental design in computational chemistry [cf. Warmuth et al., 2003].

Acknowledgments

M.S. thanks support by MEXT (17700142 and 18300057), the Okawa Foundation, and the Microsoft CORE3 Project. K.-R.M. acknowledges support by the EU (PASCAL), DFG MU 987/4-1, and BMBF. The authors are thankful for valuable discussions with Motoaki Kawanabe.

8   Covariate Shift by Kernel Mean Matching

Arthur Gretton[1]
Alex Smola[1]
Jiayuan Huang
Marcel Schmittfull
Karsten Borgwardt
Bernhard Schölkopf

Given sets of observations of training and test data, we consider the problem of reweighting the training data such that its distribution more closely matches that of the test data. We achieve this goal by matching covariate distributions between training and test sets in a high-dimensional feature space (specifically, a reproducing kernel Hilbert space). This approach does not require distribution estimation. Instead, the sample weights are obtained by a simple quadratic programming procedure. We provide a uniform convergence bound on the distance between the reweighted training feature mean and the test feature mean, a transductive bound on the expected loss of an algorithm trained on the reweighted data, and a connection to single class SVMs. While our method is designed to deal with the case of simple covariate shift (in the sense of chapter 1), we have also found benefits for sample selection bias on the labels. Our correction procedure yields its greatest and most consistent advantages when the learning algorithm returns a classifier/regressor that is "simpler" than the data might suggest.

8.1   Introduction

The default assumption in many learning scenarios is that training and test data are drawn independently and identically (i.i.d.) from the *same* distribution. When the distributions on training and test set do not match, we face the problem of *dataset shift*: given a domain of patterns $\mathcal{X}$ and labels $\mathcal{Y}$, we obtain training samples

---

1. These authors contributed equally to this work.

$Z_{\mathrm{tr}} = \left\{ (x_1^{\mathrm{tr}}, y_1^{\mathrm{tr}}), \ldots, (x_{n_{\mathrm{tr}}}^{\mathrm{tr}}, y_{n_{\mathrm{tr}}}^{\mathrm{tr}}) \right\} \subseteq \mathcal{X} \times \mathcal{Y}$ from a Borel probability distribution $\mathrm{P}_{\mathrm{tr}}(x, y)$, and test samples $Z_{\mathrm{te}} = \left\{ (x_1^{\mathrm{te}}, y_1^{\mathrm{te}}), \ldots, (x_{n_{\mathrm{te}}}^{\mathrm{te}}, y_{n_{\mathrm{te}}}^{\mathrm{te}}) \right\} \subseteq \mathcal{X} \times \mathcal{Y}$ drawn from another such distribution $\mathrm{P}_{\mathrm{te}}(x, y)$.

Although there exists previous work addressing this problem [Zadrozny, 2004; Rosset et al., 2004; Heckman, 1979; Lin et al., 2002; Dudík et al., 2005; Shimodaira, 2000; Sugiyama and Müller, 2005a], dataset shift has typically been ignored in standard estimation algorithms. Nonetheless, in reality the problem occurs rather frequently. Below, we give some examples of where dataset shift occurs (following the terminology defined by Storkey in chapter 1).

1. Suppose we wish to generate a model to diagnose breast cancer. Suppose, moreover, that most women who participate in the breast screening test are middle-aged and likely to have attended the screening in the preceding three years. Consequently our sample includes mostly older women and those who have low risk of breast cancer because they have been tested before. This problem is referred to as *sample selection bias*. The examples do not reflect the general population with respect to age (which amounts to a bias in $\mathrm{P}_{\mathrm{tr}}(x)$) and they only contain very few diseased cases (i.e., a bias in $\mathrm{P}_{\mathrm{tr}}(y|x)$).

2. Consider the problem of data analysis using a brain-computer interface, where the distribution over incoming signals is known to change as experiments go on (subjects tire, the sensor setup changes, etc.). In this case it necessary to adapt the estimator to the new distribution of patterns in order to improve performance [Sugiyama et al., 2007].

3. Gene expression profile studies using DNA microarrays are used in tumor diagnosis. A common problem is that the samples are obtained using certain protocols, microarray platforms, and analysis techniques, and typically have small sample sizes. The test cases are recorded under different conditions, resulting in a different distribution of gene expression values. In both this and the previous example, a *covariate shift* has occurred (see chapter 1).

In all cases we would intuitively want to assign more weight to those observations in the training set which are most similar to those in the test set, and less weight to those which rarely occur in the test set.

In this chapter, we use unlabeled data as the basis for a dataset shift correction procedure for various learning methods. Unlike previous work, we infer the resampling weight *directly* by nonparametric distribution matching between training and testing samples. We do not need to estimate the biasing densities or selection probabilities [Zadrozny, 2004; Dudík et al., 2005; Shimodaira, 2000], or to assume advance knowledge of the different class probabilities [Lin et al., 2002]. Rather, we account for the difference between $\mathrm{P}_{\mathrm{tr}}(x, y)$ and $\mathrm{P}_{\mathrm{te}}(x, y)$ by reweighting the training points such that the means of the training and test points in a reproducing kernel Hilbert space (RKHS) are close. We call this reweighting process kernel mean matching (KMM), following our presentation in Huang et al. [2007]. The present chapter expands on our earlier work in terms of both theoretical and experimental analysis.

Since our approach does not require density estimation, we are able to state results which apply to arbitrary domains and which do not, in principle, suffer from the curse of dimensionality that befalls high-dimensional density estimation. When the RKHS is universal [Steinwart, 2002], the population solution to this minimization is exactly the ratio $P_{te}(x, y)/P_{tr}(x, y)$; we derive performance guarantees which depend on the maximum ratio between the distributions (but not on the distributions themselves) and which show that our method is consistent. We remark that when this ratio is large, however, a large sample size would be required to ensure the bound is tight (and to guarantee a good approximation).

The required optimization is a simple quadratic program, and the reweighted sample can be incorporated straightforwardly into many regression and classification algorithms and model selection procedures, such as cross-validation. We apply our method to a variety of regression and classification benchmarks from University of California Irvine (UCI) and elsewhere, as well as to classification of microarrays from prostate and breast cancer patients. The experiments demonstrate that sample reweighting by KMM substantially improves learning performance in cases where the class of functions output by the learning algorithm is "simpler" than the true function (for instance, such a classification algorithm would estimate a decision boundary deliberately smoother than the Bayes optimal boundary that emerges as the sample size increases to infinity). Indeed, for this case, performance can be improved from close to chance level to the point of almost matching the performance of a learning algorithm with the "correct" complexity. KMM reweighting can also improve performance in cases where the complexity of the leaned classification/regression function is chosen optimally for the data, via parameter selection by cross-validation. For most such cases, however, KMM does not affect performance, or can even make it slightly worse.

In general, the estimation problem with two different distributions $P_{tr}(x, y)$ and $P_{te}(x, y)$ is unsolvable, as the two distributions could be arbitrarily far apart. In particular, for arbitrary $P_{tr}(y|x)$ and $P_{te}(y|x)$, there is no way we could infer a good estimator based on the training sample. For instance, the distributions $P_{tr}(y = 1|x)$ and $P_{te}(y = -1|x)$ could be swapped in binary classification, leading to an arbitrarily large error. The following assumption allows us to address the problem.

Assumption 8.1 *We make the simplifying assumption that* $P_{tr}(x, y)$ *and* $P_{te}(x, y)$ *only differ via* $P_{tr}(x, y) = P(y|x)P_{tr}(x)$ *and* $P_{te}(x, y) = P(y|x)P_{te}(x)$. *In other words, the conditional probabilities of* $y|x$ *remain* unchanged.

This particular case of dataset shift has been termed *covariate shift* (see examples above, chapter 1, and [Shimodaira, 2000]). We will see experimentally that even in situations where our key assumption is not valid, our method can still be useful (see section 8.6).

We begin our presentation in section 8.2, where we describe the concept of sample reweighting to match empirical distributions, and show how a reweighted sample can be incorporated easily into a variety of learning algorithms (penalized 1-norm classification, penalized logistic regression, penalized LMS (least mean square) regression, Poisson regression). In section 8.3, we describe our sample reweighting procedure, which entails matching the means of the reweighted training sample and the target (test) sample in a reproducing kernel Hilbert space. We discuss the convergence of the Hilbert space training and test means in the limit of large sample size, and provide an empirical optimization procedure to select the training sample weights (this being a straightforward quadratic program). In section 8.4, we provide transductive guarantees on the performance of learning algorithms that use the reweighted sample, subject to linearity conditions on the loss functions of these algorithms. We establish a connection between sample bias correction and novelty detection in section 8.5, with reference to the single class support vector machine (SVM). We present our experiments in section 8.6: these consist of a toy example proposed by Shimodaira [2000], a detailed analysis of performance for different classifier parameters on the UCI breast cancer dataset, a broader overview of performance on many different UCI datasets, and experiments on microarray data. We provide proofs of our theoretical results in section 8.8.

8.2 Sample Reweighting

We begin by stating the problem of risk minimization. In general a learning method aims to minimize the expected risk,

$$R[\mathrm{P}, \theta, l(x, y, \theta)] = \mathbf{E}_{(x,y) \sim \mathrm{P}} \left[l(x, y, \theta) \right] , \qquad (8.1)$$

of a loss function $l(x, y, \theta)$ depending on a parameter θ. For instance, the loss function could be the negative log-likelihood $-\log \mathrm{P}(y|x, \theta)$, a misclassification loss, or some form of regression loss. However, since typically we only observe examples (x, y) drawn from $\mathrm{P}(x, y)$ rather than $\mathrm{P}(x, y)$, we resort to computing the empirical average,

$$R_{\mathrm{emp}}[Z, \theta, l(x, y, \theta)] = \frac{1}{n} \sum_{i=1}^{n} l(x_i, y_i, \theta) . \qquad (8.2)$$

To avoid overfitting, instead of minimizing R_{emp} directly, we minimize a regularized variant,

$$R_{\mathrm{reg}}[Z, \theta, l(x, y, \theta)] := R_{\mathrm{emp}}[Z, \theta, l(x, y, \theta)] + \lambda \Omega[\theta] ,$$

where $\Omega[\theta]$ is a regularizer.

8.2.1 Sample Correction

The problem is more involved if $\mathrm{P}_{\mathrm{tr}}(x, y)$ and $\mathrm{P}_{\mathrm{te}}(x, y)$ are different. The training set is drawn from P_{tr}; however, what we would really like is to minimize $R[\mathrm{P}_{\mathrm{te}}, \theta, l]$

as we wish to generalize to test examples drawn from P_{te}. An observation from the field of importance sampling is that

$$R[P_{te}, \theta, l(x, y, \theta)] = \mathbf{E}_{(x,y) \sim P_{te}} [l(x, y, \theta)] = \mathbf{E}_{(x,y) \sim P_{tr}} \Big[\underbrace{\frac{P_{te}(x, y)}{P_{tr}(x, y)}}_{:= \beta(x,y)} l(x, y, \theta) \Big]$$

$$= R[P_{tr}, \theta, \beta(x, y) l(x, y, \theta)],$$

provided that the support of P_{te} *is contained in the support of* P_{tr}. If this does not hold, reweighting x in order to obtain a risk estimate for $P_{te}(x, y)$ is impossible. In fact, the risks could be arbitrarily different, since we have no information about the behavior of $l(x, y, \theta)$ on a subset of the domain of P_{te}.

Given $\beta(x, y)$, we can thus compute the risk with respect to P_{te} using P_{tr}. Similarly, we can *estimate* the risk with respect to P_{te} by computing the empirical risk $R_{emp}[Z, \theta, \beta(x, y) l(x, y, \theta)]$. The key problem is that the coefficients $\beta(x, y)$ are usually unknown, and must be estimated from the data. When P_{tr} and P_{te} differ in $P_{tr}(x)$ and $P_{te}(x)$ only, we have $\beta(x, y) = P_{te}(x)/P_{tr}(x)$, where β is a reweighting factor for the training examples. We thus reweight every training observation (x_i^{tr}, y_i^{tr}) such that observations that are underrepresented in P_{tr} (relative to P_{te}) are assigned a higher weight, whereas overrepresented cases are downweighted.

We could estimate P_{tr} and P_{te} and subsequently compute β based on those estimates. This is closely related to the methods of Zadrozny [2004]; Lin et al. [2002], and Sugiyama and Müller [2005a], who either have to estimate the selection probabilities, or have prior knowledge of the class distributions. While intuitive, this approach has three major drawbacks:

1. It only works whenever the estimates for P_{tr} and P_{te} (or potentially, the selection probabilities or class distributions) are good. In particular, small errors in estimating P_{tr} can lead to large coefficients β and consequently to a serious overweighting of the corresponding observations.

2. Estimating both distributions just for the purpose of computing reweighting coefficients may be overkill: we may be able to directly estimate the coefficients $\beta_i := \beta(x_i^{tr}, y_i^{tr})$ without having to perform distribution estimation. Furthermore, we can regularize β_i directly with more flexibility, taking prior knowledge into account (similar to learning methods for other problems).

3. It is well known that using the exact importance sampler weights may not be optimal, even when knowing both distributions. See e.g., Shimodaira [2000] for a discussion of the issue. The basic idea is that importance sampler weights β which deviate strongly from 1 increase the variance significantly. In fact, as we will see in lemma 8.8, the effective training sample size is $n_{tr}^2 / \|\beta\|_2^2$. Hence it may be worth accepting a small bias in return for a larger effective sample size.

8.2.2   Using the Sample Reweighting in Learning Algorithms

Before we describe how we will estimate the reweighting coefficients β_i, we briefly discuss how to minimize the reweighted regularized risk

$$R_{\text{reg}}[Z, \beta, l(x, y, \theta)] := \frac{1}{n_{\text{tr}}} \sum_{i=1}^{n_{\text{tr}}} \beta_i l(x_i^{\text{tr}}, y_i^{\text{tr}}, \theta) + \lambda \Omega[\theta], \tag{8.3}$$

in four useful settings.

Penalized 1-Norm Classification (Support Vector Classification) Using the formulation of Tsochantaridis et al. [2005] and Taskar et al. [2004] we have the following minimization problem (the original SVMs can be formulated in the same way):

$$\underset{\theta, \xi}{\text{minimize}} \ \frac{1}{2} \|\theta\|^2 + C \sum_{i=1}^{n_{\text{tr}}} \beta_i \xi_i \tag{8.4a}$$

$$\text{subject to} \ \left\langle \Phi(x_i^{\text{tr}}, y_i^{\text{tr}}) - \Phi(x_i^{\text{tr}}, y), \theta \right\rangle \geq 1 - \xi_i / \Delta(y_i^{\text{tr}}, y) \tag{8.4b}$$

$$\text{for all} \ y \in \mathcal{Y}, \ \text{and} \ \xi_i \geq 0.$$

Here, $\Phi(x, y)$ is a feature map from $\mathcal{X} \times \mathcal{Y}$ to a feature space $\mathcal{F}$, where $\theta \in \mathcal{F}$ and $\Delta(y, y')$ denote a discrepancy function between y and y'. The dual of (8.4) is

$$\underset{\alpha}{\text{minimize}} \ \frac{1}{2} \sum_{i,j=1; y, y' \in \mathcal{Y}}^{n_{\text{tr}}} \alpha_{iy} \alpha_{jy'} k(x_i^{\text{tr}}, y, x_j^{\text{tr}}, y') - \sum_{i=1; y \in \mathcal{Y}}^{n_{\text{tr}}} \alpha_{iy} \tag{8.5a}$$

$$\text{subject to} \ \alpha_{iy} \geq 0 \ \text{for all} \ i, y \ \text{and} \ \sum_{y \in \mathcal{Y}} \alpha_{iy} / \Delta(y_i^{\text{tr}}, y) \leq \beta_i C. \tag{8.5b}$$

Here $k(x, y, x', y') := \left\langle \Phi(x, y), \Phi(x', y') \right\rangle$ denotes the inner product between the feature maps. This generalizes the observation-dependent binary support vector (SV) classification described by Schmidt and Gish [1996]. Many existing solvers, such as SVMStruct [Tsochantaridis et al., 2005], can be modified easily to take sample-dependent weights into account.

Penalized Logistic Regression This is also referred to as *Gaussian process classification*. In the unweighted case [Williams and Barber, 1998], we minimize $\sum_{i=1}^{n} -\log p(y_i | x_i, \theta) + \frac{\lambda}{2} \|\theta\|^2$ with respect to θ. Using (8.3) yields the following modified optimization problem:

$$\underset{\theta}{\text{minimize}} \sum_{i=1}^{n_{\text{tr}}} -\beta_i \log p(y_i^{\text{tr}} | x_i^{\text{tr}}, \theta) + \frac{\lambda}{2} \|\theta\|^2. \tag{8.6}$$

Using an exponential families and kernel approach for

$$\log p(y | x, \theta) = \left\langle \Phi(x, y), \theta \right\rangle - g(\theta | x), \tag{8.7}$$

$$\text{where} \ g(\theta | x) = \log \sum_{y \in \mathcal{Y}} \exp \left(\left\langle \Phi(x, y), \theta \right\rangle \right)$$

we can invoke the representer theorem [Kimeldorf and Wahba, 1970] which leads to

$$\underset{\alpha}{\text{minimize}} \sum_{i=1}^{n_{\text{tr}}} \beta_i g(\alpha | x_i^{\text{tr}}) - \sum_{i,j=1; y \in \mathcal{Y}}^{n_{\text{tr}}} \alpha_{iy} \beta_j k(x_i^{\text{tr}}, y, x_j^{\text{tr}}, y_j^{\text{tr}})$$

$$+ \sum_{i,j=1; y,y' \in \mathcal{Y}}^{n_{\text{tr}}} \alpha_{iy} \alpha_{jy'} k(x_i^{\text{tr}}, y, x_j^{\text{tr}}, y'), \tag{8.8}$$

$$\text{where } g(\alpha | x_i^{\text{tr}}) := \log \sum_{y \in \mathcal{Y}} \exp \left(\sum_{j=1; y' \in \mathcal{Y}}^{n_{\text{tr}}} \alpha_{jy'} k(x_i^{\text{tr}}, y, x_j^{\text{tr}}, y') \right).$$

Penalized LMS Regression Assume $l(x, y, \theta) = (y - \langle \Phi(x), \theta \rangle)^2$ and $\Omega[\theta] = \|\theta\|^2$. Here we solve

$$\underset{\theta}{\text{minimize}} \sum_{i=1}^{n_{\text{tr}}} \beta_i (y_i^{\text{tr}} - \langle \Phi(x_i^{\text{tr}}), \theta \rangle)^2 + \lambda \|\theta\|^2. \tag{8.9}$$

Denote by $\bar{\beta}$ the diagonal matrix with diagonal $(\beta_1, \ldots, \beta_{n_{\text{tr}}})$ and by $K \in \mathbb{R}^{m \times m}$ the kernel matrix $K_{ij} = k(x_i^{\text{tr}}, x_j^{\text{tr}})$. In this case minimizing (8.9) is equivalent to solving

$$\underset{\alpha}{\text{minimize}} \quad (y - K\alpha)^\top \bar{\beta} (y - K\alpha) + \lambda \alpha^\top K \alpha$$

with respect to α. Assuming that K and $\bar{\beta}$ have full rank, the minimization yields

$$\alpha = (\lambda \bar{\beta}^{-1} + K)^{-1} y.$$

The advantage of this formulation is that it can be solved as easily as the standard penalized regression problem. Essentially, we rescale the regularizer depending on the pattern weights: the higher the weight of an observation, the less we regularize.

Poisson Regression Assume a process of discrete events, such as the distribution of species over a geographical location or the occurrence of noninfectious diseases. This process can be modeled by a conditional Poisson distribution,

$$\log p(y | x, \theta) = y \langle \Phi(x), \theta \rangle - \log y! - \exp (\langle \Phi(x), \theta \rangle) \tag{8.10}$$

as a member of the nonparametric exponential family (see e.g., Cressie [1993]), where $y \in \mathbb{N}_0$. Consequently we may obtain a reweighted risk minimization problem,

$$\underset{\alpha}{\text{minimize}} \sum_{i=1}^{n_{\text{tr}}} \beta_i \exp ([K\alpha]_i) - \beta_i y_i^{\text{tr}} [K\alpha]_i + \lambda \alpha^\top K \alpha. \tag{8.11}$$

Here K and α are defined as in the above example. The problem is convex in α.

We provided the above examples to demonstrate that it is fairly straightforward to turn most risk minimization procedures into reweighted ones. For those algorithms which cannot deal with weighted data easily, one may always resort to resampling; see, e.g., Efron and Tibshirani [1994].

8.3   Distribution Matching

8.3.1   Kernel Mean Matching and Its Relation to Importance Sampling

Let $\Phi : \mathcal{X} \to \mathcal{F}$ be a feature map into a feature space $\mathcal{F}$ and denote by $\mu : \mathcal{P} \to \mathcal{F}$ the expectation operator

$$\mu(\mathrm{P}) := \mathbf{E}_{x \sim \mathrm{P}(x)}\left[\Phi(x)\right]. \tag{8.12}$$

Clearly μ is a *linear* operator mapping the space of all probability distributions $\mathcal{P}$ into feature space. Denote by $\mathcal{M}(\Phi) := \{\mu(\mathrm{P}) \text{ where } \mathrm{P} \in \mathcal{P}\}$ the image of $\mathcal{P}$ under μ. This set is also often referred to as the *marginal polytope*. We have the following theorem, proved in section 8.8.

Theorem 8.2 *The operator μ is a* bijection *between the space of all probability measures and the marginal polytope induced by the feature map $\Phi(x)$ if $\mathcal{F}$ is an RKHS with a universal kernel $k(x,x') = \langle\Phi(x),\Phi(x')\rangle$ in the sense of Steinwart [2002] (bearing in mind that universality is defined for kernels on compact domains $\mathcal{X}$).*

The practical consequence of this (rather abstract) result is that if we know $\mu(\mathrm{P}_{\mathrm{te}})$, we can infer a suitable weighting function β by solving the following minimization problem. We first state the expectation version of the kernel mean matching (KMM) procedure:

Lemma 8.3 *The following optimization problem in β is convex.*

$$\underset{\beta}{\text{minimize}} \quad \left\|\mu(\mathrm{P}_{\mathrm{te}}) - \mathbf{E}_{x \sim \mathrm{P}_{\mathrm{tr}}(x)}\left[\beta(x)\Phi(x)\right]\right\| \tag{8.13}$$

$$\text{subject to } \beta(x) \geq 0 \text{ and } \mathbf{E}_{x \sim \mathrm{P}_{\mathrm{tr}}(x)}\left[\beta(x)\right] = 1. \tag{8.14}$$

Assume P_{te} is absolutely continuous with respect to P_{tr} (so $\mathrm{P}_{\mathrm{tr}}(A) = 0$ implies $\mathrm{P}_{\mathrm{te}}(A) = 0$), and that k is universal. The solution of (8.13) is then $\mathrm{P}_{\mathrm{te}}(x) = \beta(x)\mathrm{P}_{\mathrm{tr}}(x)$.

Proof: The convexity of the objective function follows from the facts that the norm is a convex function and the integral is a linear functional in β. The other constraints are also convex.

By virtue of the constraints, any feasible solution of β corresponds to a distribution, as $\int \beta(x) d\mathrm{P}_{\mathrm{tr}}(x) = 1$. Moreover, the choice of $\hat{\beta}(x) := \mathrm{P}_{\mathrm{te}}(x)/\mathrm{P}_{\mathrm{tr}}(x)$ is feasible as it obviously satisfies the constraints. Moreover, it minimizes the objective function with value 0. Note that such a $\beta(x)$ exists due to the absolute continuity of $P_{te}(x)$ with respect to $P_{tr}(x)$. Theorem 8.2 implies that there can be only one distribution $\beta(x)P_{tr}$ such that $\mu(\beta(x)P_{tr}) = \mu(P_{te})$. Hence $\beta(x)P_{tr}(x) = P_{te}(x)$.

8.3.2 Convergence of Reweighted Means in Feature Space

Lemma 8.3 shows that in principle, if we knew P_{tr} and $\mu[P_{te}]$, we could fully recover P_{te} by solving a simple quadratic program. In practice, however, neither $\mu(P_{te})$ nor P_{tr} is known. Instead, we only have samples X_{tr} and X_{te} of size n_{tr} and n_{te}, drawn i.i.d. from P_{tr} and P_{te}, respectively.

Naively we could just replace the expectations in (8.13) by empirical averages and hope that the resulting optimization problem will provide us with a good estimate of β. However, it is to be expected that empirical averages will differ from each other due to finite sample size effects. In this section, we explore two such effects. First, we demonstrate that in the finite sample case, for a fixed β, the empirical estimate of the expectation of β is normally distributed: this provides a natural limit on the precision with which we should enforce the constraint $\int \beta(x)dP_{tr}(x) = 1$ when using empirical expectations (we will return to this point in the next section).

Lemma 8.4 *If $\beta(x) \in [0, B]$ is some fixed function of $x \in \mathcal{X}$, then given $x_i^{tr} \sim P_{tr}$ i.i.d. such that $\beta(x_i^{tr})$ has finite mean and finite nonzero variance, the sample mean $\frac{1}{n_{tr}} \sum_i \beta(x_i^{tr})$ converges in distribution to a Gaussian with mean $\int \beta(x)dP_{tr}(x)$ and standard deviation bounded by $\frac{B}{2\sqrt{n_{tr}}}$.*

This lemma is a direct consequence of the central limit theorem [Casella and Berger, 2002, Theorem 5.5.15]. Alternatively, it is straightforward to get a large deviation bound that likewise converges as $1/\sqrt{n_{tr}}$ Hoeffding [1963]. In this case, it follows that with probability at least $1 - \delta$,

$$\left| \frac{1}{n_{tr}} \sum_{i=1}^{n_{tr}} \beta(x_i^{tr}) - 1 \right| \leq B\sqrt{\log(2/\delta)/2m}. \tag{8.15}$$

Our second result demonstrates the deviation between the empirical means of P_{te} and $\beta(x)P_{tr}$ in feature space, given $\beta(x)$ is chosen perfectly in the population sense.

Lemma 8.5 *In addition to the conditions of lemma 8.4, assume that we draw $X_{te} := \{x_1^{te}, \ldots, x_{n_{te}}^{te}\}$ i.i.d. from $\mathcal{X}$ using $P_{te} = \beta(x)P_{tr}$, and $\|\Phi(x)\| \leq R$ for all $x \in \mathcal{X}$. Then with probability at least $1 - \delta$,*

$$\left\| \frac{1}{n_{tr}} \sum_{i=1}^{n_{tr}} \beta(x_i^{tr})\Phi(x_i^{tr}) - \frac{1}{n_{te}} \sum_{i=1}^{n_{te}} \Phi(x_i^{te}) \right\|$$
$$\leq \left(1 + \sqrt{2\log 2/\delta}\right) R\sqrt{B^2/n_{tr} + 1/n_{te}}. \tag{8.16}$$

The proof is in section 8.8. Note that this lemma shows that for a *given* $\beta(x)$, which is correct in the population sense, we can bound the deviation between the mean and the importance-sampled mean in feature space. It is *not* a guarantee that we will find coefficients β_i which are close to $\beta(x_i^{\text{tr}})$, when solving the optimization problem in the next section.

Lemma 8.5 implies we have $O(B\sqrt{1/n_{\text{tr}}} + 1/n_{\text{te}}B^2)$ convergence in $n_{\text{tr}}, n_{\text{te}}$, and B. This means that for very different distributions, we need a large equivalent sample size to get reasonable convergence. Our result also implies that it is unrealistic to assume that the empirical means (reweighted or not) should match exactly. Note that a somewhat better bound could be obtained by exploiting the interplay between $P_{\text{tr}}, P_{\text{te}}$, and $\Phi(x)$. That is, it is essentially $\|\Phi(x)\| P_{\text{te}}(x)/P_{\text{tr}}(x)$ that matters, as one can see by a simple modification of the proof. For this reason, we may be able to tolerate large deviations between the two distributions at little cost, as long as the feature vector at this location is small.

8.3.3   Empirical KMM Optimization

To find suitable values of $\beta \in \mathbb{R}^{n_{\text{tr}}}$ we want to minimize the discrepancy between means subject to constraints $\beta_i \in [0, B]$ and $|\frac{1}{n_{\text{tr}}} \sum_{i=1}^{n_{\text{tr}}} \beta_i - 1| \leq \epsilon$. The former limits the scope of discrepancy between P_{tr} and P_{te} and ensures robustness by limiting the influence of individual observations, whereas the latter ensures that the corresponding measure $\beta(x)P_{\text{tr}}(x)$ is close to a probability distribution. Note that for $B \to 1$ we obtain the unweighted solution. The objective function is given by the discrepancy term between the two empirical means. Using $K_{ij} := k(x_i^{\text{tr}}, x_j^{\text{tr}})$ and $\kappa_i := \frac{n_{\text{tr}}}{n_{\text{te}}} \sum_{j=1}^{n_{\text{te}}} k(x_i^{\text{tr}}, x_j^{\text{te}})$ one may check that

$$\left\| \frac{1}{n_{\text{tr}}} \sum_{i=1}^{n_{\text{tr}}} \beta_i \Phi(x_i^{\text{tr}}) - \frac{1}{n_{\text{te}}} \sum_{i=1}^{n_{\text{te}}} \Phi(x_i^{\text{te}}) \right\|^2 = \frac{1}{n_{\text{tr}}^2} \beta^\top K \beta - \frac{2}{n_{\text{tr}}^2} \kappa^\top \beta + \text{const.}$$

Now we have all necessary ingredients to formulate a quadratic problem to find suitable β via

$$\underset{\beta}{\text{minimize}} \ \frac{1}{2} \beta^\top K \beta - \kappa^\top \beta \text{ subject to } \beta_i \in [0, B] \text{ and } \left| \sum_{i=1}^{n_{\text{tr}}} \beta_i - n_{\text{tr}} \right| \leq n_{\text{tr}} \epsilon.$$

$$(8.17)$$

In accordance with lemma 8.4, we conclude that a good choice of ϵ should be $O(B/\sqrt{n_{\text{tr}}})$. That said, even a change induced by normalizing $\sum_i \beta_i = 1$ only changes the value of the objective function by at most $\epsilon^2 R^2 + 2\epsilon L$, where L^2 is the value of the objective function at optimality.

Note that (8.17) is a quadratic program which can be solved efficiently using interior point methods or any other successive optimization procedure, such as chunking [Osuna, 1998], sequential minimal optimization (SMO) [Platt, 1999], or projected gradient methods [Dai and Fletcher, 2006]. We also point out that (8.17) resembles single class SVM [Schölkopf et al., 2001] using the ν-trick. Besides the approximate equality constraint, the main difference is the linear correction term by means of κ. Large values of κ_i correspond to particularly important observations x_i^{tr} and are likely to lead to large β_i. We discuss further connections in section 8.5.

8.4   Risk Estimates

So far we have been concerned only with distribution matching for the purpose of finding a reweighting scheme between the empirical feature space means on training X_{tr} and test X_{te} sets. We now show, in the case of *linear* loss functions, that as long as the feature means on the test set are well enough approximated, we will be able to obtain *almost unbiased* risk estimates *regardless* of the actual values of β_i vs. their importance sampling weights $\beta(x_i)$. The price is an increase in the variance of the estimate, where $n_{\text{tr}}^2/\|\beta\|^2$ will act as an effective sample size.

8.4.1   Transductive Bounds

We consider the transductive case: that is, we will make uniform convergence statements with respect to $\mathbf{E}_{y|x}$ only (recall that this expectation is the same for the training and test distributions by assumption). In addition, we will require the loss functions to be linear, as described below.

Assumption 8.6 *We require that $l(x,\theta)$ be expressible as an inner product in feature space, i.e., $l(x,\theta) = \langle \Psi(x), \Theta \rangle$, where $\|\Theta\| \leq C$. That is, $l(x,\theta)$ belongs to a reproducing kernel Hilbert space (RKHS). Likewise, assume $l(x,y,\theta)$ can be expressed as an element of an RKHS via $\langle \Upsilon(x,y), \Lambda \rangle$ with[1] $\|\Lambda\| \leq C$ and $\|\Upsilon(x,y)\| \leq R$.*

We proceed in two steps: first we show that for the expected loss

$$l(x,\Theta) := \mathbf{E}_{y|x} l(x,y,\Lambda), \tag{8.18}$$

the coefficients β_i can be used to obtain a risk estimate with low bias. Second, we show that the random variable $\sum_i \beta_i l(x_i^{\text{tr}}, y_i^{\text{tr}}, \Lambda)$ is concentrated around $\sum_i \beta_i l(x_i^{\text{tr}}, \Theta)$, if we condition $Y|X$. The first lemma is proved in section 8.8.

Lemma 8.7 *Given assumptions 8.1 and 8.6 are satisfied, and $X_{\text{tr}}, X_{\text{te}}$ i.i.d. samples drawn from P_{tr} and P_{te}, respectively. Let $\mathcal{G}$ be a class of loss-induced functions $l(x,\theta)$ with $\|\Theta\| \leq C$. Finally, assume that there exist some β_i such that*

$$\left\| \frac{1}{n_{\text{tr}}} \sum_{i=1}^{n_{\text{tr}}} \beta_i \Psi(x_i^{\text{tr}}) - \frac{1}{n_{\text{te}}} \sum_{i=1}^{n_{\text{te}}} \Psi(x_i^{\text{te}}) \right\| \leq \epsilon \,.$$

---

1. We use the same constant C to bound both $\|\Theta\|$ and $\|\Lambda\|$ for ease of notation, and without loss of generality.

In this case we can bound the empirical risk estimates as

$$
\sup_{l(\cdot,\cdot,\theta)\in\mathcal{G}} \left| \mathbf{E}_{y|x}\left[\frac{1}{n_{\mathrm{tr}}}\sum_{i=1}^{n_{\mathrm{tr}}}\beta_i l(x_i^{\mathrm{tr}},y_i^{\mathrm{tr}},\theta)\right] - \mathbf{E}_{y|x}\left[\frac{1}{n_{\mathrm{te}}}\sum_{i=1}^{n_{\mathrm{te}}}l(x_i^{\mathrm{te}},y_i^{\mathrm{te}},\theta)\right] \right| \le C\epsilon.
$$

$$(8.19)$$

The next step in relating a reweighted empirical average using $(X_{\mathrm{tr}},Y_{\mathrm{tr}})$ and the expected risk with respect to $P(y|x)$ requires us to bound deviations of the first term in (8.19). The required lemma is again proved in section 8.8.

Lemma 8.8 *Given assumption 8.6, samples y_i^{tr} drawn for each x_i^{tr} according to* $\mathrm{P}(y|x)$, *and $M := n_{\mathrm{tr}}^2/\|\beta\|_2^2$, then with probability at least $1-\delta$ over all $y|x$*

$$
\sup_{l(\cdot,\cdot,\theta)\in\mathcal{G}} \left| \frac{1}{n_{\mathrm{tr}}}\sum_{i=1}^{n_{\mathrm{tr}}}\beta_i l(x_i^{\mathrm{tr}},y_i^{\mathrm{tr}},\theta) - \frac{1}{n_{\mathrm{tr}}}\sum_{i=1}^{n_{\mathrm{tr}}}\beta_i l(x_i^{\mathrm{tr}},\theta) \right|
$$
$$
\le (2+\sqrt{2\log(2/\delta)})CR/\sqrt{M}.
$$

We can now combine the bounds from both lemmas to obtain the main result of this section.

Corollary 8.9 *Under the assumptions of lemmas 8.7 and 8.8 we have that with probability at least $1-\delta$,*

$$
\sup_{l(\cdot,\cdot,\theta)\in\mathcal{G}} \left| \frac{1}{n_{\mathrm{tr}}}\sum_{i=1}^{n_{\mathrm{tr}}}\beta_i l(x_i^{\mathrm{tr}},y_i^{\mathrm{tr}},\theta) - \mathbf{E}_{y|x}\left[\frac{1}{n_{\mathrm{te}}}\sum_{i=1}^{n_{\mathrm{te}}}l(x_i^{\mathrm{te}},y_i^{\mathrm{te}},\theta)\right] \right|
$$
$$
\le \frac{(2+\sqrt{2\log(2/\delta)})CR}{\sqrt{M}} + C\epsilon.
$$

$$(8.20)$$

This means that if we minimize the reweighted empirical risk we will, with high probability, be minimizing an upper bound on the expected risk on the test set.

Note that we have an upper bound on ϵ via lemma 8.5, although this assumes the β_i correspond to the importance weights. The encouraging news is that as *both* n_{tr} and $n_{\mathrm{te}} \to \infty$ we will obtain a minimizer of the conditional expected risk on P_{te}. That said, if the test set is small, it is very likely that the deviations introduced by the finite test set will give rise to more uncertainty, which implies that additional training data will be of limited use.

While the above result applies in the case of linear loss functions, we expect a similar approach to hold more generally. The key requirement is that the expected loss be a *smooth* function in the patterns x.

8.4.2 Bounds in Expectation and Cross Validation

There are two more important cases worth analyzing: when carrying out covariate shift correction (or transduction) we may still want to perform model selection by methods such as cross-validation. In this case we need *two* estimators of the empirical test risk — one for obtaining a regularized risk minimizer and another one for assessing the performance of the former.

A first approach is to use the reweighted training set directly for this purpose similar to what was proposed by Sugiyama et al. [2006]. This will give us an estimate of the loss on the test set, albeit biased by the deviation between the reweighted means, as described in corollary 8.9.

A second approach is to use a modification of the cross-validation procedure by partitioning first and reweighting second. That is, in tenfold cross-validation one would first partition the training set and then compute correcting weights for both the $\frac{9}{10}$th fraction used in training and the $\frac{1}{10}$th fraction used for validation. While this increases the cost of computing weights considerably (we need to compute a total of $10 + 10 + 1 = 21$ weighting schemes for model selection and final estimates in tenfold cross-validation), "transductive cross-validation" nonetheless offers a reduction in sampling bias. Again, the bounds of corollary 8.9 apply directly.

Finally, let us briefly consider the situation where we have a reference unlabeled dataset which is drawn from the same distribution as the actual test set, yet it is not identical with the test set. In this case, risk bounds similar to lemma 8.5 and corollary 8.9 can be obtained. The proof is essentially identical to that of the previous section. Hence we only state the result.

Lemma 8.10 *In addition to the conditions of Lemma 8.4, assume that* $\mathrm{P}_{\mathrm{te}} = \beta(x)\mathrm{P}_{\mathrm{tr}}$, *and* $\|\Phi(x)\| \leq R$ *for all* $x \in \mathcal{X}$. *Then, with probability at least* $1 - \delta$,

$$\left\| \frac{1}{n_{\mathrm{tr}}} \sum_{i=1}^{n_{\mathrm{tr}}} \beta(x_i^{\mathrm{tr}})\Phi(x_i^{\mathrm{tr}}) - \mathbf{E}_{\mathrm{P}_{\mathrm{te}}}\left[\Phi(x^{\mathrm{te}})\right] \right\| \leq \left(1 + \sqrt{2\log 2/\delta}\right) RB/\sqrt{n_{\mathrm{tr}}}. \quad (8.21)$$

This also can be used in combination with lemma 8.5, via a triangle inequality, to bound deviations of $\sum_i \beta_i \Phi(x_i^{\mathrm{tr}})$ from $\mathbf{E}_{\mathrm{P}_{\mathrm{te}}}\left[\Phi(x)\right]$ whenever the deviation between the two reweighted empirical samples is minimized as in (8.17).

To obtain a large deviation result with respect to the expected loss in $\mathrm{P}_{\mathrm{te}}(x, y)$, one would simply need to combine lemma 8.10 with a uniform convergence bound, e.g., the bounds by Mendelson [2003].

8.5   The Connection to Single Class Support Vector Machines

8.5.1   Basic Setting

In single class SVM estimation [Schölkopf et al., 2001] one aims to find a function f which satisfies

$$f(x) \begin{cases} \geq \rho & \text{for typical observations } x \\ < \rho & \text{for novel observations } x \end{cases} \qquad (8.22)$$

yet at the same time, f should be smooth. For functions in reproducing Kernel Hilbert spaces $f(x) = \langle \Phi(x), w \rangle$ this is obtained by solving the following optimization problem:

$$\underset{w,\xi}{\text{minimize}} \quad C \sum_{i=1}^{n} \xi_i + \frac{1}{2} \|w\|^2 \tag{8.23a}$$

$$\text{subject to } \langle \Phi(x_i), w \rangle \geq \rho - \xi_i \text{ and } \xi_i \geq 0. \tag{8.23b}$$

Since it is desirable to have an approximately *fixed* number of observations singled out as novel, it is preferable to use the ν-formulation of the problem [Schölkopf et al., 2000], which leads to

$$\underset{w,\xi,\rho}{\text{minimize}} \quad \sum_{i=1}^{n} \xi_i - \nu n \rho + \frac{1}{2} \|w\|^2 \tag{8.24a}$$

$$\text{subject to } \langle \Phi(x_i), w \rangle \geq \rho - \xi_i \text{ and } \xi_i \geq 0. \tag{8.24b}$$

The key difference is that the fixed threshold ρ has been replaced by a variable threshold, which is penalized by $\nu n \rho$. Schölkopf et al. [2000] show that for $n \to \infty$ the fraction of constraints (8.24b) being active converges to ν.

8.5.2   Relative Novelty Detection

Smola et al. [2005] show that novelty detection can also be understood as density estimation, where low-density regions are particularly emphasized, whereas high-density regions beyond a certain threshold are ignored, and normalization is discarded. This means that the formulation (8.23) is equivalent to minimizing

$$C \sum_{i=1}^{n} \max \left(0, \frac{p(x_i; w)}{p_0 \exp\left(g(w)\right)} \right) + \frac{1}{2} \|w\|^2 , \tag{8.25}$$

where $p(x; w)$ is a member of the exponential family, i.e., $p(x; w) = \exp\left(\langle \Phi(x), w \rangle - g(w)\right)$. Here $p_0 \exp(g(w))$ acts as a reference threshold. Observations whose density exceeds this threshold are considered typical, whereas observations below the threshold are viewed as novel. Note that $g(w)$ is the log-partition function which ensures that p is suitably normalized.

Having a fixed reference threshold may not be the most desirable criterion for novelty:

■ Assume that we have a density $p(x)$ on the domain $\mathcal{X}$. Now assume that we perform a variable transformation $\psi : \mathcal{X} \to \mathcal{Z}$. In this case the measure $dp(x)$ is transformed into $dp(z) = dp(x) \left| \frac{dz(x)}{dx} \right|$. Thus a simple variable transformation could render observations novel which were considered typical before and vice versa. This is clearly undesirable.

■ Assume that we already have a density model of the typical distribution of the data, e.g., a model of how stars *should* be distributed in the sky, based on prior knowledge from astrophysics. We would want to test this assumption subsequently, to discover whether and where the model has defects. This would provide us with a list of observations which are particularly *rare* with respect to this model.

Hence we would need to modify the denominator in (8.25) to reflect this modification via $p_0 \longleftarrow p_0 \left| \frac{dz(x)}{dx} \right|$ or $p_0 \longleftarrow p_{\text{model}}$.

These cases can be taken care of effectively by extending (8.23) and (8.25) to take a variable margin into account. For convenience, we do so for the variant using the ν-trick, as it is easier to parameterize the optimization problem using ν rather than C.

$$\underset{w, \xi, \rho}{\text{minimize}} \ \sum_{i=1}^{n} \xi_i - \nu n \rho + \frac{1}{2} \|w\|^2 \tag{8.26a}$$

$$\text{subject to } \langle \Phi(x_i), w \rangle \geq \rho_i + \rho - \xi_i \text{ and } \xi_i \geq 0. \tag{8.26b}$$

Here $\rho_i = \log p_0(x_i)$, i.e., ρ_i denotes a reference threshold. By using standard Lagrange multiplier techniques we see that the dual problem of (8.26) is given by

$$\underset{\alpha}{\text{minimize}} \ \frac{1}{2} \sum_{i,j=1}^{n} \alpha_i \alpha_j k(x_i, x_j) - \sum_{i=1}^{n} \rho_i \alpha_i \tag{8.27a}$$

$$\text{subject to } \sum_{i=1}^{n} \alpha_i = \nu n \text{ and } \alpha_i \in [0, 1]. \tag{8.27b}$$

The only difference from standard ν-style novelty detection is that in the objective function (8.27a) we have the additional linear term $\sum_i \rho_i \alpha_i$. This biases the solution towards nonzero α_i for which ρ_i is large. In other words, where the reference density $p_0(x_i)$ is large, the algorithm is more likely to find novel observations (where now novelty is defined with respect to $p_0(x)$). We state without proof an extension of the ν-property, as the proof is identical to that of Schölkopf et al. [2001]. Note that changing $\rho_i \rightarrow \rho_i + \text{const.}$ leaves the problem unchanged, as a constant offset in ρ_i with a corresponding change of $\rho \rightarrow \rho + \text{const.}$ does not change the optimality of the solution but merely leads to a constant shift in the objective function.

Theorem 8.11 (ν-Property) *Assume the solution of (8.26) satisfies $\rho \neq 0$. The following statements hold:*

1. *ν is an upper bound on the fraction of outliers.*

2. *ν is a lower bound on the fraction of SVs.*

3. *Suppose the data X were generated independently from a distribution $\mathrm{P}(x)$ which does not contain discrete components with respect to $p_0(x)$. Suppose, moreover, that the kernel is analytic and nonconstant. With probability 1, asymptotically, ν equals both the fraction of SVs and the fraction of outliers.*

8.5.3   From Novelty Detection to Sample Bias Correction

Note the similarity between (8.27) and (8.17). In fact, a simple reparameterization of (8.17) ($\beta_i \longrightarrow B\alpha_i$) makes the connection even more clear:

Lemma 8.12 *The problems (8.17) and (8.27) are equivalent subject to:*

- *The fraction of nonzero terms is set to $\nu = \frac{1}{B}$.*
- *The linear term ρ_i is given by*

$$\rho_i = \frac{n_{\mathrm{tr}}}{n_{\mathrm{te}}B} \sum_{j=1}^{n_{\mathrm{te}}} k(x_i^{\mathrm{tr}}, x_j^{\mathrm{te}}). \tag{8.28}$$

In other words, we typically will choose only a fraction of $1/B$ points for the covariate shift correction. Moreover, we will impose a higher threshold of "typicality" for those points which are very well aligned with the mean operator. That is, typical points are more likely to be recruited for covariate shift correction.

Remark 8.13 (Connection to Parzen Windows) *Note that ρ_i can also be expressed as $\frac{n_{\mathrm{tr}}}{B}\hat{P}_{\mathrm{te}}(x)$, that is, the Parzen window density estimate of P_{te} at location x rescaled by $\frac{n_{\mathrm{tr}}}{B}$. In keeping with the reasoning above this means that we require a higher-level estimate for observations which are relatively typical with respect to the test set, and a lower threshold for observations not so typical with respect to the test set.*

8.6   Experiments

8.6.1   Toy Regression Example

Our first experiment is on toy data, and is intended mainly to provide a comparison with the approach of Shimodaira [2000]. This method uses an information criterion to optimize the weights, under certain restrictions on P_{tr} and P_{te} (namely, P_{te} must be known, while P_{tr} can be either known exactly, Gaussian with unknown parameters, or approximated via kernel density estimation).

Our data is generated according to the polynomial regression example from Shimodaira [2000, Section 2], for which $P_{\mathrm{tr}} \sim \mathcal{N}(0.5, 0.5^2)$ and $P_{\mathrm{te}} \sim \mathcal{N}(0, 0.3^2)$ are two normal distributions. The observations are generated according to $y = -x + x^3$, and are observed in Gaussian noise with standard deviation 0.3 (see the left-hand plot in figure 8.1; the blue curve is the noise-free signal).

We sampled 100 training (darker circles) and testing (lighter crosses) points from P_{tr} and P_{te} respectively. We attempted to model the observations with a degree 1 polynomial. The black dashed line is a best-case scenario, which is shown for reference purposes: it represents the model fit using ordinary least squares (OLS) on the labeled test points. The solid gray line is a second reference result, derived

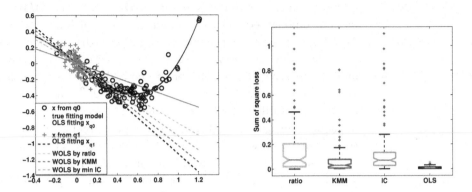

Figure 8.1 *Left:* Polynomial models of degree 1 fit with OLS and WOLS; *Right:* Average performances of three WOLS methods and OLS on this example. Labels are *ratio* for ratio of test to training density; KMM for our approach; *min IC* for the approach of Shimodaira [2000]; and *OLS* for the model trained on the labeled test points.

only from the training data via OLS, and predicts the test data very poorly. The other three dashed lines are fit with weighted ordinary least square (WOLS), using one of three weighting schemes: the ratio of the underlying training and test densities, KMM, and the information criterion of Shimodaira [2000]. A summary of the performance over 100 trials is shown in figure 8.1. In this case, our method outperforms the two other reweighting methods. Note that in this case the model (linear) is much simpler than the equation describing the underlying curve (higher-order polynomial).

8.6.2 Real World Datasets

We next test our approach on real world datasets, from which we select training examples using a deliberately biased procedure (as in Zadrozny [2004] and Rosset et al. [2004]). To describe our biased selection scheme, we need to define an additional random variable s_i for each point in the pool of possible training samples, where $s_i = 1$ means the ith sample is included, and $s_i = 0$ indicates an excluded sample. Two situations are considered: the selection bias corresponds to our key assumption 8.1 regarding the relation between the training and test distributions, and $P(s_i = 1|x_i, y_i) = P(s_i|x_i)$; or s_i is dependent only on y_i, i.e., $P(s_i|x_i, y_i) = P(s_i|y_i)$, which potentially creates a greater challenge since it violates this assumption. The training and test data were generated by splitting the original dataset at random, and then resampling the training data according to the biasing scheme. The combination of splitting and biased resampling was repeated to obtain an averaged value of test performance. Note that all data features were normalized to zero mean and unit standard deviation *before* any other procedure was applied (including training/test set splits and biased resampling of the training set).

In the following, we compare our method (labeled *KMM*) against two others: a baseline unweighted method (*unweighted*), in which no modification is made, and a weighting by the inverse of the true sampling distribution (*importance sampling*), as in Zadrozny [2004] and Rosset et al. [2004]. We emphasize, however, that our method does *not* require any prior knowledge of the true sampling probabilities. We used a Gaussian kernel $\exp(-|x_i - x_j|^2/(2\sigma^2))$ in our kernel classification and regression algorithms, except for the microarray data (in Section 8.6.3), where we used a linear kernel. For kernel mean matching, we always used a Gaussian kernel with identical size to the kernel in the learning algorithm. In the case of the microarray data, we did not have this reference value, and thus set the kernel size to the median distance between sample points. We set the parameters $\epsilon = (\sqrt{m} - 1)/\sqrt{m}$ and $B = 1000$ in the optimization (8.17). Note that using the same kernel size for the learning algorithms and the bias correction has no guarantee of being optimal. The choice of optimal kernel size for KMM remains an open question (see the conclusion, section 8.7, for a suggestion on further work in this direction). The choice of B above is likewise a heuristic, and was sufficiently large that none of the β_i reached the upper bound. When B was reduced to the point where a small percentage of the β_i reached B, we found empirically on several datasets that performance either did not change, or worsened (see table 8.1).

Breast Cancer Dataset   Before providing a general analysis across multiple datasets, we take a detailed look at one particular example: the breast cancer dataset from the UCI archive. This is a binary classification task, and includes 699 examples from two classes: benign (positive label) and malignant (negative label). Our first experiments explore the effect of varying C on the performance of covariate shift correction, in the case of a support vector classifier. This is of particular interest since C controls the trade-off between regularization and test error (see (8.4)): small values of C favor smoothness of the decision boundary over minimizing the loss. We fix the kernel size to $\sigma = \sqrt{5}$, and vary C over the range $C \in \{0.01, 0.1, 1, 10, 100\}$. Test results always represent an average over 15 trials (a trial being a particular random split of the data into training and test sets).

First, we consider a biased sampling scheme based on the input features, of which there are nine, with integer values from 0 to 9. The data were first split into training and test sets, with 25% of data reserved for training. Since smaller feature values predominate in the unbiased data, the test set was subsampled according to $P(s = 1|x \leq 5) = 0.2$ and $P(s = 1|x > 5) = 0.8$. This subsampling was repeated for each of the features in turn. Around 30% to 50% of the training points were retained by the biased sampling procedure (the exact percentage depending on the feature in question). Average performance is shown in figure 8.2.

Second, we consider a sampling bias that operates jointly across multiple features. The data was randomly split into training and test sets, where the proportion of examples used for training varied from 10% to 50%. We then subsampled the training set, selecting samples less often when they were further from the sample mean $\bar{x}$ over the training data, i.e., $P(s_i|x_i) \propto \exp(-\gamma\|x_i - \bar{x}\|^2)$ where

$\gamma = 1/20$. Around 70% of the training points were retained after the resampling. A performance comparison is given in figure 8.3.

Finally, we consider a simple biased sampling scheme which depends only on the label y: $P(s = 1|y = 1) = 0.1$ and $P(s = 1|y = -1) = 0.9$ (the data have on average twice as many positive as negative examples when uniformly sampled). Prior to this sampling, the data was again randomly split into training and test sets, with a training proportion from 10% to 50%. Around 40% of the training points were retained following the biased sampling procedure. Average performance is plotted in figure 8.4.

In all three of the above examples, by far the greatest performance advantage for both importance sampling and KMM-based reweighting is for small values of C (and thus, for classifiers which put a high priority on a smooth decision boundary). It is remarkable how great an improvement is found in these cases: the error reduces to the point where it is very close to its value for optimal choice of C, even though the unweighted error is on occasion extremely high. This advantage also holds for bias over the labels, despite this violating our key assumption 8.1. Somewhat surprisingly, we also see that covariate shift correction confers a small advantage for very large values of C. While this is seen in all three experiments, it is particularly apparent in the case of joint bias on the features (figure 8.2), where—except for the smallest training sample size—KMM consistently outperforms the unweighted and importance sampling cases.

For values $C \in \{1, 10\}$ which fall between these extremes, however, KMM does not have a consistent effect on performance, and often makes performance slightly worse. In other words, the classifier is sufficiently powerful that it is able to learn correctly over the entire input space, regardless of the weighting of particular training points.

We conclude that for the UCI breast cancer data, covariate shift correction (whether by importance sampling or KMM) has the advantage of widening the range of C values for which good performance can be expected (and in particular, greatly enhancing performance at the lowest C levels), at the risk of slightly worsening performance at the optimal C range. Our conclusions are mixed, however, regarding the effect on classifier performance of the number of training points. For small C values and label bias, the unweighted classification performance approaches the importance sampling and KMM performance with increasing training sample size (figure 8.4). No such effect is seen in the case of joint feature bias (figure 8.3), nor are there any clear trends for larger values of C.

We now address the question of cross-validating over σ, in accordance with the first procedure described in section 8.4.2: i.e., on the weighted training sample, without using a second weighting procedure on the validation set. This can be very costly due to our use of the same σ for kernel mean matching as for classification: we need to recompute the β for each new σ-value. That said, we anticipate that for close to optimal parameter settings, for a sufficiently powerful class of learning algorithms, the performance optimum for cross-validation over σ will occur at roughly the same location for the weighted and unweighted sample (we bear

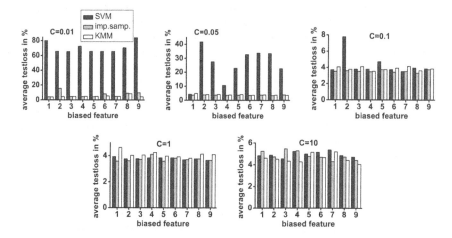

Figure 8.2 Classification performance on UCI breast cancer data. An individual feature bias scheme was used. Test error is reported on the y-axis, and the feature being biased on the x-axis.

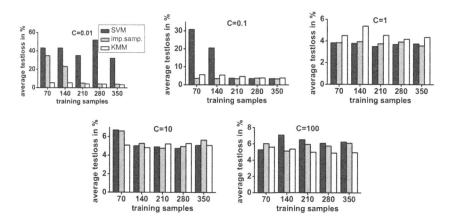

Figure 8.3 Classification performance on UCI breast cancer data. A joint feature bias scheme was used. Test error is reported on the y-axis, and the initial number of training points (prior to biased training point selection) on the x-axis.

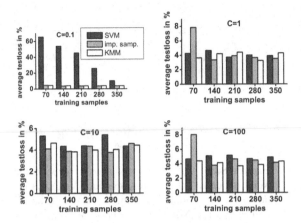

Figure 8.4   Classification performance on UCI breast cancer data. A label bias scheme was used. Test error is reported on the y-axis, and the initial number of training points (prior to biased training point selection) on the x-axis.

in mind the point made by Sugiyama et al. [2007] that cross-validation on the unweighted training data introduces an additional source of bias in the resulting test error estimate, for cases of covariate shift). We are led to this conjecture by the similar performance of the classifier at intermediate C-values for the weighted and unweighted data (figures 8.2, 8.3, and 8.4). The cross-validation (CV) performance of the classifier for fixed $C = 10$, $\sigma \in \{0.1, 1, 10, 100, 1000\}$, and a 9:1 training-validation split is shown in figure 8.5, in the case of joint bias on the features and an initial training sample size of 70 (prior to resampling; around 75% of training points were retained following resampling). We note that the optimum performance is obtained for the same value $\sigma = 10$ in all cases (unweighted, importance-weighted with unweighted CV, importance-weighted with weighted CV, KMM with unweighted CV, KMM with weighted CV), although in both KMM cases the advantage of $\sigma = 10$ over $\sigma = 1$ is negligible. Thus, in subsequent experiments, we cross-validate on the unweighted data.

Further Benchmark Datasets   A question of particular interest is whether dataset shift correction can improve performance when the learning algorithm parameters are chosen by cross-validation, rather than being chosen to be "simpler" than suggested by the data (as we saw in figures 8.2, 8.3, and 8.4 with small C-values). Thus, we compare performance of various learning algorithms on both unweighted and weighted training data from further benchmark datasets.[2] We selected training data via three biased sampling schemes. For sampling distribution bias on labels, we used either $P(s = 1|y) = \exp(a + by)/(1 + \exp(a + by))$ (denoted

---

2. Regression data from `http : //www.liacc.up.pt/` $\sim$ `ltorgo/Regression/DataSets.html`; classification data from UCI.

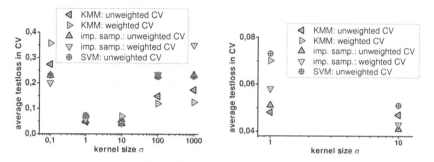

Figure 8.5 *Left:* cross-validation error vs σ for unweighted SVM, and weighted and unweighted cross-validation scores for SVM with importance sampling and KMM reweighted data; *Right:* Zoomed version of the left hand plot, showing performance for $\sigma = 1$ and $\sigma = 10$. Note: in the case of weighted cross-validation, the *weighted CV error* $\frac{1}{\sum_i \beta_i} \sum_i \beta_i I_{y_i \neq f(x_i)}$ is plotted.

label(a,b)), or the simple step distribution $P(s = 1|y = 1) = a$, $P(s = 1|y = -1) = b$ (denoted *simple label*). For the remaining datasets, we generated biased sampling schemes over the features. We first did PCA, selecting the first principal component of the training data and the corresponding projection values. Denoting the minimum value of the projection as m and the mean as $\overline{m}$, we applied a normal distribution with mean $m + (\overline{m} - m)/a$ and variance $(\overline{m} - m)/b$ as the biased sampling scheme. Detailed parameter settings are given in table 8.1. Our learning algorithms were penalized LMS for regression, and SVM for classification. We used a Gaussian kernel for both the kernel mean matching and the SVM/LMS regression. The kernel size was chosen by tenfold cross-validation on the unweighted training data over the set $\sigma \in \{0.1, 1, 10, 100, 1000\}$. This cross-validation procedure was also used to search over the remaining parameters $C \in \{0.1, 1, 10, 100, 1000\}$ (for classification) or $\lambda \in \{1e - 3, 1e - 2, 0.1, 1, 10\}$ (for regression). To evaluate generalization performance, we applied the normalized mean square error (NMSE) given by $\frac{1}{n_{\text{te}}} \sum_{i=1}^{n_{\text{te}}} \frac{(y_i^{\text{te}} - \mu_i)^2}{\text{var } y^{\text{te}}}$ for regression problems, and the average test error for classification problems. Results are listed in table 8.1.

The results from our experiments are mixed. In certain cases, both importance sampling and KMM give similar results, which improve on the performance of the unweighted case. These datasets are (7b,11,13,14). In one case (8), KMM alone improves performance; in two further cases (3,7a), importance sampling improves performance, whereas KMM does not. That said, the sampling bias for the latter two datasets violates assumption 8.1, and the result is not surprising.

In a large number of cases, however, both for classification and regression, there is very little difference between the original, importance-weighted, and KMM-corrected results. In the case of regression, these datasets are (1,4,9,10); for classification, they are (5a,6b). Performance can even worsen due to the application of KMM weighting and/or importance sampling. In some cases, the KMM correction alone gives worse results (2,6a). In the case of dataset 6a, the failure of KMM is unsurprising, since assumption 8.1 does not hold. KMM does not necessarily fail in this circumstance, however: in dataset 7a, there is little difference compared with the unweighted case (although importance sampling improves performance). In yet further instances, importance sampling worsens performance, but KMM has no effect (3,15). Finally, there exist cases where both KMM and importance sampling worsen performance (5b,12). We note that mixed results were also reported independently for KMM by Sugiyama et al. [2008, table 1], with performance being improved or unchanged for good kernel size choice (KMM(0.3) in this table), and worsening for poor kernel choice.

In comparison with the results of Huang et al. [2007, table 1], the current results are less favorable to both KMM and importance sampling: in particular, in the earlier work, KMM always improved performance. This is because our earlier experiments used parameters resulting in an overly simple classification/regression function (in particular, the kernels sizes used were relatively large: see the corresponding column in Huang et al. [2007, table 1]). We conclude from our table 8.1 results that while covariate shift can still improve performance in cases where the classification/regression parameters are chosen by cross-validation, this is not guaranteed; moreover, we have yet to determine what properties of these particular data are favorable to covariate shift. On the other hand, the application of covariate shift correction through KMM/importance sampling can decrease performance in this case, though the penalty is not generally too large.

Table 8.1 Test results for three methods on 15 datasets with different sampling schemes. The results are averages over 10 trials for regression problems (marked *) and 20 trials for classification problems. Sampling schemes: *simple label*: $P(s = 1|y = 1) = 0.1$ and $P(s = 1|y = -1) = 0.9$, *label*(a,b): $P(s = 1|y) = \exp(a + by)/(1 + \exp(a + by))$, $PCA(a,b,\sigma_{PCA})$: bias using kernel PCA with parameters a, b, σ_{PCA}. The training set size is in column n_{tr}, the number of training points after biased subsampling is in column sel, and the number of test points is in column n_{tst}.

Dataset	sampling scheme	n_{tr}	sel.	n_{tst}	NMSE/test error ± std. error		
					SVM	importance samp.	KMM
1. Abalone*	label(1,10)	2000	973	2177	0.83±0.02	0.80±0.04	0.83±0.03
2. CA Housing*	PCA(10,5,0.1)	8000	1591	12640	0.694±0.005	0.684±0.009	0.728±0.007
3. Delta Ailerons*	label(1,10)	4000	1980	3129	0.64±0.01	0.405±0.009	0.613±0.008
4. Ailerons*	PCA(1e3,4,0.1)	7154	726	6596	0.25±0.04	0.27±0.04	0.24±0.03
5a. Haberman	label(0.2,0.8)	150	68	156	0.30±0.02	0.32±0.02	0.33±0.01
5b. Haberman	PCA(2,2,0.01)	150	82	156	0.266±0.008	0.318±0.008	0.33±0.02
6a. USPS(6vs8)	simple label	500	264	1042	0.035±0.004	0.034±0.004	0.047±0.004
6b. USPS(6vs8)	PCA(3,3,1/128)	500	169	1042	0.17±0.04	0.19±0.05	0.19±0.04
7a. USPS(3vs9)	simple label	500	261	1145	0.020±0.004	0.014±0.002	0.020±0.003
7b. USPS(3vs9)	PCA(3,3,1/128)	500	165	1145	0.15±0.03	0.056±0.007	0.08±0.02
8. Bank8FM*	PCA(3,6,0.1)	4500	589	3692	0.10±0.02	0.12±0.02	0.068±0.003
9. Bank32nh*	PCA(3,6,0.01)	4500	673	3692	0.523±0.008	0.54±0.03	0.555±0.008
10. cpu-act*	PCA(4,2,1e-12)	4000	1672	4192	0.09±0.03	0.08±0.03	0.10±0.02
11. cpu-small*	PCA(4,2,1e-12)	4000	1674	4192	0.32±0.09	0.15±0.07	0.11±0.02
12. Delta Ailerons*	PCA(1e3,4,0.1)	4000	511	3129	0.38±0.02	0.41±0.03	0.44±0.03
13. Boston house*	PCA(2,4,1e-4)	300	100	206	0.63±0.08	0.5±0.2	0.50±0.04
14. kin8nm*	PCA(8,5,0.1)	5000	292	3192	1.0±0.3	0.72±0.02	0.74±0.04
15. puma8nh*	PCA(4,4,0.1)	4499	685	3693	0.75±0.03	0.83±0.06	0.75±0.02

Table 8.2 Covariate shift correction for microarray data. The notation "Gruvberger→West" indicates that we train on the data of Gruvberger and test on that of West.

Dataset	SVM	test error importance sampling	KMM
Singh	0.40±0.02	0.091±0.006	0.083±0.005
Gruvberger→West	0.061	—	0.061
West→Gruvberger	0.086	—	0.052
Dhanasekaran→Welsh	0.03	—	0.09
Welsh→Dhanasekaran	0.26	—	0.17

8.6.3 Tumor Diagnosis Using Microarrays

Our next benchmark is a dataset of 102 microarrays from prostate cancer patients [Singh et al., 2002]. Each of these microarrays measures the expression levels of 12,600 genes. The dataset comprises 50 samples from normal tissues (positive label) and 52 from tumor tissues (negative label). We simulate the realistic scenario that two sets of microarrays A and B are given with dissimilar proportion of tumor samples, and we want to perform cancer diagnosis via classification, training on A and predicting on B. As a preprocessing step, the data was normalized to have zero mean and unit variance for each feature. We selected training examples via a biased selection scheme as $P(s=1|y=1) = 0.85$ and $P(s=1|y=-1) = 0.15$; the remaining data points form the test set. We performed SVM classification using a linear SVM setting $C = 1000$ (there being too little data for cross-validation), for the unweighted, the KMM, and the importance sampling approaches. In the case of KMM, the kernel size was the median distance between training sample points. Results are given in table 8.2, and represent the average performance over 50 training/test splits. We note that both importance sampling and KMM result in a substantial performance improvement, with KMM outperforming importance sampling (despite the violation of assumption 8.1).

We now use the same setting to investigate dataset shift for microarray studies on the same tissue by different laboratories. We first consider two breast cancer microarray datasets from Gruvberger et al. [2001] and West et al. [2001], measuring the expression levels of 2166 common genes for normal and cancer patients [Warnat et al., 2005]. All settings for the data preprocessing, the SVM, and KMM, were identical to our first experiment. Results are listed in table 8.2, and describe both training on *West* and testing on *Gruvberger*, as well as training on *Gruvberger* and testing on *West*.[3] In the former case, KMM causes a performance improvement compared with the unweighted data; in the latter case, performance remains constant.

---

3. Note: Since the biasing scheme for these data is not know, there is no importance sampling result.

Finally, we study the same scenario for two prostate cancer datasets: Dhanasekaran et al. [2001] vs. Welsh et al. [2001]. Results are again in table 8.2. In this case our results are mixed: while training on *Welsh* and testing on *Dhanasekaran* demonstrates a substantial performance gain when using KMM, the reverse procedure results in a (smaller) performance reduction for KMM. We conclude that while KMM more often results in performance increases in microarray data than in the UCI benchmark sets of the previous section, this performance improvement is not guaranteed.

8.7   Conclusion

We present a new approach, kernel mean matching (KMM), for dealing with sampling bias in various learning problems. We directly estimate the resampling weights by matching training and test distribution feature means in a reproducing kernel Hilbert space. In addition, we develop bounds on the mean matching error, and transductive risk bounds, based on the maximum ratio of the distributions and the sample sizes.

In our experiments, it appears that with properly chosen parameters (via cross-validation), kernel classification and regression methods occasionally benefit from covariate shift correction, but for the most part do not. This is true both when the correction is made using KMM, and via the "optimal" reweighting given by the ratio of test and training probabilities (note that the latter is unavailable in real-world applications). We also emphasize that our results were obtained using the heuristic that the KMM kernel size was set to the kernel size of the classification/regression algorithm. Sugiyama et al. [2008, table 1] demonstrated that kernel size has a strong effect on KMM performance (though no comparison was made between the optimal KMM kernel size and that chosen by cross-validation for the learning algorithm). Thus, performance of KMM might be further improved by a more principled strategy for KMM kernel choice.[4]

Major benefits can be obtained from covariate shift correction when a simple classification/regression function is used. There are several reasons for not using a "correct" model, but rather a deliberately simpler one: these include interpretability on the one hand; and on the other hand difficulties in correct model selection by cross-validation, especially for higher-dimensional data and small sample sizes (for instance, in our microarray experiments, where we used a linear classifier, and where the performance of KMM was generally better). Covariate shift correction allows us to make use of these simpler models without too significant a performance penalty.

---

4. One approach might be along the lines of Fukumizu et al. [2008], where the variance of a kernel dependence statistic was computed via both a closed-form expression and random permutations of the sample: a good kernel size caused these quantities to match. In our case, the relevant statistic is a difference in RKHS means, so an appropriate closed-form variance expression might derive from Gretton et al. [2007].

Acknowledgements

The authors thank Patrick Warnat (DKFZ, Heidelberg) for providing the microarray datasets, and Paul von Bünau, Olivier Chapelle, Matthias Hein, Quoc Le, and Klaus-Robert Müller for helpful discussions. The work is partially supported by by the German Ministry for Education, Science, Research, and Technology (BMBF) under grant 031U112F within the Bioinformatics for the Functional Analysis of Mammalian Genomes project, which is part of the German Genome Analysis Network. NICTA is funded through the Australian Government's *Backing Australia's Ability* initiative, in part through the ARC Australian Research Council. This work was supported in part by the IST Programme of the EC, under the PASCAL Network of Excellence, IST-2002-506778.

8.8   Appendix: Proofs

Theorem 8.2

Proof: By definition μ is surjective on the marginal polytope, since the latter is defined as the set of all expectations of $\Phi(x)$. We now prove injectivity.

Let $\mathcal{F}$ be a universal RKHS, and let $\mathcal{G}$ be the unit ball in $\mathcal{F}$. We need to prove that $P_{tr} = P_{te}$ if $\mu(P_{tr}) = \mu(P_{te})$, or equivalently $\|\mu(P_{tr}) - \mu(P_{te})\| = 0$. We have

$$\|\mu(P_{tr}) - \mu(P_{te})\| = \sup_{f \in \mathcal{G}} \langle f, \mu(P_{tr}) - \mu(P_{te}) \rangle$$
$$= \sup_{f \in \mathcal{G}} \left(\mathbf{E}_{P_{tr}}[f] - \mathbf{E}_{P_{te}}[f] \right)$$
$$=: \Delta \left[\mathcal{G}, P_{tr}, P_{te} \right].$$

We use a result from Dudley [2002, lemma 9.3.2]: If P_{tr}, P_{te} are two Borel probability measures defined on a separable metric space $\mathcal{X}$, then $P_{tr} = P_{te}$ if and only if $\mathbf{E}_{P_{tr}}[f] = \mathbf{E}_{P_{te}}[f]$ for all $f \in C(\mathcal{X})$, where $C(\mathcal{X})$ is the space of continuous bounded functions on $\mathcal{X}$. If we can show that $\Delta\left[C(\mathcal{X}), P_{tr}, P_{te}\right] = D$ for some $D > 0$ implies $\Delta\left[\mathcal{G}, P_{tr}, P_{te}\right] > 0$: this is equivalent to $\Delta\left[\mathcal{G}, P_{tr}, P_{te}\right] = 0$ implying $\Delta\left[C(\mathcal{X}), P_{tr}, P_{te}\right] = 0$ (where this last result implies $P_{tr} = P_{te}$). If $\Delta\left[C(\mathcal{X}), P_{tr}, P_{te}\right] = D$, then there exists some $\tilde{f} \in C(\mathcal{X})$ for which $\mathbf{E}_{P_{tr}}\left[\tilde{f}\right] - \mathbf{E}_{P_{te}}\left[\tilde{f}\right] \geq D/2$. By definition of universality, $\mathcal{F}$ is dense in $C(\mathcal{X})$ with respect to the L_∞ norm: this means that for all $\epsilon \in (0, D/8)$, we can find some $f^* \in \mathcal{F}$ satisfying $\left\| f^* - \tilde{f} \right\|_\infty < \epsilon$. Thus, we obtain $\left| \mathbf{E}_{P_{tr}}[f^*] - \mathbf{E}_{P_{tr}}\left[\tilde{f}\right] \right| < \epsilon$ and consequently

$$\left| \mathbf{E}_{P_{tr}}[f^*] - \mathbf{E}_{P_{te}}[f^*] \right| > \left| \mathbf{E}_{P_{tr}}\left[\tilde{f}\right] - \mathbf{E}_{P_{te}}\left[\tilde{f}\right] \right| - 2\epsilon > \frac{D}{2} - 2\frac{D}{8} = \frac{D}{4} > 0.$$

Finally, using $\|f^*\| < \infty$, we have

$$\left[\mathbf{E}_{\mathrm{P_{tr}}}[f^*] - \mathbf{E}_{\mathrm{P_{te}}}[f^*]\right] / \|f^*\| \geq D/(4\,\|f^*\|) > 0,$$

and hence $\Delta\left[\mathcal{G}, \mathrm{P_{tr}}, \mathrm{P_{te}}\right] > 0$.

Lemma 8.5

Proof: Let

$$\Xi(X_{\mathrm{tr}}, X_{\mathrm{te}}) := \left\| \frac{1}{n_{\mathrm{tr}}} \sum_{i=1}^{n_{\mathrm{tr}}} \beta(x_i^{\mathrm{tr}})\Phi(x_i^{\mathrm{tr}}) - \frac{1}{n_{\mathrm{te}}} \sum_{i=1}^{n_{\mathrm{te}}} \Phi(x_i^{\mathrm{te}}) \right\|. \tag{8.29}$$

The proof follows firstly by its tail behavior using a concentration inequality, and subsequently by bounding the expectation.

For the proof we need the following result by McDiarmid [1989]:

Theorem 8.14 *Denote by $f(x_1, \ldots, x_n)$ a function of n independent random variables. Moreover let*

$$|f(x_1, \ldots, x_n) - f(x_1, \ldots, x_{i-1}, \bar{x}, x_{i+1}, \ldots, x_n)| \leq c_i \tag{8.30}$$

for all $x_1, \ldots, x_n$ and $\bar{x}$. Denote by $C := \sum_i c_i^2$. In this case

$$\mathrm{P}\left\{|f(x_1, \ldots, x_n) - \mathbf{E}_{x_1, \ldots x_n}[f(x_1, \ldots, x_n)]| > \epsilon\right\} < 2\exp(-2\epsilon^2/C). \tag{8.31}$$

To apply McDiarmid's tail bound, we need to bound the change in $\Xi(X_{\mathrm{tr}}, X_{\mathrm{te}})$ if we replace any x_i^{tr} by an arbitrary $x \in \mathcal{X}$ and likewise if we replace any x_i^{te} by some $x \in \mathcal{X}$. By the triangle inequality the replacement of x_i^{tr} by x can change $\Xi(X_{\mathrm{tr}}, X_{\mathrm{te}})$ by at most $\frac{1}{n_{\mathrm{tr}}} \|\beta(x_i^{\mathrm{tr}})\Phi(x_i^{\mathrm{tr}}) - \beta(x)\Phi(x)\| \leq \frac{2BR}{n_{\mathrm{tr}}}$. Likewise, a replacement of x_i^{te} by x changes $\Xi(X_{\mathrm{tr}}, X_{\mathrm{te}})$ by at most $\frac{2R}{n_{\mathrm{te}}}$. Since $n_{\mathrm{tr}}(2BR/n_{\mathrm{tr}})^2 + n_{\mathrm{te}}(2R/n_{\mathrm{te}})^2 = 4R^2(B^2/n_{\mathrm{tr}} + 1/n_{\mathrm{te}})$ we have

$$\mathrm{P}\left\{|\Xi(X_{\mathrm{tr}}, X_{\mathrm{te}}) - \mathbf{E}_{X_{\mathrm{tr}}, X_{\mathrm{te}}}[\Xi(X_{\mathrm{tr}}, X_{\mathrm{te}})]| > \epsilon\right\}$$
$$\leq 2\exp\left(-\epsilon^2/2R^2(B^2/n_{\mathrm{tr}} + 1/n_{\mathrm{te}})\right).$$

Hence with probability $1 - \delta$ the deviation of the random variable from its expectation is bounded by $|\Xi(X_{\mathrm{tr}}, X_{\mathrm{te}}) - \mathbf{E}_{X_{\mathrm{tr}}, X_{\mathrm{te}}}[\Xi(X_{\mathrm{tr}}, X_{\mathrm{te}})]| \leq R\sqrt{2\log\frac{2}{\delta}\left(\frac{B^2}{n_{\mathrm{tr}}} + \frac{1}{n_{\mathrm{te}}}\right)}$.

To bound the expected value of $\Xi(X_{\mathrm{tr}}, X_{\mathrm{te}})$ we use

$$\mathbf{E}_{X_{\mathrm{tr}}, X_{\mathrm{te}}}[\Xi(X_{\mathrm{tr}}, X_{\mathrm{te}})] \leq \sqrt{\mathbf{E}_{X_{\mathrm{tr}}, X_{\mathrm{te}}}[\Xi(X_{\mathrm{tr}}, X_{\mathrm{te}})^2]}.$$

Expanding out the expectation, and denoting by $\widetilde{x^{\mathrm{te}}}$ a random variable drawn from

$\mathrm{P_{te}}$ and independent of x^{te}, we get

$$\mathbf{E}_{X_{\mathrm{tr}},X_{\mathrm{te}}}\left\|\frac{1}{n_{\mathrm{tr}}}\sum_{i=1}^{n_{\mathrm{tr}}}\beta(x_i^{\mathrm{tr}})\Phi(x_i^{\mathrm{tr}})-\frac{1}{n_{\mathrm{te}}}\sum_{i=1}^{n_{\mathrm{te}}}\Phi(x_i^{\mathrm{te}})\right\|^2$$

$$=\frac{1}{n_{\mathrm{tr}}^2}\mathbf{E}_{X_{\mathrm{tr}}}\left[\sum_{i,j=1}^{n_{\mathrm{tr}}}\beta(x_i^{\mathrm{tr}})\beta(x_j^{\mathrm{tr}})k(x_i^{\mathrm{tr}},x_j^{\mathrm{tr}})\right]+\frac{1}{n_{\mathrm{te}}^2}\mathbf{E}_{X_{\mathrm{te}}}\left[\sum_{i,j=1}^{n_{\mathrm{te}}}k(x_i^{\mathrm{te}},x_j^{\mathrm{te}})\right]$$

$$-2\mathbf{E}_{X_{\mathrm{tr}},X_{\mathrm{te}}}\frac{1}{n_{\mathrm{tr}}n_{\mathrm{te}}}\left[\sum_{i=1}^{n_{\mathrm{tr}}}\sum_{i=1}^{n_{\mathrm{te}}}\beta(x_i^{\mathrm{tr}})k(x_i^{\mathrm{tr}},x_j^{\mathrm{te}})\right]$$

$$=\mathbf{E}_{\mathrm{P_{te}}}k(x^{\mathrm{te}},\widetilde{x^{\mathrm{te}}})+\frac{1}{n_{\mathrm{tr}}}\mathbf{E}_{\mathrm{P_{te}}}\left[\beta(x^{\mathrm{te}})k(x^{\mathrm{te}},x^{\mathrm{te}})\right]+\mathbf{E}_{\mathrm{P_{te}}}k(x^{\mathrm{te}},\widetilde{x^{\mathrm{te}}})$$

$$+\frac{1}{n_{\mathrm{te}}}\mathbf{E}_{\mathrm{P_{te}}}\left[k(x^{\mathrm{te}},x^{\mathrm{te}})\right]-2\mathbf{E}_{\mathrm{P_{te}}}k(x^{\mathrm{te}},\widetilde{x^{\mathrm{te}}})+O\left(n_{\mathrm{tr}}^{-2}\right)+O\left(n_{\mathrm{te}}^{-2}\right)$$

$$\lesssim R^2\left[B/n_{\mathrm{tr}}+1/n_{\mathrm{te}}\right]<R^2\left[B^2/n_{\mathrm{tr}}+1/n_{\mathrm{te}}\right].$$

The final line uses that $B<B^2$ since $B>1$ (due to the constraint (8.14)). Combining the bounds on the mean and the tail proves the claim.

Lemma 8.7

Proof: To see the claim, first note that by assumption 8.1 the conditional distributions $\mathrm{P}(y|x)$ are the same for $\mathrm{P_{tr}}$ and $\mathrm{P_{te}}$. By linearity we can apply the expectation $\mathbf{E}_{Y|X}$ to each summand individually. Finally, by assumption 8.6 the expected loss $l(x,\theta)$ can be written as $\langle\Psi(x),\theta\rangle$. Hence we may rewrite the LHS of (8.19) as

$$\sup_{l(\cdot,\theta)\in\mathcal{G}}\left|\frac{1}{n_{\mathrm{tr}}}\sum_{i=1}^{n_{\mathrm{tr}}}\beta_i l(x_i^{\mathrm{tr}},\theta)-\frac{1}{n_{\mathrm{te}}}\sum_{i=1}^{n_{\mathrm{te}}}l(x_i^{\mathrm{te}},\theta)\right|$$

$$\leq\sup_{\|\Theta\|\leq C}\left|\left\langle\frac{1}{n_{\mathrm{tr}}}\sum_{i=1}^{n_{\mathrm{tr}}}\beta_i\Psi(x_i^{\mathrm{tr}})-\frac{1}{n_{\mathrm{te}}}\sum_{i=1}^{n_{\mathrm{te}}}\Psi(x_i^{\mathrm{te}}),\Theta\right\rangle\right|.$$

By the definition of norms this is bounded by $C\epsilon$, which proves the claim.

Lemma 8.8

Proof: The strategy is almost identical to that of lemma 8.5 and of Mendelson [2003]. Let

$$\Xi(Y_{\mathrm{tr}}):=\sup_{l(\cdot,\cdot,\theta)\in\mathcal{G}}\frac{1}{n_{\mathrm{tr}}}\sum_{i=1}^{n_{\mathrm{tr}}}\beta_i\left[l(x_i^{\mathrm{tr}},y_i^{\mathrm{tr}},\theta)-l(x_i^{\mathrm{tr}},\theta)\right] \quad (8.32)$$

be the maximum deviation between empirical mean and expectation. Key is that the random variables $y_1^{\mathrm{tr}},\ldots,y_m^{\mathrm{tr}}$ are conditionally independent given X_{tr}. Replacing one y_i^{tr} by an arbitrary $y\in\mathcal{Y}$ leads to a change in $\Xi(Y_{\mathrm{tr}})$ which is bounded by

$\frac{\beta_i}{n_{\mathrm{tr}}} C \left\| \Upsilon(x_i^{\mathrm{tr}}, y_i^{\mathrm{tr}}) - \Upsilon(x_i^{\mathrm{tr}}, y) \right\| \le 2CR\beta_i/m$. Using McDiarmid's theorem we can bound

$$\mathrm{P}_{Y|X} \left\{ |\Xi(Y_{\mathrm{tr}}) - \mathbf{E}_{Y|X}\Xi(Y_{\mathrm{tr}})| > \epsilon \right\} \le 2 \exp \left(-\epsilon^2 n_{\mathrm{tr}}^2 / \left(2C^2 R^2 \left\| \beta \right\|_2^2 \right) \right). \quad (8.33)$$

In other words, $M := n_{\mathrm{tr}}^2 / \left\| \beta \right\|_2^2$ acts as an effective sample size when it comes to determining large deviations. Next we use symmetrization to obtain a bound on the expectation of $\Xi(Y_{\mathrm{tr}})$, that is,

$$
\begin{aligned}
\mathbf{E}_{Y|X}[\Xi(Y_{\mathrm{tr}})] &\le \frac{1}{n_{\mathrm{tr}}} \mathbf{E}_{Y|X} \mathbf{E}_{\tilde{Y}|X} \left[\sup_{l(\cdot,\cdot,\theta) \in \mathcal{G}} \left| \sum_{i=1}^{n_{\mathrm{tr}}} \beta_i l(x_i^{\mathrm{tr}}, y_i; \theta) - \beta_i l(x_i^{\mathrm{tr}}, \tilde{y}_i, \theta) \right| \right] \\
&\le \frac{2}{n_{\mathrm{tr}}} \mathbf{E}_{Y|X} \mathbf{E}_{\sigma} \left[\sup_{l(\cdot,\cdot,\theta) \in \mathcal{G}} \left| \sum_{i=1}^{n_{\mathrm{tr}}} \sigma_i \beta_i l(x_i^{\mathrm{tr}}, y_i, \theta) \right| \right], \quad (8.34)
\end{aligned}
$$

where the σ_i take values in $\{\pm 1\}$ with equal probability, and $\tilde{y}_i$ is drawn from $\mathrm{P}(\tilde{y}_i | x_i^{\mathrm{tr}})$ independently of y_i. The first inequality follows from convexity. The second one follows from the fact that all $y_i, \tilde{y}_i$ pairs are independently and identically distributed, hence we can swap these pairs.

For constant β_i the RHS in (8.34) is referred to as the Rademacher average. To make actual progress in computing this, we use the condition in assumption 8.6 that $l(x, y, \theta) = \langle \Upsilon(x, y), \Lambda \rangle$ for some Λ with $\| \Lambda \| \le C$. This allows us to bound the supremum. This, and the convexity of x^2 yields a series of bounds on the RHS in (8.34),

$$
\begin{aligned}
\mathrm{RHS} &\le \frac{2}{n_{\mathrm{tr}}} \mathbf{E}_{Y|X} \mathbf{E}_{\sigma} C \left\| \sum_{i=1}^{n_{\mathrm{tr}}} \sigma_i \beta_i \Upsilon(x_i^{\mathrm{tr}}, y_i) \right\| \\
&\le \frac{2}{n_{\mathrm{tr}}} C \sqrt{ \mathbf{E}_{Y|X} \mathbf{E}_{\sigma} \left\| \sum_{i=1}^{n_{\mathrm{tr}}} \sigma_i \beta_i \Upsilon(x_i^{\mathrm{tr}}, y_i) \right\|^2 } \\
&= \frac{2}{n_{\mathrm{tr}}} C \sqrt{ \sum_{i=1}^{n_{\mathrm{tr}}} \beta_i^2 \mathbf{E}_{y_i | x_i^{\mathrm{tr}}} \left\| \Upsilon(x_i^{\mathrm{tr}}, y_i) \right\|^2 } \\
&\le \frac{2}{n_{\mathrm{tr}}} CR \left\| \beta \right\|_2 = \frac{2CR}{\sqrt{M}}.
\end{aligned}
$$

Combined with the bound on the expectation and solving the tail bound for ϵ proves the claim.

9   Discriminative Learning under Covariate Shift with a Single Optimization Problem

Steffen Bickel
Michael Brückner
Tobias Scheffer

We address classification problems for which the training instances are governed by a distribution that is allowed to differ arbitrarily from the test distribution— problems also referred to as classification under covariate shift. We derive a solution that is purely discriminative: neither training nor test distribution is modeled explicitly. We formulate the general problem of learning under covariate shift as an integrated optimization problem and instantiate a kernel logistic regression and an exponential model classifier for differing training and test distributions. We show under which condition the optimization problem is convex. We study the method empirically on problems of spam filtering, text classification, and land mine detection.

9.1   Introduction

Most machine learning algorithms are constructed under the assumption that the training data is governed by the exact same distribution which the model will later be exposed to. In practice, control over the data generation process is often less than perfect. Training data may be obtained under laboratory conditions that cannot be expected after deployment of a system; spam filters may be used by individuals whose distribution of inbound emails diverges from the distribution reflected in public training corpora; image processing systems may be deployed to foreign geographic regions where vegetation and lighting conditions result in a distinct distribution of input patterns.

The case of distinct training and test distributions in a learning problem has been referred to as *covariate shift* and *sample selection bias*—albeit the term sample selection bias actually refers to a case in which each training instance is originally

161

drawn from the test distribution, but is then selected into the training sample with some probability, or discarded otherwise.

The covariate shift model and the *missing at random* case in the sample selection bias model allow for differences between the training and test distribution of instances; the conditional distribution of the class variable given the instance is constant over training and test set.

In discriminative learning tasks such as classification, the classifier's goal is to produce the correct output given the input. It is widely accepted that this is best performed by discriminative learners that directly maximize a quality measure of the produced output. Model-based optimization criteria such as the joint likelihood of input and output, by contrast, additionally assess how well the classifier models the distribution of input values. This amounts to adding a term to the criterion that is irrelevant for the task at hand.

We contribute a discriminative model for learning under arbitrarily different training and test distributions. The model directly characterizes the divergence between training and test distribution, without the intermediate – intrinsically model-based – step of estimating training and test distribution. We formulate the search for all model parameters as an integrated optimization problem. This complements the predominant procedure of first estimating the bias of the training sample, and then learning the classifier on a weighted version of the training sample. We show that the integrated optimization can be convex, depending on the model type; it is convex for the exponential model. We derive a Newton gradient descent procedure, leading to a kernel logistic regression and an exponential model classifier for covariate shift.

After formalizing the problem setting in section 9.2, we review models for differing training and test distributions in section 9.3. Section 9.4 introduces our discriminative model [Bickel et al., 2007] and section 9.5 describes the joint optimization problem. We derive primal and kernelized classifiers for differing training and test distributions in sections 9.6 and 9.7. In section 9.8, we analyze the convexity of the integrated optimization problem. Section 9.9 provides empirical results and section 9.10 concludes.

9.2   Problem Setting

In the *covariate shift* problem setting, a labeled training sample $X^{\mathrm{tr}} = \langle (\mathbf{x}_1), \ldots, (\mathbf{x}_{n_{\mathrm{tr}}}) \rangle$ with labels $Y^{\mathrm{tr}} = \langle (y_1), \ldots, (y_{n_{\mathrm{tr}}}) \rangle$ is available. This training sample is governed by an unknown distribution $p(\mathbf{x}|\lambda)$; labels are drawn according to an unknown target concept $p(y|\mathbf{x})$. In addition, an unlabeled test set $X^{\mathrm{te}} = \langle \mathbf{x}_{n_{\mathrm{tr}}+1}, \ldots, \mathbf{x}_{n_{\mathrm{tr}}+n_{\mathrm{te}}} \rangle$ becomes available. The test set is governed by a different unknown distribution, $p(\mathbf{x}|\theta)$. Training and test distribution may differ arbitrarily, but there is only one unknown target conditional class distribution $p(y|\mathbf{x})$.

The goal is to find a classifier $f : \mathbf{x} \mapsto y$ and to predict the missing labels $y_{n_{\mathrm{tr}}+1}, \ldots, y_{n_{\mathrm{tr}}+n_{\mathrm{te}}}$ for the test instances. From a purely transductive perspective, the classifier can even be seen as an auxiliary step and may be discarded after the labels $y_{n_{\mathrm{tr}}+1}, \ldots, y_{n_{\mathrm{tr}}+n_{\mathrm{te}}}$ have been conceived. The classifier should in any case perform well on the test data; that is, it should minimize some loss function $E_{(\mathbf{x},y)\sim\theta}[\ell(f(\mathbf{x}),y)]$ that is defined with respect to the unknown test distribution $p(\mathbf{x}|\theta)$.

Note that directly training f on the training data X^{tr} would minimize the loss with respect to $p(\mathbf{x}|\lambda)$. The minimum of this optimization problem will not generally coincide with the minimal loss on $p(\mathbf{x}|\theta)$.

9.3 Prior Work

If training and test distributions were known, then the loss on the test distribution could be minimized by weighting the loss on the training distribution with an instance-specific factor. Proposition 9.1 [Shimodaira, 2000] illustrates that the scaling factor has to be $\frac{p(\mathbf{x}|\theta)}{p(\mathbf{x}|\lambda)}$.

Proposition 9.1 *The expected loss with respect to θ equals the expected loss with respect to λ with weights $\frac{p(\mathbf{x}|\theta)}{p(\mathbf{x}|\lambda)}$ for the loss incurred by each $\mathbf{x}$, provided that the support of $p(\mathbf{x}|\theta)$ is contained in the support of $p(\mathbf{x}|\lambda)$:*

$$E_{(\mathbf{x},y)\sim\theta}[\ell(f(\mathbf{x}),y)] = E_{(\mathbf{x},y)\sim\lambda}\left[\frac{p(\mathbf{x}|\theta)}{p(\mathbf{x}|\lambda)}\ell(f(\mathbf{x}),y)\right]. \tag{9.1}$$

After expanding the expected value into its integral $\int \ell(f(\mathbf{x}),y)p(\mathbf{x},y|\theta)d\theta$, the joint distribution $p(\mathbf{x},y|\lambda)$ is decomposed into $p(\mathbf{x}|\lambda)p(y|\mathbf{x},\lambda)$. Since $p(y|\mathbf{x},\lambda) = p(y|\mathbf{x}) = p(y|\mathbf{x},\theta)$ is the global conditional distribution of the class variable given the instance, proposition 9.1 follows. All instances $\mathbf{x}$ with positive $p(\mathbf{x}|\theta)$ are integrated over. Hence, (9.1) holds as long as each $\mathbf{x}$ with positive $p(\mathbf{x}|\theta)$ also has a positive $p(\mathbf{x}|\lambda)$; otherwise, the denominator vanishes. This shows that covariate shift can only be compensated for as long as the training distribution covers the entire support of the test distribution. If a test instance had zero density under the training distribution, the test-to-training density ratio which it would need to be scaled with would incur a zero denominator.

Both, $p(\mathbf{x}|\theta)$ and $p(\mathbf{x}|\lambda)$ are unknown, but $p(\mathbf{x}|\theta)$ is reflected in X^{te}, as is $p(\mathbf{x}|\lambda)$ in X^{tr}. A straightforward approach to compensating for covariate shift is to first obtain estimates $\hat{p}(\mathbf{x}|\theta)$ and $\hat{p}(\mathbf{x}|\lambda)$ from the test and training data, respectively, using kernel density estimation [Shimodaira, 2000; Sugiyama and Müller, 2005b], (see also chapter 7). In a second step, the estimated density ratio is used to resample the training instances, or to train with weighted examples.

This method decouples the problem. First, it estimates training and test distributions. This step is intrinsically model-based and only loosely related to the ultimate goal of accurate classification. In a subsequent step, the classifier is derived given fixed weights. Since the parameters of the final classifier and the parameters that control the weights are not independent, this decomposition into two optimization steps cannot generally find the optimal setting of the *joint* parameter vector.

A line of work on learning under sample selection bias has meandered from the statistics and econometrics community into machine learning [Heckman, 1979; Zadrozny, 2004]. Sample selection bias relies on a model of the data generation process. Test instances are drawn under $p(\mathbf{x}|\theta)$. Training instances are drawn by first sampling $\mathbf{x}$ from the test distribution $p(\mathbf{x}|\theta)$. A selector variable s then decides whether $\mathbf{x}$ is moved into the training set ($s = 1$) or moved into the rejected set ($s = 0$). For instances in the training set ($s = 1$) a label is drawn from $p(y|\mathbf{x})$; for the instances in the rejected set the labels are unknown. A typical scenario for sample selection bias is credit scoring. The labeled training sample consists of customers who were given a loan in the past and the rejected sample are customers that asked for but were not given a loan. New customers asking for a loan reflect the test distribution.

The distribution of the selector variable maps the test onto the training distribution:

$$p(\mathbf{x}|\lambda) \propto p(\mathbf{x}|\theta)p(s = 1|\mathbf{x}, \theta, \lambda). \tag{9.2}$$

Proposition 9.2 [Zadrozny, 2004; Bickel and Scheffer, 2007] says that minimizing the loss on instances weighted by $p(s|\mathbf{x}, \theta, \lambda)^{-1}$ in fact minimizes the expected loss with respect to θ.

Proposition 9.2 *The expected loss with respect to θ is proportional to the expected loss with respect to λ with weights $p(s = 1|\mathbf{x}, \theta, \lambda)^{-1}$ for the loss incurred by each $\mathbf{x}$, provided that the support of $p(\mathbf{x}|\theta)$ is contained in the support of $p(\mathbf{x}|\lambda)$.*

$$E_{(\mathbf{x},y)\sim\theta}[\ell(f(\mathbf{x}),y)] \quad \propto \quad E_{(\mathbf{x},y)\sim\lambda}\left[\frac{1}{p(s = 1|\mathbf{x}, \theta, \lambda)}\ell(f(\mathbf{x}),y)\right]. \tag{9.3}$$

When the model is implemented, $p(s = 1|\mathbf{x}, \theta, \lambda)$ is learned by discriminating the training against the rejected examples; in a second step the target model is learned by following proposition 9.2 and weighting training examples by $p(s|\mathbf{x}, \theta, \lambda)^{-1}$. No test examples drawn directly from $p(\mathbf{x}|\theta)$ are needed to train the model; only labeled selected and unlabeled rejected examples are required. This is in contrast to the covariate shift model that requires samples drawn from the test distribution, but no selection process is assumed and no rejected examples are needed.

Propensity scores [Rosenbaum and Rubin, 1983; Lunceford and Davidian, 2004] are applied in settings related to sample selection bias; the training data is again assumed to be drawn from the test distribution $p(\mathbf{x}|\theta)$ followed by a selection process. The difference from the sample selection bias setting is that the selected *and* the rejected examples are labeled. Weighting the selected examples by the inverse of the propensity score $p(s = 1|\mathbf{x}, \lambda, \theta)^{-1}$ and weighting the rejected examples by $p(s = 0|\mathbf{x}, \lambda, \theta)^{-1}$ results in two unbiased samples with respect to the test distribution.

Propensity scoring can precede a variety of analysis steps. This can be the training of a target model on reweighted data or just a statistical analysis of the two reweighted samples. A typical application for propensity scores is the analysis of the success of a medical treatment. Patients are selected to be given the treatment and some other patients are selected into the control group. If the selection is not randomized the outcome (e.g., ratio of cured patients) of the two groups cannot be compared directly and propensity scores can be applied.

Maximum entropy density estimation under sample selection bias has been studied by Dudík et al. [2006]. Bickel and Scheffer [2007] impose a Dirichlet process prior on several learning problems with related sample selection bias. Elkan [2001] and Japkowicz and Stephen [2002] investigate the case of training data that is only biased with respect to the class ratio; this can be seen as sample selection bias where the selection only depends on y.

Kernel mean matching (Gretton et al. in chapter 8) is a two-step method that first finds weights for the training instances such that the first momentum of training and test sets—i.e., their mean value—matches in feature space. The subsequent training step uses these weights. The procedure requires a universal kernel. Matching the means in feature space is equivalent to matching all moments of the distributions if a universal kernel is used.

$\Phi(\cdot)$ is a mapping into a feature space and B is a regularization parameter. Gretton et al. in chapter 8 derive a quadratic program from (9.4) that can be solved with standard optimization tools:

$$\min_\alpha \quad \left\| \frac{1}{n_{\mathrm{tr}}} \sum_{i=1}^{n_{\mathrm{tr}}} \alpha_i \Phi(\mathbf{x}_i) - \frac{1}{n_{\mathrm{te}}} \sum_{i=n_{\mathrm{tr}}+1}^{n_{\mathrm{tr}}+n_{\mathrm{te}}} \Phi(\mathbf{x}_i) \right\|^2 \tag{9.4}$$

$$\text{subject to} \quad \alpha_i \in [0, B] \text{ and } \left| \frac{1}{n_{\mathrm{tr}}} \sum_{i=1}^{n_{\mathrm{tr}}} \alpha_i - 1 \right| \le \epsilon.$$

9.4 Discriminative Weighting Factors

In this section, we derive a purely discriminative model that directly estimates weights for the training instances. No distributions over instances are modeled explicitly. We first introduce a selector variable σ: For each element $\mathbf{x}$ of the training set, selector variable $\sigma = 1$ indicates that it has been drawn into X^{tr}. For each $\mathbf{x}$ in the test data, $\sigma = -1$ indicates that it has been drawn into the test set. The probability $p(\sigma = 1|\mathbf{x}, \theta, \lambda)$ has the following intuitive meaning: Given that an instance $\mathbf{x}$ has been drawn at random from the bag $X^{\mathrm{tr}} \cup X^{\mathrm{te}}$ of training and test set, the probability that $\mathbf{x}$ originates from X^{tr} is $p(\sigma = 1|\mathbf{x}, \theta, \lambda)$. Hence, the value of σ is observable for all training ($\sigma = 1$) and test ($\sigma = -1$) instances. The dependency between the instances and σ is undirected; neither training nor test set is assumed to be generated from the other sample.

In the following equations we will derive a discriminative expression for $\frac{p(\mathbf{x}|\theta)}{p(\mathbf{x}|\lambda)}$ which will no longer include any density on instances. When $p(\sigma = -1) \neq 0$ – which is implied by the test set not being empty – then the definition of σ allows us to rewrite the test distribution as $p(\mathbf{x}|\theta) = p(\mathbf{x}|\sigma = -1, \theta)$. Since test instances are only dependent on parameter θ but not on parameter λ, equation $p(\mathbf{x}|\sigma = -1, \theta) = p(\mathbf{x}|\sigma = -1, \theta, \lambda)$ follows. By an analogous argument, $p(\mathbf{x}|\theta) = p(\mathbf{x}|\sigma = 1, \theta, \lambda)$ when $p(\sigma = 1) \neq 0$. This implies (9.5).

In (9.6) the Bayes rule is applied twice; the two terms of $p(\mathbf{x}|\theta, \lambda)$ cancel each other out in (9.7). Since $p(\sigma = -1|\mathbf{x}, \theta, \lambda) = 1 - p(\sigma = 1|\mathbf{x}, \theta, \lambda)$, (9.8) follows. The conditional $p(\sigma = 1|\mathbf{x}, \theta, \lambda)$ discriminates training ($\sigma = 1$) against test instances ($\sigma = -1$).

$$\frac{p(\mathbf{x}|\theta)}{p(\mathbf{x}|\lambda)} = p(\mathbf{x}|\sigma = -1, \theta, \lambda)\frac{1}{p(\mathbf{x}|\sigma = 1, \theta, \lambda)} \tag{9.5}$$

$$= \frac{p(\sigma = -1|\mathbf{x}, \theta, \lambda)p(\mathbf{x}|\theta, \lambda)}{p(\sigma = -1|\theta, \lambda)}\frac{p(\sigma = 1|\theta, \lambda)}{p(\sigma = 1|\mathbf{x}, \theta, \lambda)p(\mathbf{x}|\theta, \lambda)} \tag{9.6}$$

$$= \frac{p(\sigma = 1|\theta, \lambda)}{p(\sigma = -1|\theta, \lambda)}\frac{p(\sigma = -1|\mathbf{x}, \theta, \lambda)}{p(\sigma = 1|\mathbf{x}, \theta, \lambda)} \tag{9.7}$$

$$= \frac{p(\sigma = 1|\theta, \lambda)}{p(\sigma = -1|\theta, \lambda)}\left(\frac{1}{p(\sigma = 1|\mathbf{x}, \theta, \lambda)} - 1\right). \tag{9.8}$$

The significance of (9.8) is that it shows how the optimal example weights, the test-to-training ratio $\frac{p(\mathbf{x}|\theta)}{p(\mathbf{x}|\lambda)}$, can be determined without knowledge of either training or test density. The right-hand side of (9.8) can be evaluated based on a model that discriminates training from test examples and outputs how much more likely an instance is to occur in the test data than it is to occur in the training data. Instead of potentially high-dimensional densities $p(\mathbf{x}|\theta)$ and $p(\mathbf{x}|\lambda)$, a conditional distribution of the single binary variable σ needs to be modeled.

Equation (9.8) leaves us with the problem of estimating a parametric model $p(\sigma = 1|\mathbf{x}, \mathbf{v})$ of $p(\sigma = 1|\mathbf{x}, \theta, \lambda)$. Such a model would predict test-to-training density ratios for the training data in L according to (9.8). In the following, we will derive the optimization problem that simultaneously determines parameters $\mathbf{v}$ of the test-to-training ratios and parameters $\mathbf{w}$ of the target classifier.

9.5 Integrated Model

Our goal is to find a classifier f which minimizes the expected loss under the test distribution. To this end, the best conceivable approximation is given by the Bayes decision based on all data available (9.9). For each test instance $\mathbf{x}$, the Bayes rule decides on the class which minimizes the expected loss given $\mathbf{x}$ and all available data (9.10),

$$\operatorname{argmin}_f E_{(\mathbf{x},y)\sim\theta}[\ell(f(\mathbf{x}), y)] \approx f_{\text{Bayes}}(\mathbf{x}; X^{\text{tr}}, X^{\text{te}}) \tag{9.9}$$

$$\text{with} \quad f_{\text{Bayes}}(\mathbf{x}; X^{\text{tr}}, X^{\text{te}}) = \operatorname{argmin}_{y'} \sum_y \ell(y', y)p(y|\mathbf{x}, X^{\text{tr}}, X^{\text{te}}). \tag{9.10}$$

Let $\mathbf{w}$ be the parameters of a classification function $p(y|\mathbf{x}, \mathbf{w})$ and let $\mathbf{v}$ parameterize a model $p(\sigma = 1|\mathbf{x}, \mathbf{v})$ that characterizes the training-test difference. The Bayes decision is obtained by *Bayesian model averaging*—i.e., by integrating over all model parameters in (9.11),

$$p(y|\mathbf{x}, X^{\mathrm{tr}}, X^{\mathrm{te}}) = \int \int p(y|\mathbf{x}, \mathbf{w})p(\mathbf{w}, \mathbf{v}|X^{\mathrm{tr}}, X^{\mathrm{te}})d\mathbf{v}d\mathbf{w} . \tag{9.11}$$

(9.11) exploits that class-label posterior $p(y|\mathbf{x}, \mathbf{w})$ is conditionally independent of the parameters $\mathbf{v}$ of the test-to-training ratio given $\mathbf{w}$, and also conditionally independent of the data given its parameters $\mathbf{w}$. Bayesian model averaging (9.11) is usually computationally infeasible. The integral is therefore approximated by the single assignment of values the parameters which maximizes it, the MAP estimator. In our case, the MAP estimator naturally assigns values to all parameters, $\mathbf{w}$ and $\mathbf{v}$ (9.13):

$$
\begin{aligned}
f_{\mathrm{MAP}}(\mathbf{x}; X^{\mathrm{tr}}, X^{\mathrm{te}}) &= \mathrm{argmax}_y p(y|\mathbf{x}, \mathbf{w}^{\mathrm{MAP}}) & (9.12)\\
\text{with} \quad (\mathbf{w}^{\mathrm{MAP}}, \mathbf{v}^{\mathrm{MAP}}) &= \max_{\mathbf{w}, \mathbf{v}} p(\mathbf{w}, \mathbf{v}|X^{\mathrm{tr}}, X^{\mathrm{te}}) & (9.13)\\
&= \max_{\mathbf{w}, \mathbf{v}} p(\mathbf{w}|\mathbf{v}, X^{\mathrm{tr}}, X^{\mathrm{te}})p(\mathbf{v}|X^{\mathrm{tr}}, X^{\mathrm{te}}) & (9.14)\\
&= \max_{\mathbf{w}, \mathbf{v}} p(\mathbf{w}|\mathbf{v}, X^{\mathrm{tr}})p(\mathbf{v}|X^{\mathrm{tr}}, X^{\mathrm{te}}) & (9.15)\\
&\propto \max_{\mathbf{w}, \mathbf{v}} P(X^{\mathrm{tr}}|\mathbf{w}, \mathbf{v})P(X^{\mathrm{tr}}, X^{\mathrm{te}}|\mathbf{v})p(\mathbf{w})p(\mathbf{v}) & (9.16)
\end{aligned}
$$

Equation (9.14) factorizes the joint posterior; (9.15) exploits that $\mathbf{w}$ is conditionally independent of the test data when the training-test difference $\mathbf{v}$ is given. Equation 9.16 applies the Bayes rule and shows that the posterior can be factorized into a likelihood function of the training data given the model parameters $P(X^{\mathrm{tr}}|\mathbf{w}, \mathbf{v})$, a likelihood function of the observed selection variables σ—written $P(X^{\mathrm{tr}}, X^{\mathrm{te}}|\mathbf{v})$—and the priors on the model parameters.

The class-label posterior $p(y|\mathbf{x}, \mathbf{w}^{\mathrm{MAP}})$ is conditionally independent of $\mathbf{v}^{\mathrm{MAP}}$ given $\mathbf{w}^{\mathrm{MAP}}$. However, $\mathbf{w}^{\mathrm{MAP}}$ and $\mathbf{v}^{\mathrm{MAP}}$ are dependent. Assigning a single MAP value to $[\mathbf{w}, \mathbf{v}]$ instead of integrating over all values corresponds to the common approximation of the Bayes decision rule by a MAP hypothesis. However, sequential maximization of $p(\mathbf{v}|X^{\mathrm{tr}}, X^{\mathrm{te}})$ over parameters $\mathbf{v}$ followed by maximization of $p(\mathbf{w}|\mathbf{v}, X^{\mathrm{tr}})$ with fixed $\mathbf{v}$ over parameters $\mathbf{w}$ would amount to an additional degree of approximation and will not generally coincide with the maximum of the product in (9.14).

We will now discuss the likelihood functions $P(X^{\mathrm{tr}}|\mathbf{w}, \mathbf{v})$ and $P(X^{\mathrm{tr}}, X^{\mathrm{te}}|\mathbf{v})$. Since our goal is discriminative training, the likelihood function $P(X^{\mathrm{tr}}|\mathbf{w})$ (not taking training-test difference $\mathbf{v}$ into account) would be $\prod_i p(y_i|\mathbf{x}_i, \mathbf{w})$. Intuitively, $\frac{p(\mathbf{x}|\theta)}{p(\mathbf{x}|\lambda)}$ dictates how many times, on average, $\mathbf{x}$ should occur in X^{tr} if X^{tr} was governed by the test distribution θ. When the individual conditional likelihood of $\mathbf{x}$ is $p(y|\mathbf{x}, \mathbf{w})$, then the likelihood of $\frac{p(\mathbf{x}|\theta)}{p(\mathbf{x}|\lambda)}$ occurrences of $\mathbf{x}$ is $p(y|\mathbf{x}, \mathbf{w})^{\frac{p(\mathbf{x}|\theta)}{p(\mathbf{x}|\lambda)}}$. Using a parametric model $p(\sigma|\mathbf{x}, \mathbf{v})$, according to (9.8) the test-to-training ratio $\frac{p(\mathbf{x}|\theta)}{p(\mathbf{x}|\lambda)}$ can be expressed as

$$\frac{p(\sigma = 1|\mathbf{v})}{p(\sigma = -1|\mathbf{v})} \left(\frac{1}{p(\sigma = 1|\mathbf{x}, \mathbf{v})} - 1 \right).$$

Therefore, we define the likelihood function as

$$P(X^{\mathrm{tr}}|\mathbf{w}, \mathbf{v}) = \left(\prod_{i=1}^{n_{\mathrm{tr}}} P(y_i|\mathbf{x}_i; \mathbf{w})^{\frac{p(\sigma=1|\mathbf{v})}{p(\sigma=-1|\mathbf{v})} \left(\frac{1}{p(\sigma_i=1|\mathbf{x}_i; \mathbf{v})} - 1 \right)} \right). \tag{9.17}$$

As an immediate corollary of Manski and Lerman [1977], the likelihood function of (9.17) has the property that when the true value $\mathbf{v}^*$ is given, its maximizer over $\mathbf{w}$ is a consistent estimator of the true parameter $\mathbf{w}^*$ that has produced labels for the test data under the test distribution θ. That is, as the sample grows, the maximizer of (9.17) converges in probability to the true value $\mathbf{w}^*$ of parameter $\mathbf{w}$.

The likelihood function $P(X^{\mathrm{tr}}, X^{\mathrm{te}}|\mathbf{v})$ resolves to $P(\sigma_i = 1|\mathbf{x}_i; \mathbf{v})$ for all training instances and $P(\sigma_i = -1|\mathbf{x}_i; \mathbf{v})$ for all test instances:

$$P(X^{\mathrm{tr}}, X^{\mathrm{te}}|\mathbf{v}) = \left(\prod_{i=1}^{n_{\mathrm{tr}}} P(\sigma_i = 1|\mathbf{x}_i; \mathbf{v}) \prod_{i=n_{\mathrm{tr}}+1}^{n_{\mathrm{tr}}+n_{\mathrm{te}}} P(\sigma_i = -1|\mathbf{x}_i; \mathbf{v}) \right). \tag{9.18}$$

Equation (9.19) summarizes (9.13) through (9.18). Equation (9.20) inserts the likelihood models (9.17) and (9.18) and draws constants $p(\sigma=1|\mathbf{v})$ and $p(\sigma=-1|\mathbf{v})$ out of the product.

$$p(\mathbf{w}, \mathbf{v}|X^{\mathrm{tr}}, X^{\mathrm{te}}) \propto P(X^{\mathrm{tr}}|\mathbf{w}, \mathbf{v}) P(X^{\mathrm{tr}}, X^{\mathrm{te}}|\mathbf{v}) p(\mathbf{w}) p(\mathbf{v}) \tag{9.19}$$

$$= \left(\prod_{i=1}^{n_{\mathrm{tr}}} P(y|\mathbf{x}_i; \mathbf{w})^{\frac{1}{p(\sigma_i=1|\mathbf{x}_i; \mathbf{v})} - 1} \right)^{\frac{p(\sigma=1|\mathbf{v})}{p(\sigma=-1|\mathbf{v})}} \tag{9.20}$$

$$\left(\prod_{i=1}^{n_{\mathrm{tr}}} P(\sigma_i = 1|\mathbf{x}_i; \mathbf{v}) \prod_{i=n_{\mathrm{tr}}+1}^{n_{\mathrm{tr}}+n_{\mathrm{te}}} P(\sigma_i = -1|\mathbf{x}_i; \mathbf{v}) \right) p(\mathbf{w}) p(\mathbf{v}).$$

Out of curiosity, let us briefly consider the extreme case of disjoint training and test distributions, i.e., $p(\mathbf{x}|\theta) p(\mathbf{x}|\lambda) = 0$ for all $\mathbf{x}$. In this case, the second factor is maximized by a $\mathbf{v}$ that assigns $p(\sigma = 1|\mathbf{x}; \mathbf{v}) = 1$ for all elements of X^{tr} (subject to a possible regularization imposed by $p(\mathbf{v})$). Hence, the likelihood of the training data $p(y|\mathbf{x}, \mathbf{w})^{\frac{1}{1} - 1}$ equals 1 for all possible classifiers $\mathbf{w}$. The choice of the classifier $\mathbf{w}$ is thus determined solely by the inductive bias $p(\mathbf{w})$. This result makes perfect sense because the training sample contains no information about the test distribution.

Using a logistic model for $p(\sigma = 1|\mathbf{x}, \mathbf{v})$, we notice that (9.8) can be simplified as in (9.21):

$$\frac{p(\sigma = 1|\mathbf{v})}{p(\sigma = -1|\mathbf{v})} \left(\frac{1}{1/(1 + \exp(-\mathbf{v}^{\mathsf{T}}\mathbf{x}))} - 1 \right) = \frac{p(\sigma = 1|\mathbf{v})}{p(\sigma = -1|\mathbf{v})} \exp(-\mathbf{v}^{\mathsf{T}}\mathbf{x}). \tag{9.21}$$

Optimization problem (9.3) is derived from (9.20) in logarithmic form, using linear models $\mathbf{v}^{\mathsf{T}}\mathbf{x}_i$ and $\mathbf{w}^{\mathsf{T}}\mathbf{x}_i$ and a logistic model for $p(\sigma = 1|\mathbf{x}, \mathbf{v})$. Negative log-likelihoods are abbreviated $\ell_{\mathbf{w}}(y_i \mathbf{w}^{\mathsf{T}} \mathbf{x}_i) = -\log p(y_i|\mathbf{x}_i; \mathbf{w})$ and $\ell_{\mathbf{v}}(\sigma_i \mathbf{v}^{\mathsf{T}} \mathbf{x}_i) = -\log p(\sigma_i|\mathbf{x}_i; \mathbf{v})$, respectively; this notation emphasizes the duality between likelihoods and empirical loss functions. The regularization terms correspond to Gaussian priors on $\mathbf{v}$ and $\mathbf{w}$ with variances $s_{\mathbf{v}}^2$ and $s_{\mathbf{w}}^2$.

Optimization Problem 9.3 *Over all* $\mathbf{w}$ *and* $\mathbf{v}$, *minimize*

$$\sum_{i=1}^{n_{\mathrm{tr}}} \frac{p(\sigma = 1|\mathbf{v})}{p(\sigma = -1|\mathbf{v})} \exp(-\mathbf{v}^{\mathsf{T}} \mathbf{x}_i) \ell_{\mathbf{w}}(y_i \mathbf{w}^{\mathsf{T}} \mathbf{x}_i)$$

$$+ \sum_{i=1}^{n_{\mathrm{tr}}+n_{\mathrm{te}}} \ell_{\mathbf{v}}(\sigma_i \mathbf{v}^{\mathsf{T}} \mathbf{x}_i) + \frac{1}{2s_{\mathbf{w}}^2} \mathbf{w}^{\mathsf{T}} \mathbf{w} + \frac{1}{2s_{\mathbf{v}}^2} \mathbf{v}^{\mathsf{T}} \mathbf{v}.$$

9.6 Primal Learning Algorithm

We derive a Newton gradient method that directly minimizes optimization problem 9.3 in the attribute space. To this end, we need to derive the gradient and the Hessian of the objective function. The update rule assumes the form of a set of linear equations that have to be solved for the update vector $[\Delta_{\mathbf{v}}, \Delta_{\mathbf{w}}]^{\mathsf{T}}$. It depends on the current parameters $[\mathbf{v}, \mathbf{w}]^{\mathsf{T}}$, all combinations of training and test data, and resulting coefficients. In order to express the update rule as a single equation in matrix form, we define

$$X = \begin{bmatrix} X^{\mathrm{tr}} & X^{\mathrm{te}} & \mathbf{0} \\ \mathbf{0} & \mathbf{0} & X^{\mathrm{tr}} \end{bmatrix}, \tag{9.22}$$

where X^{tr} and X^{te} are the matrices of training vectors, and test vectors respectively. We abbreviate

$$\ell_{\mathbf{v},i} = \ell_{\mathbf{v}}(\sigma_i \mathbf{v}^{\mathsf{T}} \mathbf{x}_i); \;\; \ell'_{\mathbf{v},i} \sigma_i x_{ij} = \frac{\partial \ell_{\mathbf{v}}(\sigma_i \mathbf{v}^{\mathsf{T}} \mathbf{x}_i)}{\partial v_j}; \;\; \ell''_{\mathbf{v},i} x_{ij} x_{ik} = \frac{\partial^2 \ell_{\mathbf{v}}(\sigma_i \mathbf{v}^{\mathsf{T}} \mathbf{x}_i)}{\partial v_j v_k}; \;\; (9.23)$$

$$\ell_{\mathbf{w},i} = \ell_{\mathbf{w}}(y_i \mathbf{w}^{\mathsf{T}} \mathbf{x}_i); \;\; \ell'_{\mathbf{w},i} y_i x_{ij} = \frac{\partial \ell_{\mathbf{w}}(y_i \mathbf{w}^{\mathsf{T}} \mathbf{x}_i)}{\partial w_j}; \;\; \ell''_{\mathbf{w},i} x_{ij} x_{ik} = \frac{\partial^2 \ell_{\mathbf{w}}(y_i \mathbf{w}^{\mathsf{T}} \mathbf{x}_i)}{\partial w_j w_k}; \;\; (9.24)$$

$$\omega_i = \frac{p(\sigma = 1|\mathbf{v})}{p(\sigma = -1|\mathbf{v})} \exp(-\mathbf{v}^{\mathsf{T}} \mathbf{x}_i), \tag{9.25}$$

and denote the objective function of optimization problem 9.3 by

$$F(\mathbf{v}, \mathbf{w}, X^{\mathrm{tr}}, X^{\mathrm{te}}) = \sum_{i=1}^{n_{\mathrm{tr}}} \omega_i \ell_{\mathbf{w},i} + \sum_{i=1}^{n_{\mathrm{tr}}+n_{\mathrm{te}}} \ell_{\mathbf{v},i} + \frac{1}{2s_{\mathbf{w}}^2} \mathbf{w}^{\mathsf{T}} \mathbf{w} + \frac{1}{2s_{\mathbf{v}}^2} \mathbf{v}^{\mathsf{T}} \mathbf{v}. \tag{9.26}$$

We compute the gradient with respect to $\mathbf{v}$ and $\mathbf{w}$.

$$\frac{\partial F(\mathbf{v}, \mathbf{w}, X^{\mathrm{tr}}, X^{\mathrm{te}})}{\partial v_j} = -\sum_{i=1}^{n_{\mathrm{tr}}} \omega_i \ell_{\mathbf{w},i} x_{ij} + \sum_{i=1}^{n_{\mathrm{tr}}+n_{\mathrm{te}}} \ell'_{\mathbf{v},i} \sigma_i x_{ij} + \frac{1}{s_{\mathbf{v}}^2} v_j, \quad (9.27)$$

$$\frac{\partial F(\mathbf{v}, \mathbf{w}, X^{\mathrm{tr}}, X^{\mathrm{te}})}{\partial w_j} = \sum_{i=1}^{n_{\mathrm{tr}}} \omega_i \ell'_{\mathbf{w},i} y_i x_{ij} + \frac{1}{s_{\mathbf{w}}^2} w_j. \quad (9.28)$$

The Hessian is the matrix of second derivatives.

$$\frac{\partial^2 F(\mathbf{v}, \mathbf{w}, X^{\mathrm{tr}}, X^{\mathrm{te}})}{\partial v_j \partial v_k} = \sum_{i=1}^{n_{\mathrm{tr}}} \omega_i \ell_{\mathbf{w},i} x_{ij} x_{ik} + \sum_{i=1}^{n_{\mathrm{tr}}+n_{\mathrm{te}}} \ell''_{\mathbf{v},i} x_{ij} x_{ik} + \frac{1}{s_{\mathbf{v}}^2} \delta_{jk}, \quad (9.29)$$

$$\frac{\partial^2 F(\mathbf{v}, \mathbf{w}, X^{\mathrm{tr}}, X^{\mathrm{te}})}{\partial v_j \partial w_k} = -\sum_{i=1}^{n_{\mathrm{tr}}} \omega_i \ell'_{\mathbf{w},i} y_i x_{ij} x_{ik}, \quad (9.30)$$

$$\frac{\partial^2 F(\mathbf{v}, \mathbf{w}, X^{\mathrm{tr}}, X^{\mathrm{te}})}{\partial w_j \partial w_k} = \sum_{i=1}^{n_{\mathrm{tr}}} \omega_i \ell''_{\mathbf{w},i} x_{ij} x_{ik} + \frac{1}{s_w^2} \delta_{jk}. \quad (9.31)$$

We can rewrite gradient as $X\mathbf{g} + S[\mathbf{v}, \mathbf{w}]^{\mathsf{T}}$ and Hessian as $X\Lambda X^{\mathsf{T}} + S$ using the following definitions, $\mathbf{g} = \left[\mathbf{g}^{(1)}, \mathbf{g}^{(2)}, \mathbf{g}^{(3)}\right]^{\mathsf{T}}$, $S = \begin{bmatrix} S^{\mathbf{v}} & \mathbf{0} \\ \mathbf{0} & S^{\mathbf{w}} \end{bmatrix}$ with

$$g_i^{(1)} = -\omega_i \ell_{\mathbf{w},i} + \ell'_{\mathbf{v},i} \qquad \text{for} \quad i = 1, \ldots, n_{\mathrm{tr}}, \quad (9.32)$$

$$g_i^{(2)} = -\ell'_{\mathbf{v}, n_{\mathrm{tr}}+i} \qquad \text{for} \quad i = 1, \ldots, n_{\mathrm{te}}, \quad (9.33)$$

$$g_i^{(3)} = \omega_i \ell'_{\mathbf{w},i} y_i \qquad \text{for} \quad i = 1, \ldots, n_{\mathrm{tr}}, \quad (9.34)$$

$$S_{i,i}^{\mathbf{v}} = s_{\mathbf{v}}^{-2} \qquad \text{for} \quad i = 1, \ldots, \dim(X^{\mathrm{te}}), \quad (9.35)$$

$$S_{i,i}^{\mathbf{w}} = s_{\mathbf{w}}^{-2} \qquad \text{for} \quad i = 1, \ldots, \dim(X^{\mathrm{tr}}), \quad (9.36)$$

$$\Lambda = \begin{bmatrix} \displaystyle\operatorname*{diag}_{i=1..n_{\mathrm{tr}}} \left(\omega_i \ell_{\mathbf{w},i} + \ell''_{\mathbf{v},i}\right) & \mathbf{0} & -\displaystyle\operatorname*{diag}_{i=1..n_{\mathrm{tr}}} \left(\omega_i \ell'_{\mathbf{w},i} y_i\right) \\[2ex] \mathbf{0} & \displaystyle\operatorname*{diag}_{i=1..n_{\mathrm{te}}} \left(\ell''_{\mathbf{v},n_{\mathrm{tr}}+i}\right) & \mathbf{0} \\[2ex] -\displaystyle\operatorname*{diag}_{i=1..n_{\mathrm{tr}}} \left(\omega_i \ell'_{\mathbf{w},i} y_i\right) & \mathbf{0} & \displaystyle\operatorname*{diag}_{i=1..n_{\mathrm{tr}}} \left(\omega_i \ell''_{\mathbf{w},i}\right) \end{bmatrix}. \quad (9.37)$$

The update step for the Newton gradient descent minimization of optimization problem 9.3 is $[\mathbf{v}', \mathbf{w}']^{\mathsf{T}} \leftarrow [\mathbf{v}, \mathbf{w}]^{\mathsf{T}} + [\Delta_{\mathbf{v}}, \Delta_{\mathbf{w}}]^{\mathsf{T}}$ with

$$(X\Lambda X^{\mathsf{T}} + S) \begin{bmatrix} \Delta_{\mathbf{v}} \\ \Delta_{\mathbf{w}} \end{bmatrix} = -X\mathbf{g} - S \begin{bmatrix} \mathbf{v} \\ \mathbf{w} \end{bmatrix}. \quad (9.38)$$

Given the parameter $\mathbf{w}$, a test instance $\mathbf{x}$ is classified as $f(\mathbf{x}; \mathbf{w}) = \operatorname{sign}(\mathbf{w}^{\mathsf{T}} \mathbf{x})$.

9.7 Kernelized Learning Algorithm

We derive a kernelized version of the integrated classifier for differing training and test distributions. A transformation Φ maps instances into a target space in which a kernel function $k(\mathbf{x}_i, \mathbf{x}_j)$ calculates the inner product $\Phi(\mathbf{x}_i)^\mathsf{T} \Phi(\mathbf{x}_j)$.

The update rule (9.38) thus becomes

$$(\Phi(X)\Lambda\Phi(X)^\mathsf{T} + S) \begin{bmatrix} \Delta_\mathbf{v} \\ \Delta_\mathbf{w} \end{bmatrix} = -\Phi(X)\mathbf{g} - S \begin{bmatrix} \mathbf{v} \\ \mathbf{w} \end{bmatrix}. \tag{9.39}$$

$\Phi(X)$ is defined by

$$\Phi(X) = \begin{bmatrix} \Phi(X^\mathrm{tr}) & \Phi(X^\mathrm{te}) & \mathbf{0} \\ \mathbf{0} & \mathbf{0} & \Phi(X^\mathrm{tr}) \end{bmatrix}. \tag{9.40}$$

According to the representer theorem, the optimal separator is a linear combination of examples. Parameter vectors $\boldsymbol{\alpha}$ and $\boldsymbol{\beta}$ in the dual space weight the influence of all examples:

$$\begin{bmatrix} \mathbf{v} \\ \mathbf{w} \end{bmatrix} = \Phi(X) \begin{bmatrix} \boldsymbol{\alpha} \\ \boldsymbol{\beta} \end{bmatrix}. \tag{9.41}$$

Equation 9.39 can therefore be rewritten as (9.42). We now multiply $\Phi(X)^\mathsf{T}$ from the left to both sides and obtain (9.43). We replace all resulting occurrences of $\Phi(X)^\mathsf{T}\Phi(X)$ by the kernel matrix K and arrive at (9.44); S is replaced by S' such that $\Phi(X)^\mathsf{T} S \Phi(X) = \Phi(X)^\mathsf{T}\Phi(X)S'$, i.e., $S'_{i,i} = s_\mathbf{v}^{-2}$ for $i = 1..n_\mathrm{tr} + n_\mathrm{te}$ and $S'_{n_\mathrm{tr}+n_\mathrm{te}+i, n_\mathrm{tr}+n_\mathrm{te}+i} = s_\mathbf{w}^{-2}$ for $i = 1..n_\mathrm{tr}$. Equation 9.44 is satisfied when (9.45) is satisfied. Equation 9.45 is the update rule for the dual Newton gradient descent.

$$(\Phi(X)\Lambda\Phi(X)^\mathsf{T} + S)\Phi(X) \begin{bmatrix} \Delta_\alpha \\ \Delta_\beta \end{bmatrix} = -\Phi(X)\mathbf{g} - S\Phi(X) \begin{bmatrix} \alpha \\ \beta \end{bmatrix}, \tag{9.42}$$

$$\Phi(X)^\mathsf{T}(\Phi(X)\Lambda\Phi(X)^\mathsf{T} + S)\Phi(X) \begin{bmatrix} \Delta_\alpha \\ \Delta_\beta \end{bmatrix} = -\Phi(X)^\mathsf{T}\Phi(X)\mathbf{g} - \Phi(X)^\mathsf{T} S\Phi(X) \begin{bmatrix} \alpha \\ \beta \end{bmatrix}, \tag{9.43}$$

$$(K\Lambda K + KS') \begin{bmatrix} \Delta_\alpha \\ \Delta_\beta \end{bmatrix} = -K\mathbf{g} - KS' \begin{bmatrix} \alpha \\ \beta \end{bmatrix}, \tag{9.44}$$

$$(\Lambda K + S') \begin{bmatrix} \Delta_\alpha \\ \Delta_\beta \end{bmatrix} = -\mathbf{g} - S' \begin{bmatrix} \alpha \\ \beta \end{bmatrix}. \tag{9.45}$$

Given the parameters, test instance $\mathbf{x}$ is classified by $f(\mathbf{x}; \boldsymbol{\alpha}) = \mathrm{sign}(\sum_{i=1}^{n_\mathrm{tr}} \beta_i k(\mathbf{x}, \mathbf{x}_i))$.

9.8   Convexity Analysis and Solving the Optimization Problems

The following theorem specifies the conditions for convexity of optimization problem 9.3. With this theorem we can easily check whether the integrated classifier for covariate shift is convex for specific models of the negative log-likelihood functions. The negative log-likelihood function $\ell_{\mathbf{w}}$ itself and its first and second derivatives are needed.

Theorem 9.4 *Optimization problem 9.3 is in general convex if $\ell_{\mathbf{v}}$ is convex and*

$$\ell_{\mathbf{w},i}\ell_{\mathbf{w},i}'' - \ell_{\mathbf{w},i}'^2 \geq 0. \tag{9.46}$$

Proof: Looking at optimization problem 9.3 we immediately see that the regularizers are convex and if $\ell_{\mathbf{v}}$ is convex the second term is convex as well; we only need to analyze the convexity of the last term

$$\sum_{i=1}^{n_{\mathrm{tr}}} \frac{p(\sigma = 1|\mathbf{v})}{p(\sigma = -1|\mathbf{v})} \exp(-\mathbf{v}^{\mathsf{T}}\mathbf{x}_i)\ell_{\mathbf{w}}(y_i\mathbf{w}^{\mathsf{T}}\mathbf{x}_i) \;\;=\;\; \sum_{i=1}^{n_{\mathrm{tr}}} \omega_i \ell_{\mathbf{w},i}. \tag{9.47}$$

A function is convex if the Hessian is positive semidefinite and this is the case if and only if

$$\mathbf{a}^{\mathsf{T}} H \mathbf{a} \geq 0 \tag{9.48}$$

for all vectors $\mathbf{a}$ and Hessian H.

With the notation of section 9.6 the Hessian of (9.47) is

$$\begin{bmatrix} X^{\mathrm{tr}} & \mathbf{0} \\ \mathbf{0} & X^{\mathrm{tr}} \end{bmatrix}^{\mathsf{T}} \begin{bmatrix} \displaystyle\operatorname*{diag}_{1..\dim(X^{\mathrm{tr}})} \omega_i \ell_{\mathbf{w},i} & \displaystyle\operatorname*{diag}_{1..\dim(X^{\mathrm{tr}})} -\omega_i \ell_{\mathbf{w},i}' y_i \\ \displaystyle\operatorname*{diag}_{1..\dim(X^{\mathrm{tr}})} -\omega_i \ell_{\mathbf{w},i}' y_i & \displaystyle\operatorname*{diag}_{1..\dim(X^{\mathrm{tr}})} \omega_i \ell_{\mathbf{w},i}'' \end{bmatrix} \begin{bmatrix} X^{\mathrm{tr}} & \mathbf{0} \\ \mathbf{0} & X^{\mathrm{tr}} \end{bmatrix}. \tag{9.49}$$

Using the condition of (9.48) the Hessian is positive semidefinite if the following matrix is positive semidefinite:

$$\begin{bmatrix} \displaystyle\operatorname*{diag}_{1..\dim(X^{\mathrm{tr}})} \ell_{\mathbf{w},i} & \displaystyle\operatorname*{diag}_{1..\dim(X^{\mathrm{tr}})} -\ell_{\mathbf{w},i}' y_i \\ \displaystyle\operatorname*{diag}_{1..\dim(X^{\mathrm{tr}})} -\ell_{\mathbf{w},i}' y_i & \displaystyle\operatorname*{diag}_{1..\dim(X^{\mathrm{tr}})} \ell_{\mathbf{w},i}'' \end{bmatrix}. \tag{9.50}$$

Applying (9.48) and splitting $\mathbf{a}$ into two equally sized subvectors $\mathbf{a} = [\mathbf{a}_1, \mathbf{a}_2]^{\mathsf{T}}$, the condition for convexity is

$$\ell_{\mathbf{w},i}'' \mathbf{a}_1^{\mathsf{T}}\mathbf{a}_1 - 2\ell_{\mathbf{w},i}' y_i \mathbf{a}_1^{\mathsf{T}}\mathbf{a}_2 + \ell_{\mathbf{w},i}\mathbf{a}_2^{\mathsf{T}}\mathbf{a}_2 \geq 0. \tag{9.51}$$

Multiplication of (9.51) with $\ell_{\mathbf{w},i}''$ and adding and subtracting $\ell_{\mathbf{w},i}'^2 y_i^2 \mathbf{a}_2^{\mathsf{T}}\mathbf{a}_2$ leads to (9.52). Equation 9.53 holds by the binomial theorem. For $\mathbf{a}_1 = \frac{\ell_{\mathbf{w},i}' y_i}{\ell_{\mathbf{w},i}''}\mathbf{a}_2$ the term $\left\|\ell_{\mathbf{w},i}''\mathbf{a}_1 - \ell_{\mathbf{w},i}' y_i \mathbf{a}_2\right\|^2$ takes its minimum value zero; this means (9.53) is nonnegative for arbitrary $\mathbf{a}_1$ and $\mathbf{a}_2$ if (9.54) is nonnegative.

$$\ell_{\mathbf{w},i}''^2 \mathbf{a}_1^\mathsf{T} \mathbf{a}_1 - 2\ell_{\mathbf{w},i}' \ell_{\mathbf{w},i}'' y_i \mathbf{a}_1^\mathsf{T} \mathbf{a}_2 + \ell_{\mathbf{w},i} \ell_{\mathbf{w},i}'' \mathbf{a}_2^\mathsf{T} \mathbf{a}_2 + \ell_{\mathbf{w},i}'^2 y_i^2 \mathbf{a}_2^\mathsf{T} \mathbf{a}_2 - \ell_{\mathbf{w},i}'^2 y_i^2 \mathbf{a}_2^\mathsf{T} \mathbf{a}_2 \geq 0, \quad (9.52)$$

$$\left\| \ell_{\mathbf{w},i}'' \mathbf{a}_1 - \ell_{\mathbf{w},i}' y_i \mathbf{a}_2 \right\|^2 + \mathbf{a}_2^\mathsf{T} \mathbf{a}_2 (\ell_{\mathbf{w},i} \ell_{\mathbf{w},i}'' - \ell_{\mathbf{w},i}'^2) \geq 0, \qquad (9.53)$$

$$\ell_{\mathbf{w},i} \ell_{\mathbf{w},i}'' - \ell_{\mathbf{w},i}'^2 \geq 0. \qquad (9.54)$$

∎

In order to check the optimization criterion (optimization problem 9.3) for convexity we need to choose models of the negative log-likelihood $\ell_{\mathbf{v}}$ and $\ell_{\mathbf{w}}$ and derive their first and second derivatives. These derivations are also needed to actually minimize the optimization criterion with the Newton update steps derived in the last section.

For the model of the covariate shift we use a logistic model $\ell_{\mathbf{v}}(\sigma_i \mathbf{v}^\mathsf{T} \mathbf{x}) = \log(1 + \exp(-\sigma_i \mathbf{v}^\mathsf{T} \mathbf{x}))$; the abbreviations of section 9.6 can now be expanded:

$$\ell_{\mathbf{v},i}' \sigma_i x_{ij} = -\frac{\exp(-\sigma_i \mathbf{v}^\mathsf{T} \mathbf{x}_i)}{1 + \exp(-\sigma_i \mathbf{v}^\mathsf{T} \mathbf{x}_i)} \sigma_i x_{ij}; \quad \ell_{\mathbf{v},i}'' x_{ij} x_{ik} = \frac{\exp(-\sigma_i \mathbf{v}^\mathsf{T} \mathbf{x}_i)}{(1 + \exp(-\sigma_i \mathbf{v}^\mathsf{T} \mathbf{x}_i))^2} x_{ij} x_{ik}. \quad (9.55)$$

For the model of the target classifier we detail the derivations for logistic and for exponential models of $\ell_{\mathbf{w}}$. For the logistic model the derivatives of $\ell_{\mathbf{w}}$ are the same as for $\ell_{\mathbf{v}}$, only $\mathbf{v}$ needs to be replaced by $\mathbf{w}$ and σ_i by y_i. For an exponential model with $\ell_{\mathbf{w}}(y_i \mathbf{w}^\mathsf{T} \mathbf{x}) = \exp(-y_i \mathbf{w}^\mathsf{T} \mathbf{x})$ the abbreviations are expanded as follows:

$$\ell_{\mathbf{w},i}' y_i x_{ij} = -\exp(-y_i \mathbf{w}^\mathsf{T} \mathbf{x}_i) y_i x_{ij}; \quad \ell_{\mathbf{w},i}'' x_{ij} x_{ik} = \exp(-y_i \mathbf{w}^\mathsf{T} \mathbf{x}_i) x_{ij} x_{ik}. \qquad (9.56)$$

Using theorem 9.4 we can now easily check the convexity of the integrated classifier with logistic model and with exponential model of $\ell_{\mathbf{w}}$.

Corollary 9.5 *Optimization problem 9.3 with logistic model for $\ell_{\mathbf{w}}$ is nonconvex.*

Proof: Inserting the logistic function into (9.46) we get the following solution.

$$\ell_{\mathbf{w},i}'' \ell_{\mathbf{w},i} - \ell_{\mathbf{w},i}'^2 = \frac{\exp(-y_i \mathbf{w}^\mathsf{T} \mathbf{x}_i)}{1 + \exp(-y_i \mathbf{w}^\mathsf{T} \mathbf{x})} \left(\log(1 + \exp(-y_i \mathbf{w}^\mathsf{T} \mathbf{x})) - \exp(-y_i \mathbf{w}^\mathsf{T} \mathbf{x}_i) \right) (9.57)$$

The first term of (9.57) is always positive, the difference term is always negative, thus optimization problem 9.3 with logistic model for $\ell_{\mathbf{w}}$ is nonconvex.

∎

Empirically, we find that it is a good choice to select the parameters of a regular i.i.d. logistic regression classifier as starting point for the Newton gradient search. Since i.i.d. logistic regression has a convex optimization criterion, this starting point is easily found.

One can easily show that optimization problem 9.3 is nonconvex when $\ell_{\mathbf{w}}$ are chosen as hinge loss or quadratic loss.

Corollary 9.6 *Optimization problem 9.3 with exponential model for $\ell_{\mathbf{w}}$ is convex.*

Proof: Inserting the exponential model into the above criterion results in the nonnegative expression

$$\ell_{\mathbf{w},i}'' \ell_{\mathbf{w},i} - \ell_{\mathbf{w},i}'^2 \;=\; \exp(-y_i \mathbf{w}^\mathsf{T} \mathbf{x}_i) \exp(-y_i \mathbf{w}^\mathsf{T} \mathbf{x}_i) - (-\exp(-y_i \mathbf{w}^\mathsf{T} \mathbf{x}_i)^2) \;=\; 0. \quad (9.58)$$

∎

This means the global optimum of optimization problem 9.3 with exponential model for $\ell_{\mathbf{w}}$ can easily be found by Newton gradient descent.

9.9   Empirical Results

We study the benefit of two versions of the integrated classifier for covariate shift and other reference methods on spam filtering, text classification, and land mine detection problems. The first integrated classifier uses a logistic model for $\ell_{\mathbf{w}}$ ("integrated log model"), the second an exponential model for $\ell_{\mathbf{w}}$ ("integrated exp model").

The first baseline is a classifier trained under i.i.d. assumption with logistic $\ell_{\mathbf{w}}$. All other reference methods consist of a two-stage procedure: first, the difference between training and test distribution is estimated; the classifier is trained on weighted data in a second step. The baselines differ in the first stage; the second stage is based on a logistic regression classifier with weighted examples in any case.

The first reference method is two-stage logistic regression ("two-stage LR"). The example weights are computed according to (9.8); $p(\sigma = 1|\mathbf{x}, \mathbf{v})$ is estimated by training a logistic regression that discriminates training from test examples. The second method is kernel mean matching (chapter 8); we set $\epsilon = \sqrt{n_{\mathrm{tr}} - 1}/\sqrt{n_{\mathrm{tr}}}$ as proposed by the authors. In the third method, separate density estimates for $p(\mathbf{x}|\lambda)$ and $p(\mathbf{x}|\theta)$ are obtained using kernel density estimation [Shimodaira, 2000]; the bandwidth of the kernel is chosen according to the rule of thumb of Silverman [1986]. We tune the regularization parameters of all the methods and the variance parameter of the RBF kernels on a separate tuning set. We use a maximum likelihood estimate of $\frac{n_{tr}}{n_{te}}$ for $\frac{p(\sigma=1|\theta,\lambda)}{p(\sigma=-1|\theta,\lambda)}$.

We use the spam filtering data of Bickel et al. [2007]; the collection contains nine different inboxes with test emails (5270-10964 emails, depending on inbox) and one set of training emails from different sources. We use a fixed set of 1000 emails as training data. We randomly select 32-2048 emails from one of the original inboxes. We repeat this process ten times for 2048 test emails and 20-640 times for 1024-32 test emails. As tuning data we use the labeled emails from an additional inbox different from the test inboxes. The performance measure is the rate by which the 1-AUC risk is reduced over the i.i.d. baseline [Bickel and Scheffer, 2007]; it is computed as $1 - \frac{1-AUC}{1-AUC_{iid}}$. We use linear kernels for all methods. We analyze the rank of the kernel matrix and find that it fulfills the universal kernel requirement of kernel mean matching; this is due to the high dimensionality of the data.

Figure 9.1 (top left) shows the result for various numbers of unlabeled examples. The results for a specific number of unlabeled examples are averaged over 10-640 random test samples and averaged over all nine inboxes. Averaged over all users and inbox sizes the absolute AUC of the i.i.d. classifier is 0.994. Error bars indicate standard errors of the 1-AUC risk.

The three discriminative density estimators and kernel mean matching perform similarly well. The differences from the i.i.d. baseline are highly significant. For 1048 examples the 1-AUC risk is even reduced by an average of 30% with the integrated exponential model classifier! The kernel density estimation procedure is not able to beat the i.i.d. baseline.

We now study text classification using computer science papers from the Cora dataset. The task is to discriminate machine learning from networking papers. We select 812 papers written before 1996 from both classes as training examples and 1285 papers written after 1996 as test examples. For parameter tuning we apply an additional time split on the training data; we train on the papers written before 1995 and tune on papers written 1995. Title and abstract are transformed into TFIDF vectors; the number of distinct words is 40,000. We again use linear kernels (rank analysis verifies the universal kernel property) and average the results over 20-640 random test samples for different sizes (1024-32) of test sets. The resulting 1-AUC risk is shown in figure 9.1 (top right). The average absolute AUC of the i.i.d. classifier is 0.998. The methods based on discriminative density estimates significantly outperform all other methods. Kernel mean matching is not displayed because its average performance lies far below the i.i.d. baseline. The integrated models reduce the 1-AUC risk by 15% for 1024 test examples; for a larger number of test examples (128-1024) they perform slightly better than the two-step decomposition.

In a third set of experiments we study the problem of detecting land mines using the data set of Xue et al. [2007]. The collection contains data of 29 minefields in different regions. Binary labels (land mine or safe ground) and nine dimensional feature vectors extracted from radar images are provided. There are about 500 examples for each minefield. Each of the fields has a distinct distribution of input patterns, varying from highly foliated to desert areas.

We enumerate all 29×28 pairs of minefields, using one field as training, and the other as test data. For tuning we hold out 4 of the 812 pairs. Results are increases over the i.i.d. baseline, averaged over all $29 \times 28 - 4$ combinations. We use RBF kernels with variance $\sigma^2 = 0.3$ for all methods. The results are displayed in figure 9.1 (bottom left). The average absolute AUC of the i.i.d. baseline is 0.64 with a standard deviation of 0.07; note that the error bars are much smaller than the absolute standard deviation because they indicate the standard error of the *differences* from the i.i.d. baseline.

For this problem, the integrated exponential model classifier and kernel mean matching significantly outperform all other methods on average. Integrated logistic regression and two-stage logistic regression are still significantly better than the i.i.d. baseline except for 32 test examples. We assume that the nonconvex integrated logistic regression is inferior to the convex integrated exponential model method because it runs into unfavorable local optima.

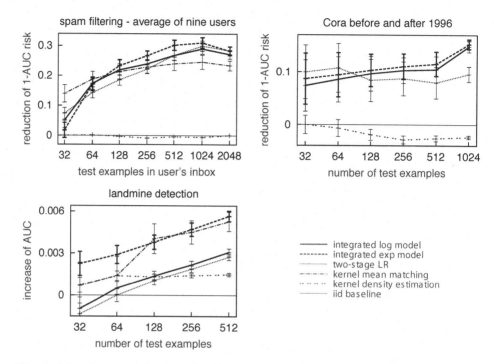

Figure 9.1 Average reduction of 1-AUC risk over nine users for spam filtering (*top left*) and Cora *Machine learning/networking* classification before and after 1996 (*top right*) and average increase of AUC for land mine detection over 812 pairs of minefields (*bottom left*) depending on the number of unlabeled test examples.

9.10   Conclusion

We derived a discriminative model for learning under differing training and test distributions. The contribution of each training instance to the optimization problem ideally needs to be weighted with their test-to-training density ratio. We show that this ratio can be expressed – without modeling either training or test density – by a discriminative model that characterizes how much more likely an instance is to occur in the test sample than it is to occur in the training sample.

When Bayesian model averaging is unfeasible and the Bayes decision is unattainable, then one can choose the joint MAP hypothesis of both the parameters of the test-to-training model and the final classifier. Optimizing these dependent parameters sequentially incurs an additional approximation compared to solving the joint optimization problem.

We derived a primal and a kernelized Newton gradient descent procedure for the joint optimization problem. Theorem 9.4 specifies the condition for the convexity of optimization problem 9.3. Checking the condition using popular loss functions as models of the negative log-likelihoods reveals that optimization problem 9.3 is only convex with exponential loss.

Empirically, we found that the models with discriminative density estimates outperform the i.i.d. baseline and the kernel density estimated model in almost all cases. For spam filtering the integrated and the two-step models perform similarly well. For land mine detection the convex integrated exponential model classifier and kernel mean matching significantly outperform all other methods.

Acknowledgment

We gratefully acknowledge support from the German Science Foundation DFG and from STRATO AG. We wish to thank Jiayuan Huang, Alex Smola, Arthur Gretton, Karsten Borgward, and Bernhard Schölkopf who provided their implementation of the kernel mean matching algorithm.

10

An Adversarial View of Covariate Shift and a Minimax Approach

Amir Globerson
Choon Hui Teo
Alex Smola
Sam Roweis

Supervised learning algorithms should ideally be robust to differences between the training and testing distributions. We consider an adversarial model where the learning algorithm attempts to construct a predictor which is robust to deletion of features at test time. The problem is formulated as finding the optimal minimax strategy with respect to an adversary that deletes features. We show that the optimal strategy may be found either by solving a quadratic program, or equivalently, using efficient bundle methods for optimization. The resulting algorithm is shown to significantly improve prediction performance on several problems including in a spam filtering challenge task.

10.1 Building Robust Classifiers

When constructing classifiers over high-dimensional spaces such as texts or images, one is inherently faced with the problem of undersampling of the true data distribution. Even so-called 'discriminative' methods which focus on minimizing classification error (or a bound on it) are exposed to this difficulty since the training objective will be calculated over the observed input vectors only, and thus may not be a good approximation of the average objective on the test data. This is especially important in settings such as document classification where features may take on certain observed values (e.g., a zero count for a particular vocabulary item) due to small sample effects. A more serious difficulty may arise when dataset shift effects are present, namely when the training and testing distributions are different. For example, the distribution of words in spam email changes very rapidly and keywords which are highly predictive of class in the training set may not be indicative or even present in the test data. As another example, consider a digital camera whose output is fed to a face recognition system. Due to hardware or transmission failures, a few pixels may "die" over the course of time. In the image processing literature, this is referred to as *pepper* noise [Bovik et al., 2000] (*salt* noise refers to the case when pixels values are clipped to some fixed value). Any classifier which attached too much weight to any single pixel would suffer a substantial performance loss in this case. As a final example, consider a network of local processing elements in an artificial sensor network or a biological network such as the cortex. The hardware/wetware of such systems is known to be extremely unreliable (thousands of neurons die each day) and yet the overall architecture maintains its function, indicating a remarkable robustness to such nonstationarities in its input.

All the above examples describe a scenario where features that were present when constructing the classifier (i.e., in the training data), are potentially *deleted* at some future point in time. Such deletion may manifest itself differently depending on the particular domain: a deleted feature may be known to be unavailable or unmeasured; it may take on random values; or its value may be set to some constant. In our formal treatment, we focus on the case where deletion corresponds to setting the feature's value to zero. Indeed, in the examples given above this is an appropriate description.

Of course, when constructing the classifier, we cannot anticipate in advance which features may be deleted in the future. One possible strategy is to analyze the performance under random deletion of features. However, this may not be a correct model of the deletion statistics. The approach we take here is to construct a classifier which is optimal in the worst-case deletion scenario, thus avoiding any modeling assumptions about the deletion mechanism. This can be formulated as a two-player game, where the action of one player (the classifier builder) is to choose robust classifier parameters, whereas the other player (the feature removal mechanism) tries to delete the features which would be most harmful given the current classifier. We note that the adversarial setting may not necessarily be an exact model of the problem (e.g., spam authors may not know the details of the spam filter, and are thus not as powerful as the adversary we model). However, considering the worst-case scenario yields a classifier that is robust to any adversarial strategy, and avoids making statistical assumptions about the deletion process. Furthermore, even if there is no true underlying adversary, robustness to feature deletion yields robustness of the resulting classifier, in the sense that it will not attach too much weight to single features, even if those appear informative at training time.

Robust minimax approaches to learning classifiers have recently attracted interest in the machine learning community [Lanckriet et al., 2004; El Ghaoui et al., 2003; Kim et al., 2006]. Our approach is related to El Ghaoui et al. [2003] where the location of sample points is only known up to an ellipsoidal region, and a classifier that is optimal in the worst-case is sought. However, in our case, the structure of uncertainty is inherently different and is related to the existence vs. nonexistence of a feature. Adversarial models have also recently been studied in the context of spam filtering by Dalvi et al. [2004]. Their formalism addresses transformations that are more general than feature deletion, and also incorporates costs for different types of mistakes. However, finding the optimal strategy in their case is a computationally hard problem, and approximations are needed.

In the context of dataset shift, our minimax approach assumes that the difference between training and testing scenarios is defined via a class of possible transformations (here we consider feature deletions), and that learning should be robust with respect to this class.

In section 10.2 we formalize the feature-dropping minimax game for classifiers such as the support vector machine [Schölkopf and Smola, 2002] in which the training objective is measured using a regularized hinge loss. We denote this optimization problem by the name FDROP. We next show that this problem can be exactly solved in polynomial time, and provide several optimization algorithms for solving it. Finally, we illustrate the method's performance on handwritten digit recognition and spam filtering tasks.

10.2   Minimax Problem Formulation

Given a labeled sample $(\mathbf{x}_i, y_i)$ $(i = 1, \ldots, n)$, with input feature vectors $\mathbf{x}_i \in \mathbb{R}^d$ and class labels[1] $y_i \in \{\pm 1\}$, we would like to construct classifiers which are robust to *deletion* of features. We focus on the case where a feature is assigned the value of zero if it is deleted, and denote by K the number of features the adversary can delete for any given sample point $\mathbf{x}$. The number K is assumed to be given and fixed in what follows, although in practice we set it using cross-validation.

In standard support vector machines (SVMs) (e.g., see Schölkopf and Smola [2002]), the goal of the learning algorithm is to find a weight vector $\mathbf{w} \in \mathbb{R}^d$ that minimizes a regularized hinge loss:

$$\frac{1}{2}\|\mathbf{w}\|^2 + C \sum_i [1 - y_i \mathbf{w} \cdot \mathbf{x}_i]_+ \ , \tag{10.1}$$

where we use the notation $[x]_+ = \max\{x, 0\}$. However, in the feature deletion case, the adversary may change the input $\mathbf{x}_i$ by deleting features from it. We would like our classifier to be robust to such deletions. Thus, we seek a classifier which minimizes the worst-case hinge loss when K features may be deleted from each data vector. In this setting, the worst-case hinge loss, for example i, is given by

$$
\begin{aligned}
h^{wc}(\mathbf{w}, y_i \mathbf{x}_i) = \ &\max \quad [1 - y_i \mathbf{w} \cdot (\mathbf{x}_i \circ (1 - \boldsymbol{\alpha}_i))]_+ \\
&s.t. \quad \boldsymbol{\alpha}_i \in \{0, 1\}^d \\
&\qquad \sum_j \alpha_{ij} = K
\end{aligned}
\tag{10.2}
$$

---

1. We focus on the binary case here. All results can be easily generalized to the multi-class case.

where α_{ij} denotes the jth element of $\boldsymbol{\alpha}_i$, and is equal to 1 if the jth feature of $\mathbf{x}_i$ is deleted (we use $\circ$ to denote the element-wise multiplication operation).

The worst-case hinge loss over the entire training set is $\sum_i h^{wc}(\mathbf{w}, y_i \mathbf{x}_i)$. The overall optimization problem, which we denote by FDROP, is then

$$\underline{\text{FDROP:}} \qquad \mathbf{w}^* = \arg\min_{\mathbf{w}} \frac{1}{2}\|\mathbf{w}\|^2 + C \sum_i h^{wc}(\mathbf{w}, y_i \mathbf{x}_i) \,. \qquad (10.3)$$

The above can be explicitly written as a minimax optimization problem:

$$
\begin{aligned}
&\min_{\mathbf{w}} \quad \max_{\boldsymbol{\alpha}_1,\dots,\boldsymbol{\alpha}_n} \ \tfrac{1}{2}\|\mathbf{w}\|^2 + C\sum_i \left[1 - y_i \mathbf{w} \cdot (\mathbf{x}_i \circ (1-\boldsymbol{\alpha}_i))\right]_+ \\
&\text{s.t.} \quad \boldsymbol{\alpha}_i \in \{0,1\}^d \\
&\qquad \textstyle\sum_j \alpha_{ij} = K \,.
\end{aligned}
\qquad (10.4)
$$

Denote the objective of the above by $f(\mathbf{w}, \boldsymbol{\alpha})$. Then (10.4) may be interpreted as finding an optimal strategy for a zero-sum game where the learning algorithm is paid $-f(\mathbf{w}, \boldsymbol{\alpha})$ and the adversary is payed $f(\mathbf{w}, \boldsymbol{\alpha})$ when the joint action $\mathbf{w}, \boldsymbol{\alpha}$ is taken.

In the next section we present two approaches to solving the optimization problem in (10.3).

10.3   Finding the Minimax Optimal Features

The minimization problem in (10.3) is closely related to the SVM optimization problem. However, in our case we have a worst-case hinge loss instead of the standard hinge loss. Since this worst-case requires maximization over $\binom{n}{k}$ possibilities per sample, it is not immediately clear how to design an efficient method for solving the overall optimization. In the following section we describe two methods for solving FDROP. The first is to use convex duality transformations to turn it into a quadratic program with $O(nd)$ variables. The second is to solve it directly in the $\mathbf{w}$ variable using the recently introduced BMRM method [Teo et al., 2007b].

10.3.1   An Equivalent Quadratic Program

In this section we show that the problem in (10.3) is equivalent to a certain convex quadratic program. We begin by analyzing the worst-case hinge loss $h^{wc}(\mathbf{w}, y_i \mathbf{x}_i)$. For a given $\mathbf{w}$, this loss can be seen to be minimized when $\boldsymbol{\alpha}_i$ is chosen to delete the K features x_{ij} with highest values $y_i w_j x_{ij}$, since these will have the strongest decreasing effect on the loss. Thus we can rewrite $h^{wc}(\mathbf{w}, y_i \mathbf{x}_i)$ as

$$h^{wc}(\mathbf{w}, y_i \mathbf{x}_i) \quad = \quad [1 - y_i \mathbf{w} \cdot \mathbf{x}_i + s_i]_+ \,,$$

where we have defined

$$s_i = \max_{\boldsymbol{\alpha}_i \in \{0,1\}^d, \sum_j \alpha_{ij} = K} y_i \mathbf{w} \cdot (\mathbf{x}_i \circ \boldsymbol{\alpha}_i) \tag{10.5}$$

as the maximum contribution of K features to the margin of sample $\mathbf{x}_i$.

To simplify the expression for s_i, we note that the integer constraint on the variables $\boldsymbol{\alpha}_i$ may be relaxed to $0 \le \boldsymbol{\alpha}_i \le 1$ without changing the optimum. This is true since the vertices of the resulting $2d + 1$ linear constraints are integral. Since the maximization (with respect to $\boldsymbol{\alpha}_i$) is over a linear function, the optimum will be at the vertices, and is therefore integral. We rewrite s_i using this relaxation, and also changing the order of multiplication

$$\begin{aligned} s_i = \quad &\max \quad y_i \left(\mathbf{w} \circ \mathbf{x}_i\right) \cdot \boldsymbol{\alpha}_i \\ &s.t. \quad 0 \le \boldsymbol{\alpha}_i \le 1 \\ &\qquad \sum_j \alpha_{ij} = K \ . \end{aligned} \tag{10.6}$$

The above expression is bilinear in $\boldsymbol{\alpha}_i$ and $\mathbf{w}$. Since this may potentially contribute a nonconvex factor to the optimization, we use a duality transformation with respect to the $\boldsymbol{\alpha}_i$ variables to avoid bilinearity. An important outcome of using a duality transformation is that a minimization problem is obtained so that the original minimax problem is turned into a minimization problem in the new variables. Note that the above problem is linear in $\boldsymbol{\alpha}_i$ so that the value of the dual will exactly equal that of s_i.[2]

Denoting the dual variables by $\mathbf{v}_i \in \mathbb{R}^d, z_i \in \mathbb{R}$, we obtain the dual of the maximization in (10.6):

$$\begin{aligned} s_i = \quad &\min \quad K z_i + \sum_j v_{ij} \\ &s.t. \quad z_i + \mathbf{v}_i \ge y_i \mathbf{x}_i \circ \mathbf{w} \\ &\qquad \mathbf{v}_i \ge 0 \ . \end{aligned} \tag{10.7}$$

To use this in the FDROP minimization problem (10.3), we introduce an auxiliary variable t_i, which at the optimum will obtain the minimum of (10.7). The resulting problem is a reformulation of the FDROP problem:

$$\begin{aligned} &\min \quad \tfrac{1}{2}\|\mathbf{w}\|^2 + C \sum_i \left[1 - y_i \mathbf{w} \cdot \mathbf{x}_i + t_i\right]_+ \\ &s.t. \quad t_i \ge K z_i + \sum_j v_{ij} \\ &\qquad \mathbf{v}_i \ge 0 \\ &\qquad z_i + \mathbf{v}_i \ge y_i \mathbf{x}_i \circ \mathbf{w} \ . \end{aligned} \tag{10.8}$$

The above problem can be easily converted into a standard quadratic program by introducing extra variables $\xi_i \ge 0$ (for $i = 1, \dots, n$) to represent the hinge function

---

2. Strong duality requires Slater's condition to hold (see Boyd and Vandenberghe [2004]), which is the case for the current problem.

via linear equalities:

$$
\begin{aligned}
\min \quad & \tfrac{1}{2}\|\mathbf{w}\|^2 + C\sum_i \xi_i \\
\text{s.t.} \quad & \xi_i \ge 1 - y_i \mathbf{w}\cdot\mathbf{x}_i + t_i \\
& \xi_i \ge 0 \\
& t_i \ge K z_i + \sum_j v_{ij} \\
& \mathbf{v}_i \ge 0 \\
& z_i + \mathbf{v}_i \ge y_i \mathbf{x}_i \circ \mathbf{w} \,.
\end{aligned}
\tag{10.9}
$$

We thus have the result that the FDROP problem in (10.3) is equivalent to the convex quadratic program (QP) in (10.9). The latter has $O(nd)$ variables and constraints, and can be solved using standard QP solvers. However, such solvers may not scale well with nd, and thus may not be usable for datasets with hundreds of thousands of variables and samples. For example, each iteration of an interior point method will require memory that is quadratic in nd and running time that is cubic in nd [Fine and Scheinberg, 2002]. In the next section we describe a method which is more suitable for these cases, and scales linearly with nd for both memory and running time.

10.3.2   Efficient Optimization Using Bundle Methods

The FDROP optimization problem in (10.3) involves minimization of a nondifferentiable (piecewise linear) function of the variable $\mathbf{w}$. Although such minimization problems cannot be solved using standard gradient methods (e.g., L-BFGS), there is a large class of subgradient methods which can be applied in this case [e.g., see Shalev-Shwartz et al., 2007; Nedic and Bertsekas, 2001]

In this section, we show how the recently introduced bundle method for regularized risk minimization, or BMRM [Teo et al., 2007b], may be applied to solving FDROP. BMRM is a generic method for solving convex regularized risk minimization problems, and does not have any tunable parameters, making it simple to implement. Furthermore, the cost of each BMRM iteration in terms of memory and running time scales linearly with the size of the problem. In what follows, we briefly review BMRM, and show how it can be applied to solve the FDROP problem.

Consider the following minimization problem:

$$
\min_{\mathbf{w}} \; J(\mathbf{w}) = \frac{1}{2}\|\mathbf{w}\|^2 + C R_{\text{emp}}(\mathbf{w})\,,
\tag{10.10}
$$

where $R_{\text{emp}}(\mathbf{w}) = \sum_{i=1}^n l(\mathbf{x}_i, y_i, \mathbf{w})$ and $l(\mathbf{x}_i, y_i, \mathbf{w})$ is a convex nonnegative loss

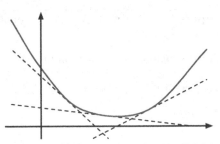

Figure 10.1 A convex function (solid line) is bounded from below by Taylor approximations of first order (dashed line). Adding more terms improves the bound.

function. The FDROP problem in (10.3) has this form with[3]

$$l(\mathbf{x}_i, y_i, \mathbf{w}) = h^{wc}(\mathbf{w}, y_i \mathbf{x}_i) \ . \tag{10.11}$$

The BMRM method solves the minimization in (10.10) by forming a piecewise linear lower bound on $R_{\text{emp}}(\mathbf{w})$, which is made tighter at each iteration. The bound relies on the fact that because of the convexity of $R_{\text{emp}}(\mathbf{w})$, the first-order Taylor expansion of $R_{\text{emp}}(\mathbf{w})$ at any point $\mathbf{w}_i$ is a (linear) lower bound on $R_{\text{emp}}(\mathbf{w})$:

$$R_{\text{emp}}(\mathbf{w}) \geq f(\mathbf{w}; \mathbf{w}_i) \ , \tag{10.12}$$

where

$$f(\mathbf{w}; \mathbf{w}_i) = R_{\text{emp}}(\mathbf{w}_i) + (\mathbf{w} - \mathbf{w}_i)\partial_{\mathbf{w}} R_{\text{emp}}(\mathbf{w}_i) \ , \tag{10.13}$$

and $\partial_{\mathbf{w}} R_{\text{emp}}(\mathbf{w}_i)$ is the subgradient of the function $R_{\text{emp}}(\mathbf{w})$ at the point $\mathbf{w}_i$. Taking the maximum of a set of such lower bounds for $\mathbf{w}_1, \ldots, \mathbf{w}_t$ also yields a lower bound on $R_{\text{emp}}(\mathbf{w})$:

$$R_{\text{emp}}(\mathbf{w}) \geq \max_{i=1,\ldots,t} f(\mathbf{w}; \mathbf{w}_i) \ , \tag{10.14}$$

and this bound becomes tighter as t grows. See figure 10.1 for an illustration. Since $R_{\text{emp}}(\mathbf{w})$ is nonnegative we may further tighten the lower bound by requiring it to be nonnegative:

$$R_{\text{emp}}(\mathbf{w}) \geq \max \left[0, \max_{i=1,\ldots,t} f(\mathbf{w}; \mathbf{w}_i)\right] \ . \tag{10.15}$$

The sequence of points $\mathbf{w}_1, \ldots, \mathbf{w}_t$ is chosen as follows: at iteration t we construct a function $J_t(\mathbf{w})$ that is a lower bound on $J(\mathbf{w})$

$$J_t(\mathbf{w}) = \frac{1}{2}\|\mathbf{w}\|^2 + C \max \left[0, \max_{i=1,\ldots,t} f(\mathbf{w}; \mathbf{w}_i)\right] \ . \tag{10.16}$$

---

3. The function $h^{wc}(\mathbf{w}, y_i \mathbf{x}_i)$ is convex in $\mathbf{w}$ since it is a maximum of functions that are linear in $\mathbf{w}$.

Inputs: A training set $\{\mathbf{x}_i, y_i\}_{i=1}^n$. Number of features to delete K. Desired precision $\epsilon > 0$.

Initialization: Set $\mathbf{w}_1 = \mathbf{0}$ and $t = 1$.

Algorithm:

- Repeat:
  - Define

  $$f(\mathbf{w}; \mathbf{w}_t) = \sum_{i=1}^n h^{wc}(\mathbf{w}_t, y_i \mathbf{x}_i) + (\mathbf{w} - \mathbf{w}_t) \sum_{i=1}^n \partial_{\mathbf{w}} h^{wc}(\mathbf{w}_t, y_i \mathbf{x}_i)$$

  where the subgradient is given in (10.20).
  - Solve the quadratic program:

  $$\begin{aligned} \min \quad & \tfrac{1}{2} \|\mathbf{w}\|^2 + C\xi \\ \text{s.t.} \quad & \xi \geq f(\mathbf{w}; \mathbf{w}_i) \quad i = 1, \ldots, t \\ & \xi \geq 0. \end{aligned}$$

  Denote the minimizer by $\mathbf{w}_{t+1}$, and the objective value by l_t.
  - Calculate upper bound $u_t = \tfrac{1}{2} \|\mathbf{w}_t\|^2 + C \sum_{i=1}^n h^{wc}(\mathbf{w}_t, y_i \mathbf{x}_i)$.
  - Halt if $u_t - l_t < \epsilon$.
  - Set $t = t + 1$.

Output: Final weight vector $\mathbf{w}_t$.

Figure 10.2 The BMRM algorithm applied to the FDROP problem.

The next point $\mathbf{w}_{t+1}$ is chosen to be the minimizer of $J_t(\mathbf{w})$, i.e.,

$$\mathbf{w}_{t+1} = \arg \min_{\mathbf{w}} J_t(\mathbf{w}) \ . \tag{10.17}$$

The minimization problem above can be expressed as a QP with t constraints by introducing an auxiliary variable ξ as follows

$$\begin{aligned} \min \quad & \tfrac{1}{2} \|\mathbf{w}\|^2 + C\xi \\ \text{s.t.} \quad & \xi \geq f(\mathbf{w}; \mathbf{w}_i) \quad i = 1, \ldots, t \\ & \xi \geq 0 \ . \end{aligned} \tag{10.18}$$

The above QP can be solved efficiently, as long as t is not too large. Teo et al. [2007b] prove that the BMRM method converges, and show that $O(\frac{1}{\epsilon})$ iterations are required to achieve a duality gap of ϵ. In practice, we have found that convergence is achieved after a few hundred iterations at most.

To apply BMRM to the FDROP problem, we need the subgradient of $R_{\text{emp}}(\mathbf{w}) = \sum_i h^{wc}(\mathbf{w}, y_i \mathbf{x}_i)$. Denote the $\boldsymbol{\alpha}_i$ that achieves the worst-case loss, for example i, by

$\boldsymbol{\alpha}_i^{\max}(\mathbf{w}, y_i\mathbf{x}_i)$ so that

$$
\begin{aligned}
\boldsymbol{\alpha}_i^{\max}(\mathbf{w}, y_i\mathbf{x}_i) = \quad &\arg\max \quad [1 - y_i\mathbf{w}\cdot(\mathbf{x}_i \circ (1-\boldsymbol{\alpha}_i))]_+ \\
&s.t. \qquad \boldsymbol{\alpha}_i \in \{0,1\}^d \\
&\qquad\qquad \textstyle\sum_j \alpha_{ij} = K \, .
\end{aligned}
\tag{10.19}
$$

In section 10.3.1 we showed that this $\boldsymbol{\alpha}_i^{\max}$ is obtained by finding the K features with maximal $y_i w_j x_{ij}$. The subgradient is then[4]

$$
\partial_{\mathbf{w}} h^{wc}(\mathbf{w}, y_i\mathbf{x}_i) = \left\{
\begin{array}{ll}
\mathbf{0} & \text{if } h^{wc}(\mathbf{w}, y_i\mathbf{x}_i) = 0 \\
-y_i\mathbf{x}_i \circ (1 - \boldsymbol{\alpha}_i^{\max}(\mathbf{w}, y_i\mathbf{x}_i)) & \text{if } h^{wc}(\mathbf{w}, y_i\mathbf{x}_i) > 0 \, .
\end{array}
\right.
\tag{10.20}
$$

The subgradient of R_{emp} is then given by

$$
\partial_{\mathbf{w}} R_{\mathrm{emp}}(\mathbf{w}) = \sum_i \partial_{\mathbf{w}} h^{wc}(\mathbf{w}, y_i\mathbf{x}_i) \, .
\tag{10.21}
$$

Finally, it is also possible to define a simple stopping criterion for BMRM. Note that the minimum value in (10.17) is a lower bound on the minimum of the FDROP problem. An upper bound may also be obtained by evaluating the FDROP objective at $\mathbf{w}_t$. Thus, the difference between these two bounds yields a measure of the accuracy of the current solution, and can be used as a stopping criterion. Pseudocode for the BMRM procedure is given in figure 10.2.

10.4   A Convex Dual for the Minimax Problem

The standard support vector machine problem is a convex quadratic problem, and has a dual convex which reveals some interesting properties and allows the use of kernel classifiers. Since our robust problem is also quadratic and convex, it is interesting to consider its dual problem. A standard duality transformation (e.g., see Boyd and Vandenberghe [2004]) can be used to show that the dual of our robust classifier construction problem is

$$
\begin{aligned}
&\min \quad \tfrac{1}{2}\| \textstyle\sum_i y_i\alpha_i\mathbf{x}_i \circ (1-\boldsymbol{\lambda}_i)\|^2 - \sum_i \alpha_i \\
&s.t. \quad 0 \le \boldsymbol{\alpha} \le C \\
&\qquad\quad 0 \le \lambda_i \le 1 \\
&\qquad\quad \textstyle\sum_j \lambda_{ij} = K \, ,
\end{aligned}
\tag{10.22}
$$

where the variables are $\boldsymbol{\alpha} \in \mathbb{R}^n$ where n is the number of samples, and $\boldsymbol{\lambda}_i \in \mathbb{R}^d$ for $i = 1,\dots,n$ where d is the dimension of the input. Furthermore, the optimal set of

---

4. Note that the subgradient is very similar to a perceptron update where the original point $\mathbf{x}_i$ has been replaced by its 'feature-deleted' version $\mathbf{x}_i \circ (1 - \boldsymbol{\alpha}_i^{\max}(\mathbf{w}, y_i\mathbf{x}_i))$.

weights $\mathbf{w}$ can be expressed as

$$\mathbf{w} = \sum_i y_i \alpha_i \mathbf{x}_i \circ (1 - \boldsymbol{\lambda}_i) \ . \tag{10.23}$$

The above problem can be written in an alternative form, where it is more clearly convex:

$$
\begin{aligned}
\min \quad & \tfrac{1}{2} \| \sum_i y_i \mathbf{x}_i \circ (\alpha_i - \boldsymbol{\lambda}_i) \|^2 - \sum_i \alpha_i \\
\text{s.t.} \quad & 0 \le \boldsymbol{\alpha} \le C \\
& 0 \le \boldsymbol{\lambda}_i \le \alpha_i \\
& \sum_j \lambda_{ij} = K \alpha_i \ .
\end{aligned}
\tag{10.24}
$$

Here the expression in the norm is an affine function of the variables, and thus the problem is convex.

Recall that the SVM dual is

$$
\begin{aligned}
\min \quad & \tfrac{1}{2} \| \sum_i \alpha_i y_i \mathbf{x}_i \|^2 - \sum_i \alpha_i \\
\text{s.t.} \quad & 0 \le \boldsymbol{\alpha} \le C \ ,
\end{aligned}
\tag{10.25}
$$

where $\mathbf{w} = \sum_i \alpha_i y_i \mathbf{x}_i$.

Thus, in our case the weight vector is not a combination of input vectors, but rather a combination of vectors weighted by elements of weight *up to* α_i where the maximal number of elements that may be set to zero is K. Interestingly, the $\boldsymbol{\lambda}_i$ values can be fractional, so that none of the features has to be completely deleted.

Note that, as opposed to the standard SVM, our dual objective will not involve dot products between $\mathbf{x}_i$, but rather between vectors $\mathbf{x}_i \circ (1 - \boldsymbol{\lambda}_i)$. Thus it is not immediately clear if and how kernel methods may be put to use in this case. This is not surprising, since the algorithm is strongly linked to the structure of the sample space $\mathbb{R}^d$, where features are dropped. Dropping such features alters the kernel function. For a given kernel function, one may consider the relevant minimax problem and try to solve for the $\mathbf{w}$ and $\boldsymbol{\alpha}$ variables, in a similar fashion to Weston et al. [2000]. However, for nonlinear kernels this would typically result in a nonconvex optimization problem, and would depend on the specific kernel used. It thus remains an interesting challenge to obtain globally optimal algorithms for this case.

10.5   An Alternate Setting: Uniform Feature Deletion

In section 10.2, we assumed that different features may be deleted for different data points. We can also consider an alternative formulation where once a feature is chosen to be deleted it is deleted uniformly from all data points simultaneously. Clearly, this scenario is subsumed by the one described in the previous section, and is thus less pessimistic.

The worst-case hinge loss is defined as in the nonuniform case in (10.2). However, now there is a single $\boldsymbol{\alpha}$ vector for all examples, whereas in the previous scenario, each sample had its own vector. The optimization thus becomes

$$\mathbf{w}^* = \min_{\mathbf{w}} \; \max_{\boldsymbol{\alpha}} \quad \|\mathbf{w}\|^2 + C \sum_i \left[1 - y_i \mathbf{w} \cdot (\mathbf{x}_i \circ (1 - \boldsymbol{\alpha}))\right]_+$$
$$\text{s.t.} \quad \boldsymbol{\alpha} \in \{0,1\}^d$$
$$\sum_j \alpha_j = K \; .$$

We first note that the above optimization problem is still convex in $\mathbf{w}$. To see why, denote by $f(\mathbf{w})$ the maximum value over all legal $\boldsymbol{\alpha}$ assignments for a given value of $\mathbf{w}$. Then $f(\mathbf{w})$ is a pointwise maximum over a set of convex functions and is thus convex [Boyd and Vandenberghe, 2004] . The problem of minimizing over $\mathbf{w}$ is therefore convex.

However, although it is convex, the current optimization problem appears more difficult than the one in the previous section, due to the presence of the $\boldsymbol{\alpha}$ in all the sum elements. As before, the integral constraints on $\boldsymbol{\alpha}$ can be relaxed, since the maximum of the inner optimization is attained at the vertices (because the target is convex). However, since the target is nonlinear (a hinge function) this maximization is not itself a convex problem, and does not seem to be efficiently solvable.

The problem *can* be solved efficiently as long as $\binom{d}{K}$ is sufficiently small so that all the feasible values of $\boldsymbol{\alpha}$ can be enumerated over. However, our experiments show that in many cases K needs to be at least 10, so that the uniform method is often not applicable.

10.6   Related Frameworks

The FDROP problem was motivated from a minimax perspective where the goal is to minimize the loss incurred by an adversary. In this section we discuss alternative interpretations of our framework, in the context of feature selection and learning with invariances.

10.6.1   Feature Selection

The adversary in the FDROP minimax problem identifies those input features whose contribution to the margin is maximal. In this sense, the adversary can be thought of as being related to feature selection algorithms which try to find the set of features which, when taken alone, would yield optimal generalization (e.g., see Yang and Pedersen [1997]). A clear illustration of this effect can be seen in figure 10.4 (section 10.7.2).

However, the current minimax setup differs from the standard feature selection approach in two important aspects. The first is that here we focus on feature *elimination*, i.e., finding the set of features whose elimination would maximally decrease performance. Intuitively, these features should also convey high information when taken on their own, but this is not guaranteed to be the case.

The other aspect which distinguishes the current approach from feature selection is that here features are selected (or eliminated to be precise), for every sample individually. The uniform feature deletion approach described in section 10.5 is more in line with the standard feature selection framework.

We can provide a somewhat more formal treatment of feature selection optimization algorithms which highlights their relation to the current approach. The standard feature selection goal is to find a set of K features which minimize generalization error. A reasonable approximation is the empirical error, or the hinge loss in our case. Thus the feature selection problem can be posed as (we omit the regularization term here)

$$\begin{aligned}
\min \quad & \sum_i [1 - y_i \mathbf{w} \cdot (\mathbf{x}_i \circ \boldsymbol{\alpha})]_+ \\
s.t. \quad & \boldsymbol{\alpha} \in \{0,1\}^d \\
& \sum_j \alpha_j = K
\end{aligned} \tag{10.26}$$

such that minimization is over both $\boldsymbol{\alpha}$ and $\mathbf{w}$. Denote by $f(\mathbf{w})$ the minimum over $\boldsymbol{\alpha}$ assignments for a given value of $\mathbf{w}$. Then $f(\mathbf{w})$ is a pointwise minimum of convex functions and is thus generally nonconvex. Thus the optimization problem in (10.26) is not convex, and is generally hard to solve. Furthermore, for a large number of features, calculating $f(\mathbf{w})$ requires enumeration over possible $\boldsymbol{\alpha}$ assignments. The problem may be approximated via different relaxations as in Gilad-Bachrach et al. [2004] or Weston et al. [2000].

The above problem may be slightly altered to resemble our current formulation by allowing the best K features to be chosen on a *per sample* basis (a single set of features might then be selected, for example, by taking the features chosen most often across samples). The resulting optimization problem is

$$\begin{aligned}
\min \quad & \sum_i [1 - y_i \mathbf{w} \cdot (\mathbf{x}_i \circ \boldsymbol{\alpha}_i)]_+ \\
s.t. \quad & \boldsymbol{\alpha}_i \in \{0,1\}^d \\
& \sum_j \alpha_{ij} = K \; .
\end{aligned} \tag{10.27}$$

This problem is easier than that in (10.26) in that the minimization over $\boldsymbol{\alpha}_i$ is always tractable: the minimizing $\boldsymbol{\alpha}_i$ is the one which has the minimum contribution to the margin. However, the function $f(\mathbf{w})$ is again nonconvex, and thus it seems that the problem remains hard.

It is interesting that these two feature selection variants, while similar in spirit to our minimax problems, seem to have considerably higher complexity, in terms of optimization efficiency. This suggests the FDROP approach may also prove useful for feature selection by finding the set of features it tends to *delete*.

10.6.2   Learning with Invariances

In some learning scenarios, it is reasonable to assume that an input point may be perturbed in certain ways without changing its class. For example, digits may undergo translations or rotations by small angles. Several recent works have addressed learning in this setting [Teo et al., 2007a; Graepel and Herbrich, 2004; Decoste and Schölkopf, 2002]. They share the common approach of assuming that the set of possible perturbations of a data point **x** generate a *cloud* of virtual data points, and that the margin of the point **x** should be measured with respect to this cloud.

Our adversarial view of feature deletion may also be interpreted in the above framework. The cloud of points in this case would be the point **x** and all points that correspond to K feature deletions on **x**. Our worst-case margin in (10.2) may then be interpreted as the worst-case margin of any point within this cloud of virtual points. Note, however, that the FDROP problem can be solved without explicitly generating the virtual points, using the methods in section 10.3. In Teo et al. [2007a] we provide a general formalism of such invariance learning, and show how algorithms such as BMRM [Teo et al., 2007b] may be applied to solving it. Under this formalism, any invariance may be used, as long as an efficient algorithm exists for finding the point with worst-case margin. One extension of FDROP which we present in Teo et al. [2007a] is to the case where features are not necessarily deleted, but scaled by some minimum and maximum factor. This new invariance is shown to improve generalization performance on a spam filtering task, when compared to both FDROP and standard SVM.[5]

10.7 Experiments

In this section we apply FDROP to synthetic and real data. We shall especially be interested in evaluating performance when features are deleted from the test set. Thus, for example, we test handwritten digit recognition when pixels are removed from the image. We first focus on relatively small training sets, such that the inherent sparseness of the problem is high, and most classification algorithms are likely to overfit. In section 10.7.3 we report results on a large-scale spam filtering experiment, with hundreds of thousands of features. In all experiments, we compare our method with a linear support vector machine algorithm.[6]

For the small-scale experiments (sections 10.7.1 and 10.7.2) we used the QP approach in section 10.3.1 (the ILOG-CPLEX package was used to solve the QPs). For the large scale experiment the BMRM method was used (see section 10.3.2).

---

5. We present results for the same spam dataset in section 10.7.3, but since different preprocessing is used, the results differ from those in Teo et al. [2007a].
6. In sections 10.7.1 and 10.7.2 both FDROP and SVM use a bias term, by adding a constant feature $x_{d+1} = 1$. The FDROP algorithm was not *allowed* to delete the bias feature $x_{d+1} = 1$. In section 10.7.3 we did not use a bias term, since this degraded the results for both algorithms.

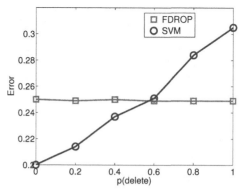

Figure 10.3   Evaluation of FDROP and SVM on a toy logistic regression example, where a highly informative feature is randomly dropped from the test sample. The value of K was set to 1. The figure shows classification error as a function of the deletion probability $p(delete)$.

10.7.1   A Synthetic Example

To illustrate the advantages of the current method, we apply it to a setting where the test data indeed differs from the training data by deleting features. We consider a feature vector in $\mathbf{x} \in \mathbb{R}^{20}$ where training examples are drawn uniformly in that space. The label is assigned according to a logistic regression rule:

$$p(y = 1|\mathbf{x}) \propto e^{\mathbf{w}\cdot\mathbf{x}+b} . \tag{10.28}$$

In our experiments, $w_1 = 5$ and all the other $w_i = -2$. The bias b was set to the mean of $\mathbf{w}$. Thus the feature x_1 is likely to be assigned a high weight by learning algorithms which do not expect feature deletion. In the test data, we delete the feature x_1, i.e., set it to zero, with a given probability $p(delete)$. We compare the performance of our FDROP minimax algorithm (with $K = 1$) to that of a standard SVM. For both methods, we choose the weight of the regularization parameter C via cross-validation.

Figure 10.3 shows the resulting error rates. It can be seen that as the probability of deletion increases, the performance of SVM decreases, while that of the minimax algorithm stays roughly constant. This constant behavior is due to the fact that the FDROP classifier is optimized for the worst-case when this feature is deleted. To understand this behavior further, we checked which feature was deleted by FDROP for every one of the samples. Indeed, on *all* the cases where $x_1 = 1$ and $y = 1$, it was x_1 that was deleted in the optimization.

10.7.2   Handwritten Digit Classification

Image classification into categories should in principle be robust to pixel deletion, or in other words deletion of parts of the image. Our game-theoretic framework captures this intuition by modeling the worst-case pixel deletion scenario.

We investigated the application of FDROP to classifying handwritten digits, and focused on robustness to pixel deletion in these images. We applied FDROP to the MNIST dataset [LeCun et al., 1995] of handwritten digits, and focused on binary problems with small training sets of 50 samples per digit. Furthermore, we only considered binary problems created by label pairs which had more than 5% error when learned using an SVM (the chosen pairs were $(4,9),(3,5),(7,9),(5,8),(3,8),(2,8),(2,3),(8,9),(5,6), (2,7),(4,7)$, and $(2,6)$). The size in pixels of each digit was (28×28). A holdout sample of size 200 was used to optimize the algorithm parameters, and a set of 300 samples was used for testing. The holdout set underwent the same pixel deletion as the test set, in order to achieve a fair comparison between SVM and FDROP. Experiments were repeated with 20 random subsets of the above sizes.

To evaluate the robustness of the algorithm to feature deletion, we trained it on the raw data (i.e., without deleted features), and then tested it on data from which K features were deleted. The values of K were $(0, 25, 50, 75, 100, 125, 150)$.

Figure 10.4 gives a visual representation of the feature deletion process. The FDROP minimax optimization deletes K features from every sample point. We can find which features were deleted from each sample by finding the K features with maximum margin contribution at the optimal $\mathbf{w}$. Figure 10.4 illustrates these features for three sample points. Each row displays the original raw input image and the same input image with the K most *destructive* features deleted (here $K = 50$). It can be seen that FDROP chooses to delete the features which maximize the resemblance between the given digit and digits in the other class. These results suggest that FDROP may indeed be useful as a feature selection mechanism.

Classification error rate should intuitively decrease as more features are deleted. The goal of FDROP is to minimize the damage incurred by such deletion. Figure 10.5 shows the dependence of classification error on the number of deleted features for both FDROP and SVM. The parameter K is taken as an unknown and is chosen to minimize error on the holdout sample for each digit pair and deletion level separately. It can be seen that FDROP suffers less degradation in error when compared to SVM. Furthermore, the optimal K grows monotonically with the number of deleted features, as is intuitively expected. The dependence on K for a specific digit pair (4 and 7) and deletion level (50 deletions) is shown in figure 10.6. It can be seen that performance is improved up to a value of $K = 25$ which supposedly matches the deletion level in the dataset (recall that FDROP considers a worst-case scenario, whereas here features are dropped randomly, so that K and the actual number of deleted features should not be expected to be close numerically).

10.7.3 Spam Filtering

One of the difficulties in filtering spam email from legitimate email is that the problem is dynamic in nature, in the sense that spam authors react to spam filters by changing content. In this sense, it is indeed a game where the two players are the spam filter and spam authors. Our formalism captures this competition, and it

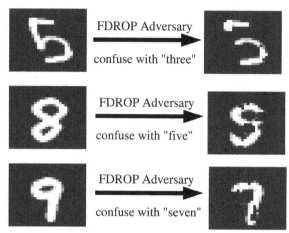

Figure 10.4 Illustration of adversarial feature (pixel) deletion for handwritten digits. Three binary classification problems were created from the MNIST digit database by discriminating the classes "five" vs. "three" (*top*), "eight" vs. "five" (*middle*), and "seven" vs. "nine." The training data consisted of 50 samples per class. The number of deleted features was $K = 50$. The images show three corresponding examples of features deleted by the FDROP adversary. The left column shows the original digit, and the right column shows the digit with the 50 pixels dropped by the FDROP algorithm. It can be seen that the worst-case against which our algorithm attempts to be robust corresponds to the deletion of extremely discriminative features for each example: the top right digit has been made to look as much as possible like a "three," the middle right digit very much like a "five" and the bottom right digit has been distorted to look very much like a "seven."

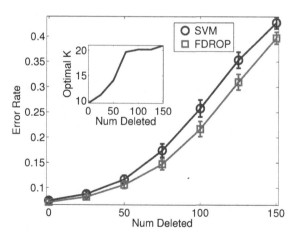

Figure 10.5 Classification error rate for the MNIST dataset, as a function of the number of features deleted from the test set. Standard errors over 20 repetitions are shown on the curve. The optimal K parameter for the FDROP algorithm was chosen per classification problem and per number of deleted features. The inset shows the optimal K for each deletion scheme.

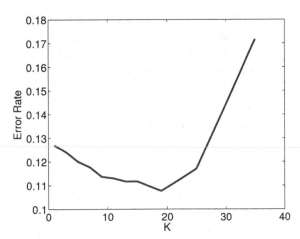

Figure 10.6 Classification error as a function of the parameter K for the digit pair $(4, 7)$ with 50 deleted features.

Table 10.1 Results on the ECML'06 spam detection task for the SVM and FDROP algorithms. The table reports classification accuracy and area under the ROC curve (AUC). The values of C and K were obtained by optimizing over a separate tuning dataset.

Method	Accuracy %	AUC %	Parameters (K, C)
SVM	77.20	90.02	(0, 1.25)
FDROP	86.63	94.03	(14, 1.25)

is therefore interesting to apply it to this case. Clearly, spam authors may change their email in ways other than removing words. For example they may add *good* words, or change the spelling of words [Lowd and Meek, 2005; Wittel and Wu, 2004; Dalvi et al., 2004]. Here we limit the adversarial strategy to word deletion, but our method may be extended to handling other strategies, using its extension in Teo et al. [2007a].

In the experiments described in previous sections, we used relatively small sample sizes and data dimensionality. In these cases, the FDROP problem could be solved using the QP in (10.8). The current section focuses on a much larger problem, where the QP in (10.8) becomes too big to solve using standard solvers. However, the problem can still be solved using the BMRM method described in section 10.3.2.

We used the ECML'06 Discovery Challenge (Task A) evaluation dataset [Bickel, 2006]. The training set consists of 4000 emails from a single inbox whereas the testing set consists of 7500 emails from three different inboxes. The vocabulary size was $d = 206,908$. We followed the approach of Drucker et al. [1999] by preprocessing the bag-of-word feature vectors into binary vectors and then normalizing them to unit norm. The values of C and K were chosen to optimize performance on a separate tuning dataset.

Performance was compared to a linear SVM, and measured in terms of classification accuracy and the area under the ROC curve (AUC). Results are reported in table 10.1. It can be seen that FDROP significantly outperforms SVM on this task, for both performance measures. We emphasize that the test data was not changed, and no features were artificially deleted, so that FDROP indeed results in robustness and improved generalization performance.

10.8　Discussion and Conclusions

We have introduced a novel method for learning classifiers which are minimax optimal under a worst-case scenario of feature deletion at test time. This is an important step toward extending statistical learning paradigms beyond the restrictive assumption that the training and testing data must come from the same distribution. An alternative view of our algorithm is as a feature selection method which seeks the features which are most crucial for performance. A key assumption of our approach is that small sets of features should not be relied upon at test time to faithfully represent the class structure. Thus, in some sense, the features available to the algorithm at training time are viewed as being subject to random, or even deliberate removal at test time. Interestingly, a recent paper by Krupka and Tishby [2006] presents a related view of features, where one considers a learning scheme where features are selected randomly from a large set, and generalization is studied with respect to unseen features.

Clearly, in some cases the adversarial model may be too strong, and thus result in decreased performance when compared to a standard SVM. For example, the data may not undergo any feature deletion, or we may have a large enough training set so that there is no need to introduce robustness via feature deletion. In these cases it may be preferable to use our model with $K = 0$. One way of addressing this issue is to use cross-validation in choosing the parameter K, so that if $K = 0$ yields lower errors on a validation set, it will be used in the final classifier. This is the approach we used in our experiments, and we indeed found that it results in lower K values in problems where fewer features are deleted.

A different game-theoretic approach to feature selection was previously suggested by Cohen et al. [2005]. Their approach is related to Shapley values in cooperative games. The Shapley value is a measure of the performance drop incurred by dropping a feature from a given set of features, where this performance is averaged over all subsets in which this feature participates. It is thus close in spirit to our feature elimination approach. However, our approach searches for multiple features simultaneously and is furthermore tractable, as opposed to exact calculation of Shapley values.

The notion of robustness to feature deletion is not limited to the classification setting. One may consider a similar setting in the context of regression or dimensionality reduction. It would be interesting to extend the method described here to these settings.

Finally, while here we focus on an adversary that deletes features, the formalism can be easily extended to other perturbations of the feature vector. In Teo et al.

[2007a] we outline such a general approach, and provide algorithms for solving the resulting optimization problem.

IV   Discussion

11   Author Comments

Hidetoshi Shimodaira
Masashi Sugiyama
Amos Storkey
Arthur Gretton
Shai-Ben David

*In the following some of the chapter authors are given the opportunity to express
their personal views about dataset shift in machine learning. The authors wrote their
comments without knowledge of what comments were being written by the others.
As a consequence this chapter is not a discussion.*

Hidetoshi Shimodaira

Covariate Shift and Misspecification
I would like to express my personal opinion on these two topics.

1. Covariate shift

Last December, a workshop on statistical machine learning was held at Tokyo
Institute of Technology. At the end of a talk given by Dr. Sugiyama on his recent
research, Prof. Shun-ichi Amari asked a question: Why is it called covariate shift?
As a member of the audience, I answered that I had thought of this term for the
purpose of making a title for a paper published in 2000. In light of the question, it
is apparent that my attempt for indicating the context was a failure.

It has been known for a long time in statistics and related fields that a sampling
mechanism changes the distribution of samples from a population. The subject is
sometimes called incomplete data or selection bias, and covariate shift is only a
special form of it. The simple structure of covariate shift made it easy to be solved
clearly; the log-likelihood is to be weighted by the ratio of the density for test
samples to that for observed samples. This importance weighting was not a main
contribution of Shimodaira [2000], but the focus was on the information criterion for

improving the inference by altering the weights as well as applying these frequentist arguments to Bayesian inference.

Selection bias without a specific structure is a difficult problem. We may have to give up unbiased estimation of model parameters. In the study of the selectivity bias, instead, we try to know how sensitively inference about the parameters depends on departures from randomness; [Copas and Eguchi, 2001].

2. Model misspecification

My talk at the December workshop was on the multiscale bootstrap [Shimodaira, 2008], which is a resampling algorithm to compute a very accurate p-value for hypothesis testing. My research has shifted to this subject since I was working on covariate shift about ten years ago, partly because I did not have a good application for covariate shift; yet I was very excited about the theory. I would like to mention my experience with model misspecification in my current research.

The multiscale bootstrap and a related testing procedure of mine are popular in the field of molecular evolution. They are used for computing a confidence level for an inferred phylogenetic tree, which is a labeled tree representing the branching order of species. The substitution of DNA along the branches, i.e., the evolution, is modeled as a Markov process. Researchers have been elaborating on complicated parametric models by incorporating several aspects of evolution. However, we are behind the rapid accumulation of DNA data, and the models are always misspecified considerably; the assumed parametric models are very distant from the true distribution with respect to the size of the data.

Covariate shift is introduced in Shimodaira [2000] by assuming model misspecification. It is also shown there that we should forget the covariate shift for the optimal estimation of parameters if the model is correctly specified. Then, someone may think that we should avoid misspecification by devising a complicated model. This is correct. In reality, however, good fitting models with a modest number of parameters are hard to obtain except for very simple applications. On the other hand, one may think that we should employ model-free methods. Practitioners, however, tend to use parametric models, because the emphasis of inference is often on the interpretation, yet it is formulated mathematically in terms of prediction error.

Masashi Sugiyama

Is Importance Weighting Needed under Covariate Shift?

Covariate shift matters in parameter learning only when the model used for function learning is misspecified (i.e., the model is so simple that the true learning target function cannot be expressed). When the model is correctly (or overly) specified, ordinary maximum likelihood estimation (MLE) is still consistent. Following this fact, there is a criticism that covariate shift adaptation by importance weighting is not needed, but just the use of a complex enough (or a nonparametric) model with ordinary MLE can settle the problem.

However, too complex models result in huge variance, so we need to choose a complex enough but not too complex a model for better generalization performance. In order to perform model selection, we often use an unbiased generalization error estimation method such as Akaike's information criterion or cross-validation. However, these generalization error estimation methods are heavily biased for misspecified models under covariate shift. Instead, importance-weighted variants can eliminate the bias and are therefore more reliable under covariate shift (see e.g., chapter 6 and chapter 7). In the model selection process, we cannot avoid computing the generalization error estimates for misspecified models since the purpose is to rule out such models from appropriate ones. For this reason, the use of (and therefore estimation of) the importance weights is indispensable when covariate shift occurs. Thus accurately estimating the importance weights (see e.g., chapter 8 and chapter 9) is very important and we need to further investigate this issue.

Amos Storkey

The problem of dataset shift is knowing precisely what shifts are possible. Without some understanding of what bias can be introduced, any sort of correspondence between the training space and test space can be introduced, and knowledge of the training data will be of no use in the test environment. The biggest difficulty in dataset shift is that the only thing we can use to infer the correspondence is the covariate distributions, and any information in the training target values that can help to characterize the structure of those distributions. This seems to be a tough problem to develop generalized or automated methods for.

There are two other fields which make the problem more manageable. The first is semisupervised learning. In most circumstances semisupervised learning is used in stationary environments. However, the use of methods in this book, combined with the valuable test-scenario target information that is available in the semisupervised context, will, I expect, provide very powerful automated approaches to dataset shift. This is also only realistic. Who is going to apply predictions obtained from a dataset shift method without ever validating the results in the test domain? Only the most foolhardy practitioner. Clearly, then, *some* information from the test domain is going to have to be available at some stage.

The second of these two fields is the general areas of multitask learning and transfer learning. Here much more contextual covariate distribution information is available. This will allow much firmer characterizations of the types of changes that can happen in a particular environment, and hence allow a firmer grasp of the likely transfer scenario. Again, many of the methods in this book can be straightforwardly generalized to multiple training scenarios. In many situations it will be fair to presume that the form of shift between the training scenarios is common to the form of shift between the training and test scenario. This is a great benefit in assessing what shift could occur.

Arthur Gretton

If the model is correct and parameters are properly set, then there may not be a benefit in covariate shift (that said, we found experimentally that it is a different story for local learning, where the "test set" has one or few points, but this is beyond the scope of our chapter: see, for instance, work by Bottou and Vapnik on this topic). In cases where we had lots of data and cross-validated carefully, the differences between using the unweighted training sample and weighted training sample were fairly small, and not always advantageous. However there are several reasons for not using a "correct" model, but rather a deliberately simpler one: these include interpretability and difficulties in effective model selection, especially for higher-dimensional data and small sample sizes, making more conservative models a safe choice (this is why, for instance, linear classifiers are so popular in fMRI studies). When these considerations cause us to choose a simpler model than suggested by cross-validation/marginal likelihood optimization, then more significant benefits can be obtained.

Shai Ben-David

My comments relate to two notions that I view as central to any theory of learning that aims to have practical implications. The first notion is that of an "Inductive bias" or some learner prior knowledge. We know very well that without restricting the class of potential predictors no reliable learning is possible. This is the famous "no free lunch" phenomenon. Such restrictions can either have the form of strong assumptions about the data generating distribution (as in the Valiant version of the PAC model), they can take the more flexible form of a prior distribution over the family of possible data generating distributions (like the classical Bayes type learning), or they can come through the use of a benchmark comparison class of predictors, aiming to perform as well as the best predictor in some fixed benchmark set of predictors (such an approach is taken by expert models for online learning as well as by the agnostic models of PAC learning).

Regretfully, some of the current work on learning in the dataset shift setting fail to make such an explicit assumption. Most notably, the common "covariate shift" assumption (stating that the change between the training data and the test data is only in the marginal data distribution and not in the conditional distribution of labels) is practically vacuous without an explicit restriction of the possible class of data labeling functions. Under the more realistic scenario, where the domain (or the support of the data generating distributions) is much larger than the training and test sample sizes, it is unlikely that the same domain point will occur in both training and test samples. Therefore, any label behavior over the training and test sample is consistent with such a "bias-free" covariate shift assumption. For example, seeing a training sample where all the labels are '1' and then a test sample where all the labels are zero can be likely if the data labeling function is one fixed function defining the test, or both the training and test data, and the only difference is that the marginal example distribution for the training data has its support over the domain points that have label '1', and the test distribution concentrates on the points labeled zero. Of course, no transfer of learning between these two domains is possible in such a scenario. In contrast, the covariate shift assumption does carry significant content once it is paired by an assumption restricting the set of potential labeling functions (say, assuming the labels are well approximated by some linear function over the data domain).

Another topic that suffers from insufficient acknowledgment of the importance of such inductive bias is the discussion of the relative virtues of "large-capacity classifiers" vs. "small-capacity classifiers." Of course, a "small-capacity" set of classifier can model only restricted families of data behavior. But the use of such small-capacity classes is inevitable if one wishes to have any finite sample size performance guarantees. "Large-capacity" classes are prone to overfitting, and no learning theory with practical aspirations should ignore this issue.

This brings me to the other central issue - the finiteness of the training data. Asymptotic analysis is a very rich fruitful field from a pure mathematical perspective, yet it bears very little significance to any real learning tasks. Consequently, some mathematically attractive notions, like "universal kernels," and the apparent "miracles" that they can do, seem to me completely detached from and irrelevant to any realistic learning task. Kernels that encode all the important knowledge of the data distributions on their means are totally useless under any finite training data setting. While the true kernel expectation may be very informative, from finite data we can only approximate it, and there exists no bound on the error in the estimation of relevant information that is associated with the approximation error of that expectation.

Not only that any reasonable learning model should assume the finiteness of training data (both labeled and unlabeled) to qualify as relevant to practical learning tasks, this finiteness assumption should be further strengthened by the realization that it is highly unlikely for the same domain point to occur in both the training and test domain sample data. Consequently, I view any method that is based on estimating the data shift distributions based on frequency counts of domain points in the available samples as a quite irrelevant highly theoretical construct.

References

N. Abe and H. Mamitsuka. Query learning strategies using boosting and bagging. In *Proceedings of the Fifteenth International Conference on Machine Learning*, pages 1–10, 1998.

H. Akaike. A new look at the statistical model identification. *IEEE Transactions on Automatic Control*, 19(6):716–723, 1974.

R. Akbani, S. Kwek, and N. Japkowicz. Applying support vector machines to imbalanced datasets. In *Machine Learning: ECML 2004*, pages 39–50, 2004.

S. Amari. *Differential-Geometrical Methods in Statistics*, volume 28 of *Lecture Notes in Statistics*. Springer Verlag, New York, 1985.

S. Amari and H. Nagaoka. *Methods of Information Geometry*, volume 191 of *Translations of Mathematical Monographs*. American Mathematical Society and Oxford University Press, 2000.

F. Bach. Active learning for misspecified generalized linear models. In B. Schölkopf, J. Platt, and T. Hofmann, editors, *Advances in Neural Information Processing Systems 19*, pages 65–72. MIT Press, Cambridge, MA, 2007.

A. Basu and B. G. Lindsay. Minimum disparity estimation for continuous models: Efficiency, distributions and robustness. *Annals of the Institute of Statistical Mathematics*, 46:683–705, 1994.

T. Batu, L. Fortnow, R. Rubinfeld, W. Smith, and P. White. Testing that distributions are close. In *FOCS*, volume 41, pages 259–269, 2000.

J. Baxter. A model of inductive bias learning. *Journal of Artificial Intelligence Research*, 12:149–198, 2000.

S. Ben-David, J. Blitzer, K. Crammer, and F. Pereira. Analysis of representations for domain adaptation. In *Advances in Neural Information Processing Systems 19*, MIT Press, Cambridge, MA, 2007.

S. Ben-David and R. Schuller. Exploiting task relatedness for multiple task learning. In *Proceedings of the Sixteenth Annual Conference on Learning Theory (COLT)*, 2003.

S. Bickel. ECML-PKDD Discovery Challenge 2006 Overview. In *Proceedings of the ECML-PKDD Discovery Challenge Workshop*, 2006.

S. Bickel, M. Brückner, and T. Scheffer. Discriminative learning for differing training and test distributions. In *Proceedings of the International Conference on Machine Learning*, 2007.

S. Bickel and T. Scheffer. Dirichlet-enhanced spam filtering based on biased samples. In *Advances in Neural Information Processing Systems 19*, MIT Press, Cambridge, MA, 2007.

C. M. Bishop. *Neural Networks for Pattern Recognition*. Clarendon Press, Oxford, 1995.

D. M. Blei, A. Ng, and M. I. Jordan. Latent Dirichlet allocation. *Journal of Machine Learning Research*, 3:993–1022, 2003.

J. Blitzer, R. McDonald, and F. Pereira. Domain adaptation with structural correspondence learning. In *Proceedings of the 2006 Conference on Empirical Methods in Natural Language Processing*, pages 120–128, 2006.

E. V. Bonilla, F. A. Agakov, and C. K. I. Williams. Kernel multi-task learning using task-specific features. In *Proceedings of AISTATS 2007*, 2007.

O. Bousquet, O. Chapelle, and M. Hein. Measure based regularization. In S. Thrun, L. Saul, and B. Schölkopf, editors, *Advances in Neural Information Processing Systems 16*, MIT Press, Cambridge, MA, 2004.

A. C. Bovik, J. D. Gibson, and A. Bovik, editors. *Handbook of Image and Video Processing*. Academic Press, Orlando, FL, 2000.

S. Boyd and L. Vandenberghe. *Convex Optimization*. Cambridge University Press, New York, 2004.

L. Breiman, J. Friedman, R. Olshen, and C. Stone. *Classification and Regression Trees*. Chapman & Hall, New York, 1984.

G. Casella and R. Berger. *Statistical Inference*, 2nd edition. Duxbury, Pacific Grove, CA, 2002.

O. Chapelle. Training a support vector machine in the primal. *Neural Computation*, 19:1155–1178, 2007.

N. V. Chawla, K. W. Bowyer, L. O. Hall, and W. P. Kegelmeyer. SMOTE: Synthetic minority over-sampling technique. *Journal of Artificial Intelligence Research*, 16: 321–357, 2002.

N. V. Chawla, N. Japkowich, and A. Kolcz. Editorial: Special issue on learning from imbalanced data sets. *SIGKDD Explorations*, 6:1–6, 2004.

N. V. Chawla and G. Karakoulas. Learning from labeled and unlabeled data: An empirical study across techniques and domains. *Journal of Artificial Intelligence Research*, 23:331–366, 2005.

S. Cohen, E. Ruppin, and G. Dror. Feature selection based on the Shapley value. In L. P. Kaelbling and A. Saffiotti, editors, *Proceedings of the Nineteenth International Joint Conference on Artificial Intelligence*, pages 665–670. Professional Book Center, 2005.

D. A. Cohn. Neural network exploration using optimal experimental design. In

Advances in Neural Information Processing Systems 6, pages 679–686, Morgan-Kaufmann, San Francisco, 1994.

D. A. Cohn, Z. Ghahramani, and M. I. Jordan. Active learning with statistical models. *Journal of Artificial Intelligence Research*, 4:129–145, 1996.

J. Copas and S. Eguchi. Local sensitivity approximation for selectivity bias. *Journal of the Royal Statistical Society: Series B*, 63:871–895, 2001.

D. Corfield. *Towards a Philosophy of Real Mathematics*. Cambridge University Press, New York, 2003.

P. Craven and G. Wahba. Smoothing noisy data with spline functions: Estimating the correct degree of smoothing by the method of generalized cross-validation. *Numerische Mathematik*, 31:377–403, 1979.

N. A. C. Cressie. *Statistics for Spatial Data*. Wiley, New York, 1993.

Y.-H. Dai and R. Fletcher. New algorithms for singly linearly constrained quadratic programs subject to lower and upper bounds. *Mathematical Programming: Series A and B Archive*, 106(3):403–421, 2006.

N. Dalvi, P. Domingos, Mausam, S. Sanghai, and D. Verma. Adversarial classification. In *Proceedings of the Tenth ACM SIGKDD International Conference on Knowledge Discovery and Data Mining*, pages 99–108, ACM Press, New York, 2004.

D. Decoste and B. Schölkopf. Training invariant support vector machines. *Machine Learning*, 46(1-3):161–190, 2002.

L. Devroye, L. Györfi, and G. Lugosi. *A Probabilistic Theory of Pattern Recognition*. Springer Verlag, New York, 1996.

S. M. Dhanasekaran, T. R. Barrette, D. Ghosh, R. Shah, S. Varambally, K. Kurachi, K. J. Pienta, M. A. Rubin, and A. M. Chinnaiyan. Delineation of prognostic biomarkers in prostate cancer. *Nature*, 412(6849):822–826, 2001.

H. Drucker, D. Wu, and V. Vapnik. Support vector machines for spam categorization. *IEEE Transactions on Neural Networks*, 10(5):1048–1054, 1999.

J. A. Dubin and D. Rivers. Selection bias in linear regression, logit and probit models. *Sociological Methods and Research*, 18:360–390, 1989.

R. O. Duda, P. E. Hart, and D. G. Stor. *Pattern Classification*. Wiley, New York, 2001.

M. Dudík, R. E. Schapire, and S. J. Phillips. Correcting sample selection bias in maximum entropy density estimation. In *Advances in Neural Information Processing Systems 17*, pages 323–330, MIT Press, Cambridge, MA, 2005.

M. Dudík, R. E. Schapire, and S. J. Phillips. Correcting sample selection bias in maximum entropy density estimation. In Y. Weiss, B. Schölkopf, and J. Platt, editors, *Advances in Neural Information Processing Systems 18*, MIT Press, Cambridge, MA, 2006.

R. M. Dudley. *Real Analysis and Probability*. Cambridge University Press, New

York, 2002.

B. Efron and R. J. Tibshirani. *An Introduction to the Bootstrap.* Chapman & Hall, New York, 1994.

L. El Ghaoui, G. R. G. Lanckriet, and G. Natsoulis. Robust classification with interval data. Technical Report UCB/CSD-03-1279, EECS Department, University of California, Berkeley, 2003.

C. Elkan. The foundations of cost-sensitive learning. In *Proceedings of the Seventeenth International Joint Conference on AI (IJCAI)*, pages 973–978, 2001.

V. V. Fedorov. *Theory of Optimal Experiments.* Academic Press, New York, 1972.

C. Field and B. Smith. Robust estimation — a weighted maximum likelihood approach. *International Statistical Review*, 62:405–424, 1994.

S. Fine and K. Scheinberg. Efficient SVM training using low-rank kernel representations. *Journal of Machine Learning Research*, 2:243–264, 2002.

K. Fukumizu. Active learning in multilayer perceptrons. In *Advances in Neural Information Processing Systems 8*, pages 295–301, MIT Press, Cambridge, MA, 1996.

K. Fukumizu. Statistical active learning in multilayer perceptrons. *IEEE Transactions on Neural Networks*, 11(1):17–26, 2000.

K. Fukumizu, A. Gretton, X. Sun, and B. Schölkopf. Kernel measures of conditional dependence. In D. Koller and Y. Singer, editors, *Advances in Neural Information Processing Systems 20*, pages 489–496, MIT Press, Cambridge, MA, 2008.

M. N. Gibbs and D. J. C. MacKay. Efficient implementation of Gaussian processes. Unpublished manuscript, 1997.

R. Gilad-Bachrach, A. Navot, and N. Tishby. Margin based feature selection – theory and algorithms. In *Proceedings of the Twentyfirst International Conference on Machine Learning*, pages 43–50. ACM Press, New York, 2004.

N. Goodman. *Fact, Fiction, and Forecast.* Harvard University Press, Cambridge, MA, 1955.

N. Goodman and C. Elgin. *Reconceptions in Philosophy.* Routledge, Florence, KY, 1998.

T. Graepel and R. Herbrich. Invariant pattern recognition by semidefinite programming machines. In S. Thrun, L. Saul, and B. Schölkopf, editors, *Advances in Neural Information Processing Systems 16*, pages 33–40. MIT Press, Cambridge, MA, 2004.

P. J. Green. Iteratively reweighted least squares for maximum likelihood estimation, and some robust and resistant alternatives. *Journal of the Royal Statistical Society: Series B*, 46:149–192, 1984.

A. Gretton, K. Borgwardt, M. Rasch, B. Schölkopf, and A. J. Smola. A kernel method for the two-sample-problem. In B. Schölkopf, J. Platt, and T. Hofmann, editors, *Advances in Neural Information Processing Systems 19*, pages 513–520,

MIT Press, Cambridge, MA, 2007.

S. Gruvberger, M. Ringner, Y. Chen, S. Panavally, L. H. Saal, C. Peterson A. Borg, M. Ferno, and P. S. Meltzer. Estrogen receptor status in breast cancer is associated with remarkably distinct gene expression patterns. *Cancer Research*, 61, 2001.

F. R. Hampel, E. M. Ronchetti, P. J. Rousseeuw, and W. A. Stahel. *Robust Statistics: The Approach Based on Influence Functions*. Wiley, New York, 1986.

L. K. Hansen. Bayesian averaging is well-tempered. In S. A. Solla, T. K. Leen, and K.-R. Müller, editors, *Advances in Neural Information Processing Systems 12*, pages 265–271, MIT Press, Cambridge, MA, 2000.

L. K. Hansen. How useful are unlabeled examples for supervised learning? Technical report, Informatics and Mathematical Modelling Department, Technical University of Denmark, 2001.

T. Hastie, R. Tibshirani, and J. Friedman. *The Elements of Statistical Learning: Data Mining, Inference, and Prediction*. Springer Verlag, New York, 2001.

D. Haussler and M. Opper. Mutual information, metric entropy and cumulative relative entropy risk. *Annals of Statistics*, 45:2451–2492, 1997.

T. He, S. Ben-David, and L. Tong. Nonparametric change detection and estimation in large scale sensor networks. *IEEE Transactions on Signal Processing*, 54(4): 1204–1217, 2006.

J. J. Heckman. Shadow prices, market wages, and labor supply. *Econometrica*, 42 (4):679–694, 1974.

J. J. Heckman. Sample selection bias as a specification error. *Econometrica*, 47: 153–161, 1979.

J. J. Heckman. Varieties of selection bias. *American Economic Review*, 80(2): 313–318, 1990.

M. Hein. Uniform convergence of adaptive graph-based regularization. In G. Lugosi and H. Simon, editors, *Proceedings of the Nineteenth Conference on Learning Theory (COLT)*, pages 50–64, 2006.

W. Hoeffding. Probability inequalities for sums of bounded random variables. *Journal of the American Statistical Association*, 58:13–30, 1963.

J. L. Horowitz and C. F. Manski. Identification and estimation of statistical functionals using incomplete data. *Journal of Econometrics*, 132:445–459, 2006.

J. Huang, A. Smola, A. Gretton, K. M. Borgwardt, and B. Schölkopf. Correcting sample selection bias by unlabeled data. In B. Schölkopf, J. Platt, and T. Hofmann, editors, *Advances in Neural Information Processing Systems 19*, pages 601–608, MIT Press, Cambridge, MA, 2007.

R. A. Jacobs, M. I. Jordan, S. J. Nowlan, and G. E. Hinton. Adaptive mixtures of local experts. *Neural Computation*, 3:79–87, 1991.

N. Japkowicz and S. Stephen. The class imbalance problem: A systematic study.

Intelligent Data Analysis, 6:429–449, 2002.

M. I. Jordan and R. A. Jacobs. Hierarchical mixtures of experts and the EM algorithm. *Neural Computation*, 6:181–214, 1994.

T. Kanamori. Statistical asymptotic theory of active learning. *Annals of the Institute of Statistical Mathematics*, 54(3):459–475, 2002.

T. Kanamori. Pool-based active learning with optimal sampling distribution and its information geometrical interpretation. *Neurocomputing*, 71(1–3):353–362, 2007.

T. Kanamori and H. Shimodaira. Active learning algorithm using the maximum weighted log-likelihood estimator. *Journal of Statistical Planning and Inference*, 116:149–162, 2003.

D. Kifer, S. Ben-David, and J. Gehrke. Detecting change in data streams. In *Very Large Databases (VLDB)*, 2004.

S. Kim, A. Magnani, and S. Boyd. Robust Fisher discriminant analysis. In Y. Weiss, B. Schölkopf, and J. Platt, editors, *Advances in Neural Information Processing Systems 18*, pages 659–666. MIT Press, Cambridge, MA, 2006.

G. S. Kimeldorf and G. Wahba. A correspondence between Bayesian estimation on stochastic processes and smoothing by splines. *Annals of Mathematical Statistics*, 41:495–502, 1970.

E. Krupka and N. Tishby. Generalization in clustering with unobserved features. In Y. Weiss, B. Schölkopf, and J. Platt, editors, *Advances in Neural Information Processing Systems 18*, pages 683–690. MIT Press, Cambridge, MA, 2006.

G. R. G. Lanckriet, N. Cristianini, P. L. Bartlett, L. El Ghaoui, and M. I. Jordan. Learning the kernel matrix with semidefinite programming. *Journal of Machine Learning Research*, 5:27–72, 2004.

P. Latinne, M. Saerens, and C. Decaestecker. Adjusting the outputs of a classifier to new a priori probabilities may significantly improve classifiction accuracy: Evidence from a multi-class problem in remote sensing. In *Proceedings of the Eighteenth International Conference on Machine Learning*, pages 298–305, Morgan Kaufmann, San Francisco, 2001.

N. D. Lawrence and M. I. Jordan. Gaussian processes and the null-category noise model. In O. Chapelle, B. Schölkopf, and A. Zien, editors, *Semi-Supervised Learning*, chapter 8. MIT Press, Cambridge, MA, 2005.

N. D. Lawrence, J. C. Platt, and M. I. Jordan. Extensions of the informative vector machine. In J. Winkler, N. D. Lawrence, and M. Niranjan, editors, *Deterministic and Statistical Methods in Machine Learning*, pages 56–87. Springer Verlag, New York, 2005.

Y. LeCun, L. Jackel, L. Bottou, A. Brunot, C. Cortes, J. Denker, H. Drucker, I. Guyon, U. Müller, E. Sackinger, P. Simard, and V. N. Vapnik. Comparison of learning algorithms for handwritten digit recognition. In F. Fogelman and P. Gallinari, editors, *International Conference on Artificial Neural Networks,*, pages 53–60. North-Holland, Amsterdam, 1995.

L. Lee. Some approaches to the correction of selectivity bias. *Review of Economic Studies*, 49:355–372, 1982.

J. Leskovec and J. Shawe-Taylor. Linear programming boosting for uneven datasets. In *ICML 2003*, 2003.

Y. Lin, Y. Lee, and G. Wahba. Support vector machines for classification in nonstandard situations. *Machine Learning*, 46:191–202, 2002.

B. G. Lindsay. Efficiency versus robustness: The case for minimum Hellinger distance and related methods. *Annals of Statistics*, 22:1081–1114, 1994.

D. Lowd and C. Meek. Good word attacks on statistical spam filters. In *Proceedings of the Second Conference on Email and Anti-Spam (CEAS)*, 2005.

J. Lunceford and M. Davidian. Stratification and weighting via the propensity score in estimation of causal treatment effects: A comparative study. *Statistics in Medicine*, 23(19):2937–2960, 2004.

D. J. C. MacKay. Bayesian interpolation. *Neural Computation*, 4(3):415–447, 1992a.

D. J. C. MacKay. Information-based objective functions for active data selection. *Neural Computation*, 4(4):590–604, 1992b.

C. F. Manski. The estimation of choice probabilities from choice based samples. *Econometrica*, 45:1977–1988, 1977.

C. F. Manski. Anatomy of the selection problem. *Journal of Human Resources*, 18:343–360, 1989.

C. F. Manski and S. Lerman. The estimation of choice probabilities from choice based samples. *Econometrica*, 45(8):1977–1988, 1977.

C. McDiarmid. On the method of bounded differences. In *Survey in Combinatorics*, pages 148–188. Cambridge University Press, New York, 1989.

S. Mendelson. A few notes on statistical learning theory. In S. Mendelson and A. J. Smola, editors, *Advanced Lectures on Machine Learning*, number 2600 in Lecture Notes in Artificial Intelligence, pages 1–40. Springer Verlag, Heidelberg, 2003.

A. Nedic and D. P. Bertsekas. Incremental subgradient methods for nondifferentiable optimization. *SIAM Journal on Optimization*, 12(1):109–138, 2001.

K. Nigam, A. McCallum, S. Thrun, and T. Mitchell. Text classification from labeled and unlabeled documents using EM. *Machine Learning*, 30(3), 2000.

E. Osuna. *Support Vector Machines: Training and Applications*. PhD thesis, Massachusetts Institute of Technology, Cambridge, MA, 1998.

J. Pearl. *Causality: Models, Reasoning, and Inference*. Cambridge University Press, New York, 2000.

D. Pfeffermann, C. J. Skinner, D. J. Holmes, H. Goldstein, and J. Rasbash. Weighting for unequal selection probabilities in multilevel models. *Journal of the Royal Statistical Society: Series B*, 60:23–56, 1998.

J. Platt. Fast training of support vector machines using sequential minimal optimization. In B. Schölkopf, C. J. C. Burges, and A. J. Smola, editors, *Advances in Kernel Methods — Support Vector Learning*, pages 185–208, MIT Press, Cambridge, MA, 1999.

G. Pólya. *Mathematics and Plausible Reasoning.* Princeton University Press, Princeton, NJ, 1954.

C. E. Rasmussen and Z. Ghahramani. Infinite mixtures of Gaussian process experts. In *Advances in Neural Information Processing Systems 14*, MIT Press, Cambridge, MA, 2002.

C. E. Rasmussen and C. K. I. Williams. *Gaussian Processes for Machine Learning.* MIT Press, Cambridge, MA, 2006.

J. Rissanen. Modeling by shortest data description. *Automatica*, 14(5):465–471, 1978.

P. Rosenbaum and D. Rubin. The central role of the propensity score in observational studies for causal effects. *Biometrika*, 70(1):41–55, 1983.

S. Rosset, J. Zhu, H. Zou, and T. Hastie. A method for inferring label sampling mechanisms in semi-supervised learning. In *Advances in Neural Information Processing Systems 17*, MIT Press, Cambridge, MA, 2004.

M. Schmidt and H. Gish. Speaker identification via support vector classifiers. In *Proceedings of ICASSP'96*, pages 105–108, Atlanta, May 1996.

B. Schölkopf, J. Platt, J. Shawe-Taylor, A. J. Smola, and R. C. Williamson. Estimating the support of a high-dimensional distribution. *Neural Computation*, 13(7):1443–1471, 2001.

B. Schölkopf and A. J. Smola. *Learning with Kernels.* MIT Press, Cambridge, MA, 2002.

B. Schölkopf, A. J. Smola, R. C. Williamson, and P. L. Bartlett. New support vector algorithms. *Neural Computation*, 12:1207–1245, 2000.

G. Schwarz. Estimating the dimension of a model. *Annals of Statistics*, 6:461–464, 1978.

H. S. Seung, M. Opper, and H. Sompolinsky. Query by committee. In *Proceedings of the Fifth Workshop on Computational Learning Theory*, pages 287–294, Morgan Kaufmann, San Francisco, 1992.

S. Shalev-Shwartz, Y. Singer, and N. Srebro. Pegasos: Primal estimated subgradient solver for SVM. In *Proceedings of the Twentyfourth International Conference on Machine Learning.* ACM, New York, 2007.

H. Shimodaira. Improving predictive inference under covariate shift by weighting the log-likelihood function. *Journal of Statistical Planning and Inference*, 90:227–244, 2000.

H. Shimodaira. Testing regions with nonsmooth boundaries via multiscale bootstrap. *Journal of Statistical Planning and Inference*, 138:1227–1241, 2008.

B. Silverman. *Density Estimation for Statistics and Data Analysis.* Chapman &

Hall, London, 1986.

D. Singh, P. Febbo, K. Ross, D. Jackson, J. Manola, C. Ladd, P. Tamayo, A. Renshaw, A. DAmico, and J. Richie. Gene expression correlates of clinical prostate cancer behavior. *Cancer Cell*, 1(2), 2002.

C. J. Skinner, D. Holt, and T. M. F. Smith. *Analysis of Complex Surveys*. Wiley, New York, 1989.

A. Smith and C. Elkan. A Bayesian network framework for reject inference. In *Proceedings of the Tenth ACM SIGKDD International Conference on Knowledge Discovery and Data Mining*, pages 286–295, ACM Press, New York, 2004.

A. J. Smola, S. V. N. Vishwanathan, and T. Hofmann. Kernel methods for missing variables. In R. G. Cowell and Z. Ghahramani, editors, *Proceedings of International Workshop on Artificial Intelligence and Statistics*, pages 325–332. Society for Artificial Intelligence and Statistics, 2005.

P. Sollich. Probabilistic interpretations and Bayesian methods for support vector machines. In *ICANN99*, pages 91–96, 1999.

P. Sollich. Bayesian methods for support vector machines: Evidence and predictive class probabilities. *Machine Learning*, 46:21–52, 2002.

I. Steinwart. Support vector machines are universally consistent. *Journal of Complexity*, 18:768–791, 2002.

M. Stone. Cross-validatory choice and assessment of statistical predictions. *Journal of the Royal Statistical Society: Series B*, 36:111–147, 1974.

A. J. Storkey and M. Sugiyama. Mixture regression for covariate shift. In *Advances in Neural Information Processing Systems 19*, MIT Press, Cambridge, MA, 2007.

M. Sugiyama. Active learning in approximately linear regression based on conditional expectation of generalization error. *Journal of Machine Learning Research*, 7:141–166, Jan. 2006.

M. Sugiyama. Generalization error estimation for non-linear learning methods. *IEICE Transactions on Fundamentals of Electronics, Communications and Computer Sciences*, E90-A(7):1496–1499, 2007.

M. Sugiyama, B. Blankertz, M. Krauledat, G. Dornhege, and K.-R. Müller. Importance weighted cross-validation for covariate shift. In K. Franke, K.-R. Müller, B. Nickolay, and R. Schäfer, editors, *DAGM 2006*, volume 4174 of *Lecture Notes in Computer Science*, pages 354–363, Springer Verlag, New York, 2006.

M. Sugiyama, M. Kawanabe, and K.-R. Müller. Trading variance reduction with unbiasedness: The regularized subspace information criterion for robust model selection in kernel regression. *Neural Computation*, 16(5):1077–1104, 2004.

M. Sugiyama, M. Krauledat, and K.-R. Müller. Covariate shift adaptation by importance weighted cross validation. *Journal of Machine Learning Research*, 8: 985–1005, May 2007.

M. Sugiyama and K.-R. Müller. The subspace information criterion for infinite dimensional hypothesis spaces. *Journal of Machine Learning Research*, 3:323–359, Nov. 2002.

M. Sugiyama and K.-R. Müller. Input-dependent estimation of generalization error under covariate shift. *Statistics & Decisions*, 23(4):249–279, 2005a.

M. Sugiyama and K.-R. Müller. Model selection under covariate shift. In *Proceedings of the International Conference on Artificial Neural Networks*, 2005b.

M. Sugiyama, S. Nakajima, H. Kashima, P. von Bünau, and M. Kawanabe. Direct importance estimation with model selection and its application to covariate shift adaptation. In D. Koller and Y. Singer, editors, *Advances in Neural Information Processing Systems 20*, pages 1433–1440, MIT Press, Cambridge, MA, 2008.

M. Sugiyama and H. Ogawa. Incremental active learning for optimal generalization. *Neural Computation*, 12(12):2909–2940, 2000.

M. Sugiyama and H. Ogawa. Subspace information criterion for model selection. *Neural Computation*, 13(8):1863–1889, 2001.

M. Sugiyama and H. Ogawa. Optimal design of regularization term and regularization parameter by subspace information criterion. *Neural Networks*, 15(3): 349–361, 2002.

M. Sugiyama and H. Ogawa. Active learning with model selection—Simultaneous optimization of sample points and models for trigonometric polynomial models. *IEICE Transactions on Information and Systems*, E86-D(12):2753–2763, 2003.

H. G. Sung. *Gaussian Mixture Regression and Classification*. PhD thesis, Rice University, Houston, 2004.

K. Takeuchi. Distribution of information statistics and criteria for adequacy of models. *Mathematical Sciences*, 153:12–18, 1976. in Japanese.

B. Taskar, C. Guestrin, and D. Koller. Max-margin Markov networks. In S. Thrun, L. Saul, and B. Schölkopf, editors, *Advances in Neural Information Processing Systems 16*, pages 25–32, MIT Press, Cambridge, MA, 2004.

C. H. Teo, A. Globerson, S. Roweis, and A. Smola. Convex learning with invariances. In D. Koller and Y. Singer, editors, *Advances in Neural Information Processing Systems 20*, pages 1489–1496. MIT Press, Cambridge, MA, 2007a.

C. H. Teo, Q. Le, A. Smola, and S. V. N. Vishwanathan. A scalable modular convex solver for regularized risk minimization. In *Proceedings of the Thirteenth ACM SIGKDD International Conference on Knowledge Discovery and Data Mining*, pages 727–736. ACM Press, New York, 2007b.

V. Tresp. Mixtures of Gaussian processes. In *Advances in Neural Information Processing Systems 13*, pages 654–660, MIT Press, Cambridge, MA, 2001.

I. Tsochantaridis, T. Joachims, T. Hofmann, and Y. Altun. Large margin methods for structured and interdependent output variables. *Journal of Machine Learning Research*, 6:1453–1484, 2005.

V. N. Vapnik. *Statistical Learning Theory*. Wiley, New York, 1998.

F. Vella. Estimating models with sample selection bias: A survey. *Journal of Human Resources*, 33:127–169, 1998.

K. Veropoulos, N. Cristianini, and C. Campbell. Controlling the sensitivity of support vector machines. In *Proceedings of the International Joint Conference on Artificial Intelligence (IJCAI99)*, Stockholm, 1999.

G. Wahba. *Spline Model for Observational Data*. Society for Industrial and Applied Mathematics, Philadelphia, 1990.

M. K. Warmuth, J. Liao, G. Rätsch, M. Mathieson, S. Putta, and C. Lemmen. Active learning with SVMs in the drug discovery process. *Chemical Information and Computer Sciences*, 43(2):667–673, 2003.

P. Warnat, R. Eils, and B. Brors. Cross-platform analysis of cancer microarray data improves gene expression based classification of phenotypes. *BMC Bioinformatics*, 6:265, Nov 2005.

S. Watanabe. Algebraic analysis for nonidentifiable learning machines. *Neural Computation*, 13(4):899–933, 2001.

J. B. Welsh, L. M. Sapinoso, A. I. Su, S. G. Kern, J. Wang-Rodriguez, C. A. Moskaluk, J. R. Frierson HF, and G. M. Hampton. Analysis of gene expression identifies candidate markers and pharmacological targets in prostate cancer. *Cancer Research*, 61(16):5974–5978, 2001.

M. West, C. Blanchette, H. Dressman, E. Huang, S. Ishida, R. Spang, H. Zuzan, J. A. Olson Jr, J. R. Marks, and J. R. Nevins. Predicting the clinical status of human breast cancer by using gene expression profiles. *Proceedings of the National Academy of Sciences*, 98(20), 2001.

J. Weston, S. Mukherjee, O. Chapelle, M. Pontil, T. Poggio, and V. N. Vapnik. Feature selection for SVMs. In *Advances in Neural Information Processing Systems 13*, pages 668–674. MIT Press, Cambridge, MA, 2000.

D. P. Wiens. Robust weights and designs for biased regression models: Least squares and generalized M-estimation. *Journal of Statistical Planning and Inference*, 83 (2):395–412, 2000.

C. K. I. Williams and D. Barber. Bayesian classification with Gaussian processes. *IEEE Transactions on Pattern Analysis and Machine Intelligence PAMI*, 20(12): 1342–1351, 1998.

M. P. Windham. Robustifying model fitting. *Journal of the Royal Statistical Society: Series B*, 57:599–609, 1995.

C. Winship and R. D. Mare. Models for sample selection bias. *Annual Review of Sociology*, 18:327–350, 1992.

G. Wittel and S. Wu. On attacking statistical spam filters. In *Proceedings of the First Conference on Email and Anti-Spam (CEAS)*, 2004.

Y. Xue, X. Liao, L. Carin, and B. Krishnapuram. Multi-task learning for classification with Dirichlet process priors. *Journal of Machine Learning Research*, 8: 35–63, 2007.

Y. Yang and J. O. Pedersen. A comparative study on feature selection in text categorization. In *Proceedings of the Fourteenth International Conference on Machine Learning*, pages 412–420, Morgan Kaufmann, San Francisco, 1997.

B. Zadrozny. Learning and evaluating classifiers under sample selection bias. In R. Greiner and D. Schuurmans, editors, *Proceedings of the Twentyfirst International Conference on Machine Learning (ICML)*, pages 114–122, 2004.

B. Zadrozny and C. Elkan. Learning and making decisions when costs and probabilities are both unknown. In *Proceedings of the Seventh International Conference on Knowledge Discovery and Data Mining*, pages 204–213, 2001.

D. Zhou, O. Bousquet, T. N. Lal, J. Weston, and B. Schölkopf. Learning with local and global consistency. In S. Thrun, L. Saul, and B. Schölkopf, editors, *Advances in Neural Information Processing Systems 16*, pages 321–328, MIT Press, Cambridge, MA, 2004.

X. Zhu, Z. Ghahramani, and J. Lafferty. Semi-supervised learning using Gaussian fields and harmonic functions. In T. Fawcett and N. Mishra, editors, *Proceedings of the Twentieth International Conference on Machine Learning (ICML)*, pages 912–919, 2003a.

X. Zhu, J. Lafferty, and Z. Ghahramani. Combining active learning and semi-supervised learning using Gaussian fields and harmonic functions. In *Proceedings of the ICML 2003 Workshop on the Continuum from Labeled to Unlabeled Data in Machine Learning and Data Mining*, pages 58–65, 2003b.

Notation and Symbols

Sets of Numbers

$\mathbb{N}$	the set of natural numbers, $\mathbb{N} = \{1, 2, \dots\}$
$\mathbb{R}$	the set of reals
$[n]$	compact notation for $\{1, \dots, n\}$
$x \in [a, b]$	interval $a \leq x \leq b$
$x \in (a, b]$	interval $a < x \leq b$
$x \in (a, b)$	interval $a < x < b$
$|C|$	cardinality of a set C (for finite sets, the number of elements)

Data

$\mathcal{X}$	the input domain
d	(used if $\mathcal{X}$ is a vector space) dimension of $\mathcal{X}$
M	number of classes (for classification)
n	number of data examples
n_{tr}	number of training examples
n_{te}	number of test examples
i, j	indices, often running over $[n_{\mathrm{te}}]$ or $[n_{\mathrm{tr}}]$
x_i	input patterns $x_i \in \mathcal{X}$
x_i^{tr}	input training patterns $x_i^{\mathrm{tr}} \in \mathcal{X}$
x_i^{te}	input test patterns $x_i^{\mathrm{te}} \in \mathcal{X}$
y_i	classes $y_i \in [M]$ (for regression: target values $y_i \in \mathbb{R}$)
y_i^{tr}	training data classes $y_i^{\mathrm{tr}} \in [M]$ (for regression: target values $y_i^{\mathrm{tr}} \in \mathbb{R}$)
y_i^{te}	test data classes $y_i^{\mathrm{tr}} \in [M]$ (for regression: target values $y_i^{\mathrm{te}} \in \mathbb{R}$)
X	sample of input patterns, $X = (x_1, \dots, x_n)$
X^{tr}	sample of training input patterns, $X^{\mathrm{tr}} = (x_1^{\mathrm{tr}}, \dots, x_n^{\mathrm{tr}})$
X^{te}	sample of test input patterns, $X^{\mathrm{te}} = (x_1^{\mathrm{te}}, \dots, x_n^{\mathrm{te}})$
Y	sample of output targets, $Y = (y_1, \dots, y_n)$
Y^{tr}	sample of training output targets, $Y^{\mathrm{tr}} = (y_1^{\mathrm{tr}}, \dots, y_n^{\mathrm{tr}})$
Y^{te}	sample of training output targets, $Y^{\mathrm{te}} = (y_1^{\mathrm{te}}, \dots, y_n^{\mathrm{te}})$

Kernels

$\mathcal{H}$	feature space induced by a kernel
Φ	feature map, $\Phi : \mathcal{X} \to \mathcal{H}$
k	(positive definite) kernel
K	kernel matrix or Gram matrix, $K_{ij} = k(x_i, x_j)$

Vectors, Matrices, and Norms

$\mathbf{1}$	vector with all entries equal to 1
$\mathbf{I}$	identity matrix
$A^\top$	transposed matrix (or vector)
A^{-1}	inverse matrix (in some cases, pseudoinverse)
$\mathbf{tr}\,(A)$	trace of a matrix
$\mathbf{det}\,(A)$	determinant of a matrix
$\langle \mathbf{x}, \mathbf{x}' \rangle$	dot product between $\mathbf{x}$ and $\mathbf{x}'$
$\mathbf{x} \circ \mathbf{x}'$	Elementwise multiplication of vectors $\mathbf{x}$ and $\mathbf{x}'$
$\lVert \cdot \rVert$	2-norm, $\lVert \mathbf{x} \rVert := \sqrt{\langle \mathbf{x}, \mathbf{x} \rangle}$
$\lVert \cdot \rVert_p$	p-norm , $\lVert \mathbf{x} \rVert_p := \left(\sum_{i=1}^{N} \lvert x_i \rvert^p \right)^{1/p}$, $N \in \mathbb{N} \cup \{\infty\}$
$\lVert \cdot \rVert_\infty$	∞-norm , $\lVert \mathbf{x} \rVert_\infty := \sup_{i=1}^{N} \lvert x_i \rvert$, $N \in \mathbb{N} \cup \{\infty\}$

Functions

$\ln$	logarithm to base e
$\log_2$	logarithm to base 2
f	a function, often from $\mathcal{X}$ or $[n]$ to $\mathbb{R}$, $\mathbb{R}^M$ or $[M]$
$\mathcal{F}$	a family of functions
$L_p(\mathcal{X})$	function spaces, $1 \leq p \leq \infty$

Probability

$\mathrm{P}\{\cdot\}$	probability of a logical formula
$\mathrm{P}_{\mathrm{tr}}\{\cdot\}$	probability of a logical formula associated with training data distribution
$\mathrm{P}_{\mathrm{te}}\{\cdot\}$	probability of a logical formula associated with test data distribution
$\mathrm{P}(C)$	probability of a set (event) C
$p(x)$	density evaluated at $x \in \mathcal{X}$
$p_{\mathrm{tr}}(x)$	density associated with training data distribution evaluated at $x \in \mathcal{X}$
$p_{\mathrm{te}}(x)$	density associated with test data distribution evaluated at $x \in \mathcal{X}$
$\mathbf{E}\,[\cdot]$	expectation of a random variable
$\mathbf{Var}\,[\cdot]$	variance of a random variable
$\mathcal{N}(\mu, \sigma^2)$	normal distribution with mean μ and variance σ^2

Graphs

g	graph $\mathbf{g} = (V, E)$ with nodes V and edges E
$\mathcal{G}$	set of graphs
W	weighted adjacency matrix of a graph ($W_{ij} \neq 0 \Leftrightarrow (i,j) \in E$)
D	(diagonal) degree matrix of a graph, $D_{ii} = \sum_j W_{ij}$
$\mathcal{L}$	normalized graph Laplacian, $\mathcal{L} = D^{-1/2} W D^{-1/2}$
L	unnormalized graph Laplacian, $L = D - W$

SVM-related

$\rho_f(x, y)$	margin of function f on the example (x, y), i.e., $y \cdot f(x)$
ρ_f	margin of f on the training set, i.e., $\min_{i=1}^m \rho_f(x_i, y_i)$
h	VC-dimension
C	regularization parameter in front of the empirical risk term
λ	regularization parameter in front of the regularizer
$\mathbf{w}$	weight vector
b	constant offset (or threshold)
α_i	Lagrange multiplier or expansion coefficient
β_i	Lagrange multiplier
$\boldsymbol{\alpha}, \boldsymbol{\beta}$	vectors of Lagrange multipliers
ξ_i	slack variables
$\boldsymbol{\xi}$	vector of all slack variables
Q	Hessian of a quadratic program

Miscellaneous

I_A	characteristic (or indicator) function on a set A i.e., $I_A(x) = 1$ if $x \in A$ and 0 otherwise
δ_{ij}	Kronecker δ ($\delta_{ij} = 1$ if $i = j$, 0 otherwise)
δ_x	Dirac δ, satisfying $\int \delta_x(y) f(y) dy = f(x)$
$O(g(n))$	a function $f(n)$ is said to be $O(g(n))$ if there exist constants $C > 0$ and $n_0 \in \mathbb{N}$ such that $|f(n)| \leq Cg(n)$ for all $n \geq n_0$
$o(g(n))$	a function $f(n)$ is said to be $o(g(n))$ if there exist constants $c > 0$ and $n_0 \in \mathbb{N}$ such that $|f(n)| \geq cg(n)$ for all $n \geq n_0$
rhs/lhs	shorthand for "right/left hand side"
$\blacksquare$	the end of a proof

Contributors

Shai Ben-David
David R. Cheriton School of Computer Science
University of Waterloo
Waterloo, Ontario, Canada
shai@cs.uwaterloo.ca

Steffen Bickel
Max Planck Institute for Computer Science
Saarbrücken, Germany
bickel@mpi-inf.mpg.de

Karsten Borgwardt
Department of Engineering
University of Cambridge
Cambridge, U.K.
kmb51@eng.cam.ac.uk

Michael Brückner
Max Planck Institute for Computer Science
Saarbrücken, Germany
brum@mpi-inf.mpg.de

David Corfield
Philosophy, School of European Culture and Languages
University of Kent, Canterbury
Kent, U.K.
D.Corfield@kent.ac.uk

Amir Globerson
Computer Science and Artificial Intelligence Laboratory
Massachussetts Institute of Technology
Cambridge, MA
gamir@csail.mit.edu

Arthur Gretton
Max Planck Institute for Biological Cybernetics
Tübingen, Germany
arthur.gretton@tuebingen.mpg.de

Lars Kai Hansen
Informatics and Mathematical Modelling
Technical University of Denmark
Lyngby, Denmark
lkh@imm.dtu.dk

Matthias Hein
Department of Computer Science
Saarland University
Saarbrücken, Germany
hein@cs.uni-sb.de

Jiayuan Huang
School of Computer Science
University of Waterloo
Waterloo, Ontario, Canada
j9huang@cs.uwaterloo.ca

Takafumi Kanamori
Department of Computer Science and Mathematical Informatics
Nagoya University
Nagoya, Japan
kanamori@is.nagoya-u.ac.jp

Klaus-Robert Müller
Technical University of Berlin
Faculty IV - Institute for Software Engineering and Theoretical Computer Science
Berlin, Germany
krm@cs.tu-berlin.de

Sam Roweis
Department Computer Science
University of Toronto
Toronto, Ontario, Canada
roweis@cs.toronto.edu

Neil Rubens
Department of Computer Science
Tokyo Institute of Techonology
Tokyo, Japan
neil@hrstc.org

Tobias Scheffer
Max Planck Institute for Computer Science
Saarbrücken, Germany
scheffer@mpi-inf.mpg.de

Marcel Schmittfull
Max Planck Institute for Biological Cybernetics
Tübingen, Germany
marcel.schmittfull@tuebingen.mpg.de

Bernhard Schölkopf
Max Planck Institute for Biological Cybernetics
Tübingen, Germany
bernhard.schoelkopf@tuebingen.mpg.de

Hidetoshi Shimodaira
Department of Mathematical and Computing Sciences
Tokyo Institute of Technology
Tokyo, Japan
shimo@is.titech.ac.jp

Alex Smola
RSISE, Australian National University
Statistical Machine Learning, NICTA
Canberra, Australia
alex@smola.org

Amos Storkey
School of Informatics
University of Edinburgh
Edinburgh, U.K.
a.storkey@ed.ac.uk

Masashi Sugiyama
Department of Computer Science
Tokyo Institute of Technology
Tokyo, Japan
sugi@cs.titech.ac.jp

Choon Hui Teo
RSISE, Australian National University
Statistical Machine Learning, NICTA
Canberra, Australia
choonhui.teo@anu.edu.au

Index

Printed in the United States
by Baker & Taylor Publisher Services